THE WORD OF GOD
AND TRADITION

By the same author

THEOLOGY AND PROCLAMATION

THE NATURE OF FAITH

(Fontana Library of Theology and Philosophy)

THE WORD OF GOD
AND TRADITION

HISTORICAL STUDIES
INTERPRETING THE DIVISIONS
OF CHRISTIANITY

GERHARD EBELING

Translated by S. H. Hooke

Collins
ST JAMES'S PLACE
LONDON
1968

First published by Vandenhoeck & Ruprecht
Göttingen, 1964, as Wort Gottes und Tradition

Contents

ACKNOWLEDGEMENTS

The author, translator and publishers wish to acknowledge their indebtedness for permission to use copyright material contained in this volume as follows: for extracts from *Theological Investigations*, Vols. III, IV and V, by Karl Rahner, S.J., translated by Karl-H and Boniface Kruger, Kevin Smyth, published by Darton, Longman & Todd, London and Helicon Press, Baltimore, U.S.A.

Abbreviations

AAS	*Acta Apostolicae Sedis*
AKG	Arbeiten zur Kirchengeschichte
BHTh	Beiträge zur historischen Theologie
BoA	M. Luther, *Werke in Auswahl*, ed. O. Clemen ('Bonner' Ausgabe), 1912ff.
BSLK	*Die Bekenntnisschriften der evang.-luth. Kirche*, ed. Deutscher Evangelischer Kirchenausschuss, 1956[3]
Cath	Catholica. Vierteljahrschrift für Kontroverstheologie, herausgegeben vom Adam Mohler-Institut, Paderborn.
ChrW	*Christliche Welt*
CSEL	*Corpus scriptorum ecclesiasticorum Latinorum*
Denz	Denzinger-Rahner, *Enchiridion Symbolorum*, 1953
DThC	*Dictionnaire de Théologie Catholique*, 1903ff
EvTh	*Evangelische Theologie*
FGLP	Forschungen zur Geschichte und Lehre des Protestantismus.
HUTh	Hermeneutische Untersuchungen zur Theologie.
KD	K. Barth, *Die kirchliche Dogmatik* (English translation, *Church Dogmatics*, Edinburgh, T. & T. Clark, 1936ff)
KuD	*Kerygma und Dogma*
MdKI	*Materialdienst des Konfessionskundlichen Instituts*
Mirbt	C. Mirbt, *Quellen zur Geschichte des Papstums und des römischen Katholizismus*, 5th ed., 1934
MPL	J. P. Migne, *Patrologiae cursus completus*, series Latina

Abbreviations

RAC	*Reallexikon für Antike und Christentum*, 1941ff
RGG³	*Die Religion in Geschichte und Gegenwart*, 1927ff.: 1957ff³
SgV	Sammlung gemeinverständlicher Vorträge und Schriften aus dem Gebiet der Theologie und Religionsgeschichte
S.Th	*Studia Theologica*
ThQ	*Theologische Quartalschrift*
Theol.Rev.	*Theologische Revue*
WA	M. Luther, *Werke. Kritische Gesamtausgabe* (Weimarer Ausgabe), 1883ff
WAB	M. Luther, *Werke. Kritische Gesamtausgabe, Briefwechsel* (Weimarer Ausgabe), 1906ff
WADB	M. Luther, *Werke. Kritische Gesamtausgabe. Die Deutsche Bibel* (Weimarer Ausgabe), 1906ff
WATR	M. Luther, *Werke. Kritische Gesamtausgabe.* Tischreden (Weimarer Ausgabe), 1912ff
ZKG	*Zeitschrift für Kirchengeschichte*
ZThK	*Zeitschrift für Theologie und Kirche*
WuG	G. Ebeling, *Wort und Glaube*, 1962² (English translation, *Word and Faith*, London, SCM Press, 1963)

Author's Foreword to the English Edition

It will perhaps be of some help to the readers of this translation of my volume of essays on the Confessional problem if I put my intention in a few sentences. And I should like to hope that my self-interpretation will be confirmed by the reader when he comes to the various essays themselves.

My concern is with understanding. In the age of the ecumenical movement this looks like a triviality. The old style of theological controversy has in general given way to an extraordinarily eirenical readiness to understand. It is unnecessary for me to describe the change in climate, especially in regard to the relationship between Roman Catholic and Protestant theology; nor need I emphasize how gratifying this development is.

But the cause of proper understanding can only be served if we are ready to examine the actual differences as thoroughly as possible. I do not claim that in the following essays I have succeeded in doing this. They are just individual sallies towards a distant goal, yet I hope that some of them at least may indicate the way that further work will have to be done. It can only help better understanding if one makes the task more difficult, by, as it were, building in the oppositions, than might seem necessary or desirable in the present confessional thaw. But of course this making difficulties must not be an artificial matter, but must proceed from a sober view of the true state of affairs. For me this means that the various aspects of confessional studies—the historical, the hermeneutical and the Reformed-theological—must all be allowed to play their part.

We must continually keep in mind to what an extent our Confessional differences are due to extremely complicated historical events. We must exercise the discipline of strict historical methods in order to defend ourselves from the inclination to define or to bridge over our

9

differences by means of doctrinal systematization. For this inclination tends to underrate the conditioned historical nature of this kind of systematization. So it is important not just to take account of the non-theological factors, which are so much discussed in ecumenical circles, but above all to note the difference between the various standard texts and our present situation with its responsibilities. For Protestantism in particular it is very salutary to be confronted in this way by the theological relevance of the problem of tradition, and to deal with history in such a way that its burden as well as its richness can be experienced.

This leads us to the hermeneutical problem. In the confrontation of the Confessions, it is true, the matter does not only have this general form of demanding critical consideration, in such historical investigations, of the conditions of understanding. For the significance of the hermeneutical question touches the very nature of the great Confessions. In these Confessions we are faced with comprehensive entities which have to be understood as a whole. That is why it is such a difficult and inexhaustible task to investigate the 'essence' of Protestantism or Catholicism: indeed, one might almost conclude that it is a hopeless undertaking to be concerned about reaching an understanding. For even the means of understanding, namely, the languages used on either side, are caught up in the opposition.

For this reason a great deal has already been achieved when we can get rid of preliminary mutual misunderstandings and press forward to the point where we can agree about what it is that really separates us.

Hence I am convinced that it does not help to weaken the oppositions which have arisen in the history of the Church. We should rather make it our business to sharpen and clarify the question of truth that is concealed in these oppositions. It would be a disservice to genuine understanding within Christendom for a theologian who is pledged to the heritage of the Reformation not to affirm this heritage as decisively and clearly as possible in an encounter between the Confessions. At a time like the present, when the Reformation is unexpectedly producing certain fruits within the Roman communion, the ecumenical significance of the legacy of the Reformation deserves the most careful consideration.

I

Church History is the History of the Exposition of Scripture

The task of laying a methodological foundation for the study of Church history confronts us with a number of intricate problems. As a branch of theological science, Church history must account for its place in theology as a whole, that is, for its basis and the results of its character as a theological discipline. As a specialized area of historiography, Church history involves the basic problems of the human sciences in general, and those of history and the philosophy of history in particular. In view of Church history's close relationship to theology on the one hand, and to the human sciences on the other, the whole problem of theology as a science comes alive in the question of the relationship between Church history and secular history.

The problem raised by Church history as a theological discipline—a problem roughly outlined in the preceding paragraph in terms which can be disputed—must be considered from every angle. Only then can positive statements be made about the matter and method of Church history. Any attempt to avoid the intricate problems involved and to propose a biblicist or speculative concept of Church history would be an act of self-deception. The accumulated burden of our own history is an ever-present factor in the problem indicated above. The questions and solutions of past generations have seeped into our speech and permeated our thinking in countless ways. And the very history which we neglect takes its revenge upon us by binding us in its fetters. It is only through dialogue with our past that we can free (though not completely dissociate) ourselves from the past. In any case, while history enriches us immeasurably, it remains a heavy burden. When we pay attention to it, however, history may become a fruitful burden. This observation is valid for our whole existence and its involvement in history. It is also valid when we attempt to lay a methodological foundation for Church history as a theological discipline. Neither can history, as the course of events (*Historie*) nor in its written form as the systematic foundation of history, escape the historical nature of existence and thereby dispense with conscious reference to history as past event (*Geschichte*). The core of the whole problem lies in our quest for a methodological foundation for Church history as a theological discipline. We shall begin, therefore, by tracing out the pattern of our problem along the lines indicated at the outset.

The place of Church history as a theological discipline is neither historically nor factually obvious or undisputed. When we look at the history of Church history as a discipline within the theological curriculum rather than at the history of the writing of Church history, we find that Church history is by far the youngest branch of theological study. Church history as an independent subject goes back only to the middle of the seventeenth century. The University of Helmstedt led the way: others followed slowly. Tübingen, for example, did not take the first step until 1720 when an honorary professor of ecclesiastical history was appointed. Status as an independent branch of theology was achieved in three stages. The Renaissance and Humanism paved the way for an approach to history which contrasted with the scholastic educational system. It was largely due to Melanchthon's influence that this interest in history, which at first had been restricted chiefly to the history of antiquity, extended to universal history. As such history took its place in the arts curriculum along with poetry, rhetoric or ethics, Church history came under the faculty of philosophy as a branch of universal history, which still followed the pattern of theological dispensationalism, i.e., six periods of a thousand years each and four world monarchies. The next stage saw the separation of purely political world history from this pattern and from its close association with Church history. In this way the study of history passed over into the field of jurisprudence, while Church history was discarded and relegated to the theological faculty. This classification of Church history as a theological discipline, however—and this was the third step—was not accomplished as an apologetic theological reaction in face of the process of secularization in modern thought, but as the invasion by this modern thought of the fortress of the orthodox system.

This meant that the element of unrest and of criticism, which has provided the decisive impulses to the present day, was taken into theology. The historical method, which took possession of biblical studies in a violent storm of conquest, and even touched dogma itself, the real region of systematic theology, seemed to be from the first a dissolvent power in theology, against which dogmatic thinking took up a defensive posture. Since that time the movement in theological thought has been kept going by means of the opposition between historical and dogmatic methods. Extreme historicism on the one hand, and extreme dogmatism on the other hand, with a wealth of compromise solutions in between—these are the structural marks of theological development till our own day. In the inevitable swing of the pendulum, the predominant position of historical theology at the turn of the century was succeeded by an enthusiastic turning to systematic theology and a sudden decline of historical theology. While Harnack regarded works on systematic theology as *belles lettres*, Barth does not concede an independent status to Church history as a subject of study, but only admits its usefulness as an aid, if an indispensable one, to study.

It would certainly be completely erroneous to regard the tensions and oppositions in Protestant theology as due to the temporary predominance of one or other method, and in continuation of the old party strife between liberal and positive, to think that one can, in contrast to the secular historical method with its revolutionary effect on dogma, extol the dogmatic method as a definitely theological means of preserving dogma. The derivation of the name 'systematic' theology from idealistic German philosophy with its high-handed treatment of history, betrays a no less suspect origin of the systematic method than that of the preceding historical method from the Enlightenment, the Romantic movement, and Positivism. And the history of theology shows, not only in the last two centuries, but in the earlier flowering period of a systematic theology in Scholasticism as well as in Protestant orthodoxy, the immense threat to theology presented by the systematic method.

If, reviewing the course of theological activity since the Enlightenment, we attempt to reach an estimate of its results, it can be frankly stated that the distinctive gain for theology during this period has been the result of historical work, both in the field of exegesis and in the field of Church history and the history of dogma. Indeed, the facts revealed in the course of accurate historical research, even against the convictions of the historians themselves, have brought theology back so forcibly to the recognition of its real subject that it has been able to guard against the alien influence of secular philosophical schools of thought. When, beneath the superficial aspects of the developments of the last twenty-five years, the really operative motives and influences are recognized, it becomes apparent that, apart from the preceding historical research undertaken by theology, they are not only unthinkable, but they owe to it their best work, namely, the turning to the historicity of the revelation in Jesus Christ. It also becomes apparent that contemporary theological development is in danger of degenerating into Scholasticism, speculative Gnosticism, or apologetic, to the extent to which it allows the connection with the tradition of historical theology to be broken, and that it withstands this danger to the extent to which it takes historical studies seriously.

It is questionable whether the usual modern division of theological studies into five main departments is wholly justifiable. It is mainly determined by the different view-points of Method, Subject-matter, and Purpose, and needs clearer methodological consideration. Even if we bracket practical theology as a separate subject, and divide the remaining branches of study into historical and systematic, the problem is not made any easier; nor is it any better if we bracket off Church history and the history of dogma as non-independent auxiliary branches of study, and only retain the division between exegesis and dogmatic.

The separate lines of theological studies are to such an extent interdependent, that it is impossible to treat them in isolation. The exegete must not only know the history of the interpretation, but must also realize to the full what the systematic theologian's task involves in the exposition of the text, namely, the encounter of theology in its totality with human existential totality. Similarly, the systematic theologian can only fulfil his task when he has mastered exegesis and

Church history in the broadest sense, that is, when he has really taken the historical nature of existence seriously. Not only does the practice of systematic theology show that it must go hand in hand with history, but also the recognition that theology does not admit of an *a priori* approach makes it impossible to formulate an absolute systematic method independent of the historical method. Finally, that the Church historian cannot dispense either with exegetic or systematic theology should already have become apparent through our methodological approach to Church history, and should be further clarified by what follows.

If then, even for reasons of natural human limitations, we propose a division of tasks between biblical theology, Church history, and systematic theology, we shall do well not to assign a predominant role to any of them, but to allow them each to serve one another. Hence, if any attempt is made to arrange the theological disciplines in order of precedence and value in general, the most that can be said is that every aspect of theological study must subserve the interpretation of Holy Scripture. Nevertheless, at this point we must beware of the mistake of supposing that a specialization in Old or New Testament studies can be of less auxiliary value than, from our point of view, the study of Church history and of systematic theology unquestionably are. Further consideration will reveal what is involved for theology as a whole in assigning this position to Church history as a branch of study.

We must, however, first consider the second group of problems: the relation of Church history as a branch of study to the science of history in general. There can be no doubt that, from the point of view of historical method, Church history is a special department of historiography. This connection with secular intellectual disciplines is, however, not peculiar to Church history as a branch of study. To partition science as a whole only from the point of view of formal methods would be to deny the standing of theology as an independent discipline. For if 'Method' necessitates rationality and directed thinking, it follows that there is no specific theological method, nor any specific method in exegetic or dogmatic studies. On the other hand, the concept of a purely formal method is extremely problematical. Not only is it subject to the influence of the subject handling it, a source of error which must be vigorously resisted, though it cannot be entirely eliminated, but above all it is subject to the demands of the object to which it is applied; thus every department of learning is compelled to think through afresh the question of its methodology in relation to an understanding of the real nature of its object.

The impossibility of a formal general methodology of science has become apparent in the efforts to establish a methodology in the human sciences, in the struggle with the Kantian epistemology which in the end has been applied exclusively to the logic of mathematics and physics. The theologian, however, cannot be too definitely warned against attempting to take advantage of this situation by seeking release from the demand for the strict exercise of rational and controlled thinking in his own method. No less can he dispense with accurate historical study on the ground that an absolute objective knowledge is impossible, nor would it be right for him to take advantage, say, of the present critical situation in physics to make an unwarranted apologetic use of it. The fact that theological studies to a considerable extent interlock with other fields of study, and can at no point be completely detached from them, involves a healthy discipline, and the timid shirking of it can only harm theology.

Hence the Church historian must go to school with historical science in general, not merely to become familiar with its results, but above all to learn its methods of work. This does not, however, release him from the necessity of thinking through afresh and independently the question of the methodology of historical study as it concerns the field of his material. Not only because this, like other special branches of history, such as the history of art, requires specialization and modifications of historical method, but also because historical method in due course runs up against its own limit, where the problem of the philosophy of history renders any naïve self-sufficiency with regard to the study of history impossible. This limit is not an external one, separating the different fields of study from one another, but an internal limit which exists at present in every activity of historical science; it compels the historian to arrive at philosophical judgements, but also compels the Church historian to exercise the watchfulness which, as a theologian, he needs when confronted by any philosophical problems. Nevertheless the factual situation is not so simple; it does not imply that where the historian runs up against the problems of the philosophy of history, the Church historian finds that historical theology provides him with ready-made solutions. Rightly understood, theology gives no answer to any genuine philosophical questioning. Hence theology in no way relieves the Church historian of the perplexities in which his study involves him; it compels him, rather, to face up to the problems raised by the philosophy of history, and instils in him a sober estimate of the relative character of the solutions which it proffers.

Accordingly, we shall proceed to give an outline of the methodological situation in which the study of Church history as a branch of historiography now stands; we shall do this, however, more by way of illustration than as providing a comprehensive account. At the core of the study of history, and implicit in the German word '*Geschichte*', is the dialogue between the objective event in the past and the subjective understanding of the past event in the present; it is this which makes criticism an essential requirement in historical studies: and that in a double sense, exposing not only the manifold distortions of the sources, but also the manifold causes of error in the presuppositions of the historian. The Church historian must bring into operation every form of historical criticism, undeterred by apologetic considerations. So-called hypercriticism is self-contradictory, and should be critically exposed as the negation of criticism. There is no other legitimate limit of criticism than the often strange or even wholly unintelligible evidence of historical facts. Herein lies the incontestable vindication of Ranke's ideal attitude to history: the obliteration of the historian's personality, allowing the events themselves to speak.

Criticism, however, does not produce understanding, but only the preconditions for it. With the aim of interpretation in view, the historian must leave himself free to make use of every available method, the pragmatic method, the history of ideas, and so forth, excluding no method on principle, and allowing none to predominate. The respective value of these methods of interpretation will be determined by the nature of the subject-matter to be dealt with; it will thus depend, in the case of Church history, upon the definition of what is meant by Church history. Here is the point where historical methodology in general comes up against its limit, and where the Church historian, according to his existential understanding of the subject-matter to be dealt with, must adopt a standpoint which brings him into relation with the event. For it is impossible to understand history without a standpoint and a perspective. Hence the historian should endeavour to take up a position, not arbitrarily chosen, but as far as possible appropriate to the subject-matter, and above all, within his horizon, to observe the laws of perspective, distorting nothing.

This peculiarity of historical interpretation enables us to understand the essential unfinished nature of historical research and the necessity of constant renewal, as well as the fact that the history of historiography itself is a reflection of the history of the spirit, and, apart from noteworthy progress in individual instances, makes no attempt to arrive at a final definite completion of its task. It is a further consequence of this peculiarity of the understanding of history that the significance of historical knowledge is not a product, as it once was, of merely knowing the facts, or of any kind of political, ethical, universal, apologetic, or polemical measures aiming at present or future advantage; these are only more or less the by-product of historical knowledge. The significance of history is only to be found in the fact that in his encounter with history (*Geschichte*) man learns to understand himself. To say that man understands himself in his encounter with history does not simply mean that he realizes that he is a product of his own past, but that in the encounter in the broadest sense with the reality of human nature, man becomes conscious of himself. This knowledge may so far degenerate as to become an almost desperate meaninglessness, and a hindrance to the full experience of life. Nevertheless it is still true that history (*Historie*) is an advantage or a disadvantage for life to the extent to which self-knowledge is regarded as advantageous or disadvantageous for life.

To what extent the import of the study of Church history reaches finality in this definition of history (*Historie*), and whether the description of Church history as 'A medley of mistakes and violence' is perhaps the last word on the subject, depends on whether we find in Church history nothing other than is to be found in general history. In any case, it can be seen that the significance of the study of history is inseparable from the question of the nature and meaning of history (*Geschichte*) itself. Here we are faced with a question which emerges, not only on the margin of the study of history as its possible limit, but which accompanies all historical activities. It depends on this question, whether we regard history (*Geschichte*) as a waste heap of trivial facts, or as a designed self-realization of the world-spirit; whether we consider it as essentially political history, history of ideas, economic history, or the history of important personalities; whether we estimate the course of history mainly as a causal chain of events, or as a teleological development, either in the direction of progress or decadence, or as an endless secular revolution in ever-recurring periods; whether we venture to conceive of it in its totality as world-history, or remain content with snippets and fragments. Church history is, as we have said, deeply involved in this problem. In respect of history (*Historie*) as such, it is advisable to avoid one-sided conclusions in this or that direction. Relativism and scepticism are more appropriate attitudes for the historian than dogmatism. How far that also holds good for the study of Church history depends on what differentiates it from world-history.

This brings us to the third of the problems indicated at the outset of our study: the relation between secular and Church history. This problem can be divided into two closely interconnected questions. First, is the division of secular and Church history into two separate fields of study justified in reality; secondly, how far is it possible to make a distinction between writing secular history and writing the history of the Church? If we begin with the second question and turn our attention first to the actual origin of this distinction, we are forced to the conclusion that it is not to be found in Christian, but in secular western ideas of history, and possibly at a stage of compromise, when history had not yet become definitely and completely secularized. Then, instead of setting up, in accordance with the Christian conception, a secular conception of history, and subordinating the field of Church history to this, the historians came to a stop before Church history, and contented themselves with establishing in contrast to it a supposedly autonomous field of secular events; in this way they contrived to bring together two contradictory and opposed conceptions of history in a more or less peaceful juxtaposition of two spheres of history existing side by side. If we leave out of account for the present the fact that this process of secularization actually developed within theology into a secular form of Church history, it must however be conceded that we have evidence for the division of written history into two separate fields in the great historical prototypes, the historical works of classical antiquity, and the *Ecclesiastical History* of Eusebius whose methodological influence lasted down through the Middle Ages up to the threshold of the modern age.

Hence we must go further back and enquire what is the significance of Christianity for the history of historiography. The characteristic feature of classical historiography in antiquity, in contrast with the preceding mythological poetic history, was the radical demythologization of history. If we pause to consider that period of ancient history following the rise of Christianity and dominated by it, and the medieval period, we are struck by the unreliable chronology and the uncritical mythology which characterize its historical writing. How is this fact to be explained? It is still more surprising when we realize the unique relation between the Christian faith and history (*Geschichte*). It is not as the founder of a religion alone that Jesus Christ is the source and inspiration of the Christian faith, but the historicity and unrepeatability of his passion, death, and resurrection constitute the indefectible foundation of the Christian faith. This historicity of Jesus Christ links the Christian conception of the world and history to the Old Testament conception of history which is fundamentally opposed to the Greek conception. History (*Geschichte*) has a beginning and an end, and therefore unrepeatability and irreversibility; it has a continuity and a totality, a dualistic movement and presses on to a predetermined and certain goal. This view of history produces in Augustine the grand conception of an indissoluble bond between world history and Church history. It also initiates, in contrast to ancient historiography, the great forward step of viewing history as a whole, instead of treating it as a mere succession of natural happenings.

What is the explanation, in contrast to this, of the sterility of historical writing of early and medieval Christianity? It lies in the fact that the living apprehension of the historical revelation had been transformed from an historical activity into a thing, a mere state of affairs. The reality of Christ had been transformed into a sacramental event; relics had taken the place of the reality of past history; the living interpretation of the Scriptures had been replaced by an apostolically guaranteed tradition; the vital eschatological dualism of the *civitas dei* and the *civitas terrena* had become the visible juxtaposition of Church and not-Church, replacing faith based on history by an immediate experience; the critical search for historical truth had been replaced by a simple acceptance of tradition; the vision of the dialectical multiplicity of phenomena had been replaced by a schematized and mythological view of a wholly black and white universe. World history had lost all interest because the Church had finally filled the horizon. Church history was essentially uninteresting because in its contemporary form its whole past had become contemporary.

Not until the Reformation did the reality of the revelation find expression through the rediscovery of the historicity of the revelation in Jesus Christ; but, in addition, through a unique involvement with the history of ideas, it experienced a new encounter with antiquity; finally, as the result of a protracted process of interaction, the relation with history rooted in Christian modes of thought became linked with a critical, demythologizing conception of history. It is essential to recognize in this rediscovery of history (*Geschichte*) by modern thought, not only its anti-christian tendencies, but its Christian roots.

As the result of this process the question of the relation between secular and Church history has revived. Protestant theology is still striving towards a clarification of the problem. It should, at least, however, be clear that the distinction between secular and Church history is no longer tenable. For Church history is not in its own right sacred history, and so-called secular history is only such because of our conception of what is meant by secular. Everything is the result of divine activity; but God does not reveal his activity everywhere; on the contrary, he conceals his activity everywhere. Nowhere in history may we recognize his Yea and his Nay, his willing and his refusal, his mercy and his judgement. Nowhere may it be recognized save in Christ, in his Word. That is why there may well be a proclamation of his Word in history, but not a knowledge of his Word from history as such. That is why there is no historical writing which discloses in history (*Geschichte*) the traces of divine decisions. There can be only one kind of theological historical writing, namely, one which traces out the proclamation of God's Word in history (*Geschichte*). But this kind of theological history does not rest on the separation of the respective spheres of world and Church history, for where would the boundary be drawn? It rests on the distinction between a recognizable relation of the Word of God to history and one which cannot be recognized. Briefly, it would be the history of the witness of Jesus Christ in history (*Geschichte*).

Thus far we have discussed the three groups of problems indicated at the outset of our study: the place of Church history as a branch of study in theology in general; the relation of Church history as a branch of study to the science of history in general; and the relation between secular and Church history. We have now come to the point where we may and must venture, on the basis of the questions so far faced and the results so far established, to reach definite conclusions about the subject and method of Church history. We have no intention of replacing the conception of Church history whose problematic nature we have recognized, simply by another. Our task is rather to interpret its relevance to our situation.

II

The conception of Church history has, in its course, developed three main forms: the Catholic, the Enthusiastic, and the Reformed. Each of these three types has originated in a different conception of the nature of the Church.

The Roman Catholic conception of the Church provides an unambiguous starting-point for the definition of the essential nature of Church history. The identification of the Church with the mystical Body of Christ on the one hand, and with the historically verifiable Roman Catholic Church on the other, makes the history of the Church the direct continuation of the Incarnation and therefore of the history of Jesus Christ. In this way both the theological and the historical character of Church history remain free from ambiguity. The sanctity and unity attaching to the Church belong also to its history in time. From this relational point of view all the manifold aspects of Christianity fall clearly into order. Everything appertains to Church history in so far as it is related to the Roman Catholic Church. Nevertheless, this conception of Church history is not without its internal difficulty. To what changes is its actual history liable? The Church can only grow, its doctrine can only develop, by maintaining inviolate its identity and continuity. Any change which it undergoes is a purely biological one, there is no real historical development. Such actual historical development as there is assumes the merely marginal form of persecution and heresy. Hence the Roman Catholic Church exhibits no burning theological urge to concern itself with Church history. Its aim is predominantly apologetic or edifying. The critical situation for this conception of Church history emerges wherever it comes into conflict with the historical facts themselves, as over the question of the origin of the Roman Catholic Church. It is exactly here that the strength of the Catholic conception of the history of the Church appears, namely, its unambiguous dogmatic conception of the Church, enabling it to anticipate objections by putting forward a definite picture of the course of the Church's history. On the other hand the weakness of the Catholic conception of Church history also appears, namely, its vulnerability in the face of the historical method.

It is this situation which calls forth the full strength of the Enthusiastic conception of Church history. It is certainly an extremely problematic undertaking to attempt to include under a single conception of Church history all the different aspects which are usually covered by the term 'Enthusiasm'. It seems to me, however, that a certain apprehension of the relation between Church and history (*Geschichte*) does make possible, and justifies, the use of such a comprehensive concept as 'Enthusiasm'—provided we put it in inverted commas. The characteristic feature of Enthusiasm consists in its spiritualizing severance of the correlation between the Church and the historicity of the revelation in Jesus Christ. The Enthusiastic concept of the Church is marked by its immediate experience of God. The basic significance of this lies in the fact that the historicity of the Church disappears in the essential conception of an invisible Church. Although the attempt may be made by using certain features of Enthusiasm to give the Church an appearance of visibility by representing it as a community of saints, it will nevertheless lack any real connection with history. For the Enthusiastic type of Church lives only in the vertical plane of metaphysics and not in the horizontal plane of history. Hence Church history in the positive sense as the history of the true Church becomes an impossible conception. Ultimately Church history only exists in the negative sense as a caricature of a Church. Hence, while Enthusiasm is theologically entirely uninterested in history as such, it can nevertheless take a very lively interest in Church history, to wit, a polemical and critical interest in it as disclosing its destructive effect on the conception of the Church, and hence on Church history as such. The incredible stimulus which modern thought has imparted to an interest in Church history, raising the question whether this is not at bottom a form of Enthusiasm, can be traced back to this motive. Its ultimate result is the critical dissolution of the conception of the Church. The radical application of the historical method has placed theology in a state of confusion as to what Church history really is. Protestant theology today is faced by the question whether this is the necessary result of the application of the historical method to Church history. This explains both the Catholicizing and the Confessional Lutheran Romanticism in the theology of our time. It is nevertheless a flight from the still unsolved problem of the relation of the Reformation to Enthusiasm. Here the modern issues lie. For Enthusiasm confronts us with a real theological question, for the answer to which Protestantism still remains responsible, namely, the relation between Church and history.

It is misleading to speak of a Reformed type of the conception of Church history, because we are here faced by a problem which has so far found no fundamental solution, and in consequence has reached hitherto no clear expression in history. The dialectic in the Reformed idea of the Church which has assumed the form of the antithesis between an invisible and a visible Church, a formula, fateful and capable of manifold interpretations as it has been, but not to be rejected out of hand, has not yet reached any satisfactory settlement. The effect of this has been devastating, especially in the field of Protestant canon law, whose function it is, like that of the study of Church history, to deal with the relation between Church and history. Here a struggle is taking place between Enthusiastic docetism on the one hand, and historical positivism on the other. Victory will regularly rest with the latter, inasmuch as Enthusiasm, as the result of its dissipation of the visibility of the Church, contrary to its original concern, must abandon the question of the form of the Church in history to purely positivist points of view which do not derive from the nature of the Church.

Hence, if, in the study of Church history, a conception of the Church based on the idea of its invisibility were adopted, it would appear that not only are we deprived of the possibility of knowing the subject under discussion, but also of its historicity in general. The Church thus loses not only any historical basis of knowledge, but also any historical ground for its existence. From such premises it would be possible to arrive at a conclusion resembling Sohm's well-known thesis, that Church history is a contradiction of the nature of the Church. But this brings us back to the Enthusiastic conception of Church history.

If, however, we take our stand at the opposite extreme, amid the complexities of the Reformed conception of the Church, attested by history, then Church history as a branch of study would seem to be relegated to particular historical bodies, such as individual State or Free Churches, of varying size, presenting Confessional contrasts and well-defined local and temporal characteristics. The impossibility of writing universal Church history from such a point of view is obvious. Yet even the record of Church history associated with some particular Confessional Church does not confine itself to the history of that particular Church, beginning for instance with the period of the Reformation. Nor on the other hand can the conception of witnesses to the truth (which is in any case unable to do justice to the total phenomenon of Church history) master the preceding five hundred years, far less the parallel development, since the Reformation, of different Confessional churches. Hence the confused gropings after unity amid the multiplicity of appearances, and after substitute conceptions, such as History of the Christian Churches, History of Christianity, History of the Christian Religion, and so on.

Nevertheless, Protestant theology need not have fallen into this perplexity if it had not been trapped in emergency solutions which became permanent, and so came to a full stop in its development of the Reformation of the Church; but it could have gone on to develop and shape this idea from article VII of the Augsburg Confession. The lead which this article could have provided lies in the linking of Church and history, as guided by the interpretation of Holy Scripture, finding its fulfilment in the actual assembly obedient to the Word, and thus constituting that assembly ever anew. The communication of the Word of God is not a continuous process, but is only given in the constantly renewed interpretation of Holy Scripture. This interpretation is not to be separated from its relation to the actual assembly of those who hear it, and as hearers fulfil it. Herein lies the genuine historical character of the Church founded on the historical character of the Word of God.

Men have been led astray because, in opposition to article VII of the Augsburg Confession, they have sought the unity of the Church in external matters such as unity of locality, of historical tradition and ritual conformity. This has led to a position in which 'Church' has come to mean mainly the organization binding the community together; this, again, has had, to say the least, a strong tendency to produce an independent existence nourished not by the Word of God itself but by the historical objectifications of the Word of God, if not entirely by purely secular elements; this in opposition to the actual fulfilment of the interpretation of Holy Scripture in the Community. In this way the Reformers' position was lost, a position in which the idea of the Church was based on the proclamation of the Word of God, which alone establishes the communities and binds up with the Church. To begin once more at this point would open the way to a clear theological definition of the concept of Church history: Church history as the history of the interpretation of Holy Scripture.

III

What can this definition accomplish?

1. It defines the sphere of Church history. Church history fulfils its function where the witness of Jesus Christ is heard in the interpretation of Holy Scripture. The objection to this definition that it places the

Scriptures at the beginning of the history of the Church, whereas, in fact, the origin of the New Testament canon is a product of Church history, does not hold water. The fact still holds good that, from the moment of the Church's birth in the Easter event, it has entered into history, and exists in history by virtue of the witness of Jesus Christ fulfilled in the interpretation of Holy Scripture, which means in the first place the Old Testament. To that extent at any rate the study of the origins of the New Testament writings belongs, strictly speaking, to the study of Church history, since it is nothing else but the witness of Jesus Christ in the interpretation of Holy Scripture. Nevertheless, in so far as the formation of the New Testament canon is a single and finally settled fact, and, as the continuation of the living voice of the Apostles, has come to possess as its actual basis a constitutive and normative significance, it is not only justifiable but imperative to distinguish the interpretation of the New Testament from Church history as a branch of study and to place them in a contrasting relationship. Hence the witness to Jesus Christ contained in the New Testament must be fundamentally distinguished from all subsequent interpretation of Holy Scripture, since the latter is, strictly speaking, only the interpretation of the Apostolic interpretation, the attestation of the Apostolic witness to Jesus Christ. What distinguishes the New Testament canon from all subsequent facts of Church history is a historical facticity which can be explained by no historical researches into its origin, any more than the unique character of the history of Jesus Christ can be explained by such means.

Hence, to abandon the term 'Holy Scripture' in order to define Church history as the history of the Word of God, or of the witness to Christ, or in some other way, is not a course to be recommended, since it immediately introduces a critical element into the definition. Failure to recognize that the unity of Holy Scripture by itself and with Church history constitutes an entity which is full of tensions is as much to be avoided as the other extreme of somehow or other getting rid of this tension as a precondition of the historian's work. The acceptance of the unity of the whole of the Old and New Testament writings, a unity which is by no means on the surface, does not militate against the dogmatic presupposition, indispensable for the Church historian, of the recognition of the revelation of God in Jesus Christ, since, apart from this presupposition, it is not possible to perceive the essential nature of Church history. It is, however, as much a relevant historical presupposition, as it is an incontestable historical fact, that in all its varied aspects, Church history has as its presupposition the unity of the entire canon, however it may be interpreted.

Another objection to the proposed definition is that the concept of 'interpretation' seems too restricted and intellectual to embrace the wide range of manifestations whose part in Church history cannot be denied. But interpretation of Holy Scripture does not find expression only in preaching and doctrine, and certainly not primarily in commentaries; but also in doing and suffering. Interpretation of Holy Scripture finds expression in ritual and prayer, in theological work and in personal decisions, in Church organization and ecclesiastical politics, in the temporal power of the Papacy, and in the ecclesiastical pretensions of rulers, in wars of religion, and in works of compassionate love, in the promotion of a Christian culture and in a cloistered renunciation of the world, in martyrdoms and witch-burnings. By the term 'interpretation' we are to understand a relation to Holy Scripture which is not only spoken but unspoken, not only conscious but also unconscious, not only positive but also negative. For, wherever a relation to Holy Scripture exists—a situation which is almost universal for the West— there premonitory signs indicate that historical events stand in such a way under the influence of this historical principle that they invariably become events of Church history.

The concept of interpretation has therefore a range whose extent cannot be grasped, in so far as even phenomena which are apparently entirely secular and lie outside the ecclesiastical sphere, in virtue of an existing, if hidden, relation to Holy Scripture, become phenomena in Church history. On the other hand, the concept of interpretation is a very restricted one, in so far as it is exclusively in virtue of this spoken or unspoken, conscious or unconscious, positive or negative relation to Holy Scripture, that an event becomes an event of Church history. It is the task of the Church historian to uncover this relation of the event to Holy Scripture, and to assign its place and estimate its significance. Activity of this kind presupposes in those who engage in it that they have their own specific understanding of Holy Scripture. It is thus, to a certain extent, denominationally determined, although in no way denominationally limited; that is to say, this encounter of Church history with Scripture cannot annul the authoritative claims of Tradition. The work of the Church historian is not therefore free from signs of tendentious subjectivity if he refrains as far as possible from displaying his own theological knowledge; but only if he strives to the utmost to reach a satisfactory interpretation of Holy Scripture. In so far as he is and remains a disciplined historian he will be in no danger, in view of the vast company of witnesses to Christ in the history of the Church, of supposing himself to be in possession of a final and exclusive understanding of Holy Scripture; this need not imply that he should renounce any exercise of his individual judgement and relapse into mere relativism.

Hence the work of the Church historian involves certain consequences. In the first place, his horizon must be as wide as possible, calling for the closest contact with secular historical studies. On the other hand, the guiding principle in his researches must always be the specifically theological viewpoint of the interpretation of Holy Scripture. The consequence will be that the Church historian must pay a greater attention to the history of the interpretation of Holy Scripture in a stricter sense than has hitherto been the case; this may be either by a more thoroughgoing use of Church history in the interpretation of individual passages, or by throwing light on the history of the understanding of individual sections or thought-patterns; this may possibly take place, not only in theological literature, but also in its practical interpretation of the event itself. Even a slight attempt to sketch the outlines of a history of the interpretation of the Old Testament, or of the conception of the imitation of Jesus Christ, or of New Testament eschatology in Church history, should make us realize how fruitful, yet how immense, are the tasks here involved. The one-sidedness which the study of Church history has hitherto displayed in emphasizing the history of dogma must therefore be corrected by a fresh attention to the history of hermeneutics and the exegesis of Scripture.

2. The proposed definition also defines the nature of Church history. Church history is that which lies between us and the revelation of God

in Jesus Christ. It separates and unites, obscures and illuminates, accuses and enriches. Through it alone has the witness to Jesus Christ come down to us. To that extent it belongs to the event of revelation. It no more gives us a direct approach to Holy Scripture, than it gives us a direct approach to Jesus Christ. In any case, the fact that Church history as Tradition lies between us and Jesus Christ has a part to play in the understanding and interpretation of Holy Scripture, even if and when we are unconscious of it. This role of Tradition becomes fatal when it replaces the understanding and interpretation of Holy Scripture and becomes a substitute for Scripture itself. The legitimate function of Tradition in the interpretation of Holy Scripture is to serve as a sign-post to Jesus Christ. This means that Tradition is genuine when it does not foreclose the point of decision, and when understanding does not mean remembering but representation, in virtue of the complete self-realization of Christ in present living union with the believer through the proclamation of the Word. Where this understanding of faith takes place, the time element in Church history disappears, and present living union with Jesus Christ is established; not in virtue of some clever method of interpretation, but in virtue of the fact that the witness to Jesus Christ is the living and creative Word of God himself, here and now. Thus, at the same time, Church history becomes irrelevant, at any rate for the believer, yet not as though it had never existed. In present living union with Jesus Christ the believer becomes contemporary with the whole history of the Church and enters into the communion of saints, which transcends not only space but time.

Church history as the history of the interpretation of Holy Scripture is thus the history of the continued living presence of that same Jesus Christ who was crucified under Pontius Pilate and rose again. We cannot escape the paradoxical assertion of the contemporaneity of the past if we would avoid tearing asunder the two sides of the Church's nature, in that she is at the same time both a historical and an eschato-logical entity. An interpretation of the New Testament statements about the Church will demonstrate the futility of any attempt to set history and eschatology, as they appear in the history of the Church, in opposition to one another, and to explain Church history as a substitute for the delayed Parousia. In view of the fact that in the

Church is to be found the full meaning of the interpretation of Holy Scripture, she is, as a historical entity, also an eschatological entity. The Word of God, being at the same time both a historical and an eschatological event, is the sole basis of the continuity and unity of Church history; it does not, however, guarantee the permanence of any kind of organization, institution, religious group or system.

It is not the Word of God which, in the history of the Church, is subject to change and movement—Jesus Christ is the same yesterday, today, and for ever—but the interpretation of this same Word of God in all the heights and depths of the world and human existence. This movement finds its expression in the manifold developments of recessions and recoveries, of which we cannot fathom the all-comprehending design. It is not moving towards some immanent goal of development, but can only be understood as awaiting that point of time, known only to God, when the course of the Word of God through the world and the number of the elect are completed. From the theological point of view the remarkable thing about this course of events is that the Church, although she remains one and the same, undergoes a manifold change of form; thus the witness to Jesus Christ in the history of the Church does not consist in the mere repetition of Holy Scripture and in imitation of the way in which the disciples followed him; but in interpretation, that is, in ever new usages and forms, thoughts and decisions, sufferings and victories, and hence in an unfolding of the richness and power of the Word of God, and in ever new victories for the hidden kingdom of God.

3. Finally, the proposed definition defines the theological character of Church history as a discipline. The work of the Church historian operates as the radical critical destruction of all that, in the course of Church history, has interposed a barrier between us and Christ, instead of being an interpretation of Holy Scripture pointing to him. It serves, moreover, as a demonstration of the limitless wealth of the Word of God in its interpretation in the world during its passage through history. It therefore ministers to the Church's understanding of itself and its witness, to the extent that we cannot gain this from Scripture alone, but can only discern it from Scripture in history.

2

Confessional Study: Task and Method[1]

I

It is the business of Confessional Study to make a comprehensive survey of the differences existing in contemporary Christendom.

There are three things which need to be emphasized with regard to this very incomplete definition of the task of Confessional study.

1. In the first place, the task of such a study is a *descriptive* one, though it is not confined to that. It is necessary to guard against speculative explanations of differences existing between Confessional groups built on any preconceived ideas; against arbitrary systematization and schematization; and against exaggerating differences for apologetic reasons, or minimizing them for the sake of conciliation. It is rather a matter of getting acquainted with actual situations, from which a concrete, living, and at the same time a distinctive point of view may be obtained. The ideal condition for a study of this kind calls for the closest contact with the life of other Christian communions. It is regrettable that we are able to get information, for instance, about the Russian Orthodox Church, or American Protestantism, only from books; without taking an actual part in their worship, or getting an immediate impression of their beliefs and manner of life. At the same time, the value of direct contact should not be over-estimated. The distance which separates us from one who worships before an ikon is far more than spatial. It would not be diminished, but in some respects actually increased, if we were to find ourselves in personal contact with such a believer. A direct impression is of no use unless one can grasp intelligently the unfamiliar elements in such an impression, and comprehend them in a larger synthesis. World-travel in pursuit of material for Confessional study cannot be a substitute for a basic study of

accessible documents and literary evidence. Nevertheless, an impression gained from immediate contact is of undeniable value in deepening and correcting ideas.

2. In the second place, attention must be directed to the impression created by the term 'differences existing in Christendom'. I have already spoken of the danger of imposing arbitrary systems and schemes, and must also point out that, just as it is part of the task to arrive at a comprehensive view of the essence of the main Confessional types, so, too, must the difficulties presented by the facts be taken seriously. Anyone who has even a superficial idea of the nature of the most circumscribed of the Confessional churches, the Roman Catholic Church, is to some extent aware of the difficulty of comprehending the multiplicity of its aspects under one descriptive epithet. Catholicism in its German expression—not to mention the variations we find in Italian, Spanish or North American Catholicism—does not display the full extent of its manysidedness. The wide variety, moreover, is to be seen in what we designate as 'Protestant', or 'Lutheran', or 'Reformed'. Confessional study of the differences between the communions also involves the internal differences in individual communions.

3. It is the task of Confessional study to make a comprehensive survey of the differences between the communions in *contemporary* Christendom. This involves a limitation. Confessional study is not concerned with every doctrinal controversy and the formation of every religious body in the course of Church history. It is not the business of Confessional study to portray the Marcionite or the Novatianist churches, since these are phenomena which belong only to the past. But concentration on contemporary denominations and ecclesiastical fellowships does not only mean a lightening of the task, but also an increase of its difficulty. For we are not concerned with describing historically complete phenomena. A Confessional study of the Eastern Church, for example, which does not take into consideration its present situation and problems, and hence leaves out of its purview the present ecclesiastical situation in Soviet Russia, is, to say the least, incomplete. It would be just as unsatisfactory to confine the study of Roman Catholicism to the situation at the time of the Council of Trent, or that of the Reformation Churches to the character which

they had developed in the sixteenth century. Yet such a glance at the contemporary situation discloses difficulties—in the first place—of a purely informatory nature. I need only refer again to Russia for a reminder of the limitations which impede any kind of reliable insight into contemporary denominational problems. Nor is this only the case in Russia. The difficulties are of a universal nature. To arrive at a comprehensive grasp of what is going on and of the changes in the Ecumenical movement and to keep up to date with them is a task which exceeds the ability of any single individual. Even when conditions are most favourable for obtaining information, the mere assemblage of a mass of isolated details does not necessarily yield a satisfactory picture of the whole. When attention is directed to our own contemporary scene, the task of distinguishing between essentials and non-essentials, and of recognizing the really dominating trends and arriving at a satisfactory estimate of the situation as a whole, is one whose accomplishment is difficult because the lack of sources prevents us from getting sufficiently close to our subject. Furthermore, it would be a distortion and a simplification of the task of Confessional study to confine it to a mere statistical analysis of church conditions on the Ecumenical scene. However, it is still worth while to try to understand the contemporary state of historically conditioned entities, their contemporary forms of expression of life, growth, and processes of change. Even though a communion presents the appearance of being a completely closed and unchangeable community, it would have ceased to live if the contemporary understanding of how it had reached that condition were not able to be the object of Confessional study. But this opens up for us another aspect of Confessional study.

II

Confessional study has the task of communicating a historical understanding of the differences in contemporary Christendom.

The Church is a historical entity. Its division into various denominational churches is the result of historical events. In order to understand the nature of modern denominations it is necessary to be acquainted with their historical origins. And this is not just because it is a matter of historical education to know the history of confessions as well as their contemporary form. Rather, strictly speaking, only historical study can make possible a real understanding of the denominations as they exist at present. Moreover, the history of the denominations does not only provide the panorama which illuminates their timeless nature; it is only a knowledge of their origin and development that reveals the real nature of the individual denominations. To take a highly important example, unless the historical factors which led to the special development of the West are studied, it will never be possible to understand the nature of the separation between the Eastern Orthodox Churches and the Roman Catholic Church, nor the essential character of either. Nowhere as in the study of the Confessions is the reason so obvious why theologians pursue the study of the history, both of the Church and theology, not as a hobby, but for the sake of theology, and that means for the sake of the Church as well. Through Confessional study even one who is uninterested in history can recognize the inescapable significance of their history for both Church and theology today. Such study is, however, concerned with the results of Church history operative in the contemporary scene. To their own traditions the individual denominations owe their unity and permanence, but they fall too easily into the danger of being fettered by their own past. It is a disturbing question whether the churches are in a position to confront modern man with the question of truth, since they parade in the more or less outmoded dress of bygone centuries.[1]

The problem of the relation between Church and History obtrudes itself in various ways. In the first place when we consider the individual churches themselves. Embedded in the general history of the Church, each Confessional church has its own history, to which it owes its own special character. This involves the question of the origin and beginnings of the churches in question. With regard to the Reformation churches this question seems to be easily answered by a reference to the sixteenth century; but the origin of Catholicism raises a far more difficult question. Taking only rough milestones as examples, are we to assign its origin to the pontificate of Leo I; or to the third century under Cyprian; or to the turn of the second century with Ignatius of Antioch, or in the First Epistle of Clement; or are we to find the origins of Catholicism in the New Testament itself? It is clear that on the answer to this question depends the answer to the question of the nature of Catholicism. But no Confessional church can remain content with a more or less plausibly determined point of origin somewhere in the general history of the Church. Limiting our enquiry to the churches of the Reformation, it is clear that they regard themselves as the Church of Jesus Christ, but not, however, as a new foundation of the sixteenth century. That is to say, they know themselves to be inseparably linked with the founding of the Church in the Apostolic age. Thus, if each of the Confessional churches regards itself as sprung from the same historical origin, then the critical point of the problem of the relation between Church and history is the necessity of understanding its relation to the one historical origin of the Church. The divergences in the Confessional churches are the result, therefore, of the formation of traditions which cause the one historical origin of the Church to be seen in a different light. Hence it is in the historically conditioned increasing proliferation of traditions that the specific characteristics which differentiate the Confessional churches are revealed. This raises the question of the development of the Church in history; it raises the question of a normative conclusion to that development, together with the possibility of further change; and it raises the question of a barrier against uncontrolled changes, and of the guarantees of the permanent identity of the Church in history. To all these problems a different answer is given by the individual Confessional churches, and their doctrine and discipline depend upon these different answers.

III

It is the aim of Confessional study to give an account of the nature of the individual contemporary denominations, both with reference to their inner unity and their manysidedness, and to their mutual relations, their differences and their common ground.

What we have said in Section I about the descriptive task with regard to the differences in contemporary Christendom, and in Section II about the importance of taking the historical aspect into consideration, may help towards a conception of the essential nature of the denominations. This permits, and indeed requires, a purposive selection from the vast mass of historical and contemporary denominational material. Completeness is not attainable, either from ecclesiastical or from historical analysis. The ideal of completeness would be meaningless even in a separate study of the nature and history of a single contemporary church. In a Confessional study the only kind of contemporary and historical material which calls for examination is that which throws light on the nature of individual churches. Of course this leaves open a wide range of selection; but the guiding aim must be an understanding of the whole. In its presentation the selected material must not appear as a collection of isolated facts, but should allow the inner connection to appear. We must now continue our study of the nature of the individual churches from two angles.

1. It would be a mistake to conceive of the task of Confessional study as only concerned with the differences between the churches. Such a study presupposes a much more difficult problem, and one which, from the point of method, must not be separated from it, namely, the task of discovering the essential inner unity of the individual churches, with all their manysidedness. While keeping this aim in view, it is always necessary to consider the contemporary aspect of the situation, as well as the aspect of church history involved. The difficulty of defining the historical character of a Confessional church without violating history or adopting an uncritical attitude towards one's own position, may be somewhat clearer in the case of Lutheranism than, for example, in the case of Roman Catholicism. In spite of the considerable development which Lutheranism has undergone, together with Protestantism as a whole, since the Reformation, how is it possible to define its character—if it is not going to be done in a merely positivistic way from the *Book of Concord*—by entirely ignoring the problems and changes which the modern age has introduced? If it is wrong for this reason to limit oneself to the development of the doctrine of a church with reference to the classical dogmatic definitions and symbols, such a limitation of the task of denominational study should be rejected for another reason as well.

2. What is involved is a comprehensive understanding of the individual Confessional churches, and not merely a description and comparison of different doctrinal systems. Denominational study can only avoid the danger of erroneously describing churches whose distinguishing characteristic may not be a doctrinal one, if it takes into consideration all the ways in which the life of the churches finds expression, that is to say, their worship, constitution, piety, morality, and culture, instead of merely paying attention to doctrine. When denominational study succeeds in throwing light on the inner connection between dogma, worship, constitution, piety, morality, and culture, there may be some hope of arriving at an understanding of the essential character of the individual churches. In no other way can a proper understanding of the gravity of the differences between the denominations be reached; at the same time, however, the way can be opened to a critical discussion of them, enabling the question to be faced which is raised by the contradiction between the existence of exclusive Confessional Churches and the common credal confession of one Holy, Catholic, and Apostolic Church.

IV

It is the task of Confessional study to approach the problem, both in its totality and in detail, from the question of the origin of Confessional differences.

In Section II it was suggested that the root of the Confessional problem lies in the relation between the Church and history. In order to derive value from this proposition from the point of view of method, and to establish a conception of Confessional study as a theological discipline, we must look more closely at this relation between the Church and history.

Its connection with history is an essential element in the nature of the Church. As the Church of Jesus Christ it stands or falls by its once-for-all origin which, as the eschatological revelational activity of God in history, stands out as superior to all subsequent Church history. The Church continues to exist in history in virtue of its witness to this once-for-all revelation event, and its interpretation of it as continuing in its own contemporary history in the present. The significance which the Person of Jesus Christ and the Holy Scriptures possess for the Church, and which is summed up in the epithet applied to the Church in the Creed, 'Apostolic', is fundamental for the Church's own and inalienable connection with history. Since the relation of the Church to its origin is absolutely decisive for its existence in the world today, the problem of the relation between the Church and history clearly ranks as the main problem for any attempt to describe the Confessional churches and the Confessional question in general. The nature of the Eastern churches, of Roman Catholicism, and of the Protestant churches, has its roots in a relation to the origin of the Church which has differed from time to time, and hence in a basic conception of the relation between Church and history which has similarly varied from time to time.

The central theological importance of this question becomes clear when we recognize that it is concerned with the actual realization of the once-for-all revelation of God in Jesus Christ in its relation to the origin of the Church as the event upon which the very existence of the Church as such depends. It is here that the question of the relation of the Church to history is presented in its sharpest form. It is over the idea of the actual realization of the historical once-for-all revelation event that the different churches are divided. It is therefore understandable that the meaning of the Eucharist should be a central feature of the discussions between the churches. Here the question of the actual realization of the revelation event assumes its most acute form. The answer to it affects the very existence of the Church in the world; it is decisive for its influence upon world-history and the dialogue with world-history.

The depth of the problem of 'Church and history' reveals the close connection between the Confessional and the hermeneutic problem.

What is Christian and what is not, and what, therefore, is true for Christian belief, and what is not true, must be shown by its connection with the event which, as revelation, constitutes the beginning of Christianity. If, then, this connection is a historical one, its realization is not to be found in repetition, but in interpretation. The truth of this can be seen most clearly in the task of proclamation. This does not consist in the repetitive recitation of sacred texts, but in interpretation, that is to say, in translation into another language, into another age with other modes of thought, into continually different situations. This is why sermons must be continually renewed, and the work of theology be carried on unceasingly. The conception of truth as historically conditioned is thus bound up with the variable element inseparable from the category of interpretation. Hence Christianity is historical, that is, subject to continual change. How the fundamental question of truth is presented and how it is answered in actual individual cases, will be decided by a more exact definition of the pattern of interpretation, making clear the relation between the variability of the interpretation and the identity of that which is interpreted.

The bearing of these considerations upon the Confessional problem should be clear. Not every change, alteration, or difference, is, as such, a departure from the truth. Apart from such possibility of change the Church could not exist in history, nor could preaching and theology be possible. At the same time this involves the consequence that, not only without a historical, but also without a contemporary manysidedness, the existence of the Church in the world is impossible. This variability and manysidedness is not a regrettable concession to an imperfect world, but is implicit in the nature of the historically determined truth by which the Church lives. It is a matter of dispute to what extent this manysidedness and variability should be allowed to operate within the hermeneutic process; under dispute is the question of the standards which should determine the necessary degree of adherence to the truth in view of the inevitable historical changes; and which should decide the relevance of interpretation, and where the boundaries should be drawn between the true Church and heresy. In the nature of things it is a difficult task to decide these questions, and to reach a clear understanding of the point where, for the sake of truth, differences within Christianity may be regarded as wholly relevant; where they may be regarded as irrelevant but tolerable; and where, finally, they are a divisive element. We shall not be mistaken in accepting the conclusion that not only in the differences themselves, but in our judgements concerning them, error and sin have been operative. From the outset, then, we must accept the possibility that not all Confessional decisions have been made for the sake of the truth, and that, conversely, in the course of the Church's history many decisions which, for the sake of the truth, ought to have been made, have not been made. This leads to the simple point, that exactly when the Confessional problem is looked at in relation to the question of truth, we should be cautious in accepting the view that a Confessional separation is always a simple decision made in the interest of the truth, and that, from the historical point of view, the struggle for the truth is the sole motive in the formation of a Confessional church. What makes the Confessional problem so difficult is the fact that the question of truth itself can only be decided in the course of interpretation, and hence may assume many forms. Moreover, this question of truth is itself overlaid and concealed by a multitude of other historical factors which, rightly or wrongly, are operative in the rise and development of Confessional churches.

The connection between the hermeneutic and the Confessional problem must be still further amplified. The process of interpretation is not wholly confined to the activities of preaching and theology. In all the manifestations of its life the Church shares in the process of interpretation. Even its laws and constitution give expression to a specific view of the revelation. I know of no other means of arriving at an understanding of the special problem presented by Church history and the history of the Confessional churches than the category of interpretation. It embraces the problem of the relation between the Church and history, and that in their theological aspect. It seems to me that from this inner connection between the hermeneutic and the Confessional problem, the way lies open to a theologically relevant investigation of the essential nature of the main Confessional types. In this way it is possible to avoid a mere external, more or less incidental, collection of material relating to denominational study. An insight into the pattern of the Confessional problem throws light on the special pattern of each individual church. From this it becomes clear that, whatever the differences, each Confession has in the last resort the same questions, and hence their problems present a similar pattern. Thus, while the account based on denominational studies is strictly concerned with what unites the Confessions in so far as it is a divisive factor, and with what separates them in so far as it is a unitive factor, we find ourselves at the critical point where the encounter must be carried through with the utmost seriousness, and where the account itself involves the question of decision, and thus where the study of the Confessions and their historical form is driven to Holy Scripture itself.

Thus any description resulting from denominational studies presupposes that the following points of view have been taken into account in the study of the individual Confessions:

1. In the first place, the historical character of the church under consideration must be firmly kept in mind, in order that we may have a clear view of its history and of the basic features of the contemporary situation resulting therefrom.

2. Next, it is necessary to emphasize the conception which the church under consideration holds of the historical unrepeatability of the revelation, and by what historical standards it regards the historicity of the revelation as assured. Above all, its understanding of the revelation and of the relation of Scripture to tradition must be stated.

3. Since its relation to that once-for-all revelation is fulfilled in interpretation, an interpretation that is a translation into another language, and other modes of thought, each church must be asked what are its prevailing language and thought-categories, that is to say, principally, what is its position with regard to metaphysical and meta-historical problems. Above all, this involves the relation in the church under consideration of theology and philosophy, and its general picture of the world and of history.

4. For every church the central problem is its conception of the way in which from time to time the once-for-all historical revelation may be actually realized. Here something needs to be said about the connection between Christology and Soteriology, of the Word and sacraments, as well as the question of the cultus and of piety.

5. Nevertheless, the Church does not merely exist from time to time. Duration and permanence are of the essence of history; in the historical time-succession something remains constant. Hence every church is concerned with its continuity in history. This determines what the church in question thinks about the nature of the Church,

about the nature of office and constitution, and about the fundamental questions of church law and its pattern in details.

6. Finally, every church must be asked what it thinks about the interaction of church- and world-history, and what form the relation between them takes in its own life. Under this head come the questions about the existence of individual believers in the secular world, about the relation between Church and State, about the interchange between Church and politics, Church and culture, and finally the attitude of the Church in question towards eschatology.

Such an outline of Confessional studies has the merit of presenting the whole picture from one central point of view. We need not fear that what is here suggested might result in the arbitrary imposition upon individual churches of a pattern which does not correspond to their real character, because this analysis is the result not of a generalization from one particular Confessional pattern, but of an insight into the nature of the Confessional problem as such, based on an enquiry into the relation between Church and history. Of course, while the general similarity of these insights remains constant, the special emphases and aspects must suit the Confession under discussion. The pattern of enquiry outlined above is, nevertheless, sufficiently flexible to allow room for these differences; on the other hand, it is firm enough to ensure that the variety of material and of problems to be dealt with does not get out of control; it also ensures that by keeping our attention always fixed on this central problem, our concern should always be directed towards what really matters. It must certainly be acknowledged that the conceptions upon which this pattern of analysis is based are derived from a study of the Confessional problem from a Protestant point of view. From this point of view alone is it possible to get the full significance of the relation between Church and history into clear perspective; and similarly it is only from the Protestant point of view that the full implication of the Confessional problem can be clearly seen. When it is understood in this way, it raises the demand for a non-partisan, completely factual study.

V

*It is the business of Confessional study to show that no attempt to define the
nature of the Confessional churches can dispense with the exercise of criticism,
and therefore such a study involves decisions ranging over the internal life of
the churches, and over the Ecumenical, secular, and eschatological fields.*

Confessional study needs to make use of criticism from two points of
view. The need for critical decisions arises both from the existence of
the churches alongside and in opposition to one another, and from the
task of understanding aright the essential nature of the individual
churches. This does not exclude Confessional decision which has been
made before the Confessional studies are undertaken. On the contrary,
such a basic decision is essential.

It is conceivable that a determined opponent of every kind of
Christian organization might make his own basic decision of a kind
which was radically critical of all Confessional studies, and produce a
study which would be worthy of attention. It is also conceivable that an
inter-Confessional position might be adopted by someone who, impressed both by the deficiencies and the attractions which he found in
all the churches, might feel himself compelled to suspend judgement,
and to renounce any decision for one of the churches. Such a basic
decision could entail the presentation of a clearly envisaged and decisive
standpoint for a denominational study, so far as a thoroughgoing
critical attitude was involved. In this case the question would arise
whether anyone who thought that Christian faith required him to
adopt an anti-Confessional position was not unaware of the meaning
of the Church for the Christian life, and whether his separation from
any Confessionally characterized church did not indicate that he was
unaware of the relevance of Confessional study for the Christian faith.
For how can it be supposed that anyone is concerned with the Christian
faith, but that the Church is a matter of indifference to him, and that
therefore as a Christian, in face of the diametrical contrast between
Catholicism and Protestantism, he can adopt a position of neutrality?
An anti-Christian, anti-Confessional study might possibly be more

useful than a Christian anti-Confessional one. Anyhow it is impossible to conceive of a Confessional study whose author again and again changed his position to accord with the denomination under study. This would involve that each denomination was so exclusively described from its own standpoint that the entire study would fall apart into a series of descriptions of individual denominations. Such an apparently ideal objectivity, apart from its psychological impossibility, would be an undesirable presupposition for any denominational study. It would lead to an uncritical description which misunderstood the real task.

Under normal conditions a basic decision for a specific church is presupposed. This need not prejudice the factuality of the description given of other churches, although this danger is always present when, in its description, a church only applies criticism to other churches, but remains wholly uncritical of itself. Such a Confessional study lays itself open to the charge of being wholly polemical or apologetic. It may abound in material and ideas, but necessarily ignores the problems involved and will ultimately prove unfruitful.

Only such a form of basic decision is completely in accord with the purpose of Confessional study as is open to the test of self-criticism. A Confessional study with a basic Confessional decision, but which is at the same time capable of critical decisions, can only be Protestant; and as Protestant it *must* be a critical study. A Protestant Confessional study will make no secret of the criticism of other churches which the facts demand. Its criticism will be as thoroughgoing as possible, so far as is consistent with justice to other churches; although Protestantism cannot receive similar treatment from them. This means that a Protestant denominational study will at the same time allow the criticism of other churches to be directed against itself. It will, therefore, be supremely critical of itself, realize that from the essential nature of its own position it must attach the highest importance to criticism. A Protestant Confessional study is capable of the task of criticism if, and so far as, it subjects its own Confession to the judgement of the Word of God.

The range of such critical studies is indicated by such descriptive titles as 'the internal life of the Church', 'Ecumenical', 'Secular', and 'Eschatological'. A study of this kind is concerned with the internal decisions of the Church in so far as it considers its own position in the light of its relation to truth, and recognizes what is inconsistent in its own Churchliness. It is concerned with Ecumenical decisions in so far as it reveals the factors which both divide and unite the churches, undistracted by illusions; in so far, too, as it takes into account with all seriousness that hostility to Christ, not to be overcome by human endeavour, which exists in Christendom today, and in this way prepares for Ecumenical openness. It is concerned with secular decisions in so far as they throw light on the Confessional background of the great ideological controversies and brutal struggles for power on the contemporary scene. Of these movements, beside Catholic Rome, North America in virtue of its Protestant origins, and Soviet Russia, so strangely involved in the heritage of the Eastern Church with its contradictions and solidarity, are the leading representatives. Finally, it is concerned with an eschatological decision in so far as it has to do with questions which, in spite of human error and guilt, relate to eternal salvation for the individual and for the world.

3

The Problem of the Confessions

I

The necessity of struggling with the various deviationist forms of the Christian faith is as old as Christianity itself, and is an essential feature of the existence of the Church in history. The Christian proclamation has always been in danger of falsification, and the unity and purity of the Church have been threatened by the rise of heretical and schismatic communions. This situation is already reflected in the New Testament. It would give us an entirely false picture of the beginnings of the Christian Church to represent its development as starting from a clear and undisputed understanding of Christian orthodoxy, and a period of untroubled unity and purity, followed later by a decline owing to heresies whose unorthodoxy had been established in principle from the outset. Such a picture of the history of the early Church is the result of reading back into the past the Church's idealization of its own beginnings, and it has subsequently exercised a considerable influence on Church history. This view of the early history of the Church was especially challenged by Walter Bauer.[1] His argument that certain features of Christianity which were later condemned as heretical were in many cases older than so-called orthodoxy, may be unconvincing and disputable in many details; nevertheless it is undoubtedly true that the beginnings of Church history exhibit a bewildering process of fermentation, resulting in a definite clarification of the orthodox position, and a decision concerning those forms of belief which should be regarded and treated as heretical.

This consolidation of the early Catholic Church and of its basic standards could not prevent the continuing existence and growth of rival Christian communities, nor the rise of new ones. Christian Gnosticism, the subject of the earliest controversies, may not have possessed suffi-

47

cient strength to create early ecclesiastical communities. Nevertheless the early Catholic Church found itself in conflict with other numerous, and so far as their expansion was concerned important, rival churches, namely, the Marcionite, Montanist, Novatianist, Donatist, and other schismatic churches. The fact that the mother Church, after the Constantinian turning-point, was completely victorious over the rival heretical churches, and obliterated as far as possible all traces of them, has made it difficult to arrive at a satisfactory picture of the actual situation of the Church in the second and third centuries. It is hardly possible to overestimate the extent and importance of the separated church communities at that period. Moreover the development under and after Constantine shows clearly enough that, even with the help of the State, it was far from easy to cope with this situation. The old heretical and schismatic communities displayed a remarkably tough resistance in their conflict with the State so closely bound up with the mother Church. Finally, in spite of more or less skilful measures on the part of the Establishment to ensure the unity of the Church, new important separated churches came into existence, such as the Arian Germanic provincial churches, and the Monophysite and Dyophysite national churches.

In its endeavour to preserve its unity, the Empire may have succeeded in remaining actually free at its centre from fresh ecclesiastical divisions; it was not able, however, to prevent the characteristic conjunction of ecclesiastical and national secession taking place in its outlying provinces. As a result of the Constantinian conversion the concept and actuality of the Ecumenical unity of Christendom were so closely bound up with and limited to the Empire, that the churches which grew up beyond the Empire, or which existed in the provinces that had broken away from the Empire, inevitably developed a doctrinal opposition to the imperial Church. The unity of the imperial Church was preserved at the cost of a considerable diminution of its geographical extent. Moreover, the imperial Church did not, in any case, owe its unique predominance in the subsequent history of the Church solely to its spiritual strength, but also to its political and cultural connections. The disappearance, that is to say, the conversion to Catholicism, of the Arian provincial churches, was part of the development of the states which had emerged from the migrations of peoples within the Empire. The Frankish kingdom, breaking away from this conglomeration of states, opened the way for the triumphant progress of the Catholic Church in the West. On the other hand, the extirpation or decay of the heretical churches in the east and south of the Empire was the result of the great Arabian movements of peoples. The connection between these events must be kept in mind if we are to understand why the Church in the rest of the Empire was no longer seriously threatened by the emergence of separatist heretical churches, and why, as the result of the great struggle for the unity of the Church, the future confirmed her claim to be the sole successor of the ancient Church. To that extent then it is clear that in no small degree something like a Confessional problem existed in the ancient Church.

What effect did this have on the theological treatment of this problem in the ancient Church? Considered in detachment, there would have been abundant opportunity and material for a Confessional study. But the very idea of Confessional study at that time would be an anachronism. It is our firm presupposition that no form of Confessional study could have been possible at that period. But it may be instructive to examine the reasons for this.

1. Of course there is no lack of controversial literature. A considerable amount of early church writing was devoted to the refutation of heresies, and hence provides to some extent a description of their characteristics. Nevertheless these activities were, without exception, directly controversial.

2. The conception of the Church which prevailed in the early Church did not admit of a Confessional problem in the modern sense. In the first place, it was sufficiently flexible and unfettered by centripetal institutional factors to prevent the lines between internal matters of dispute and doctrinal causes of division from being too sharply drawn. By no means all so-called heresies in the early Church led to the formation of schismatic communions. On the other hand, the concept of the Church was so absolute that the plural ἐκκλησίαι could only mean individual churches, and could not imply the existence of separated Confessional churches. It was impossible to call anything a church that lay outside the Catholic Church. Separation from the one Church

could only be the work of Satanic powers. From such a standpoint it could not be admitted that the Church was actually divided, and hence the theological problem involved in such a possibility did not come into view.

3. This absoluteness of the conception of the Church was reinforced by the ecclesiastical policy and legislation of the Christianized Empire. In spite of the fact that the Great Church was the only one legally recognized, and that membership of it was compulsory, heretical communions did not immediately cease to exist; but their diminution was the result of their illegality. They were driven into hiding. Thus the original doctrinal conception of heresy became imbued with both a sociological and a political element. By its very nature the heretical church community seemed to have lost its vital connection with the people and the State, and became a proscribed and politically suspect minority. Conversely, the conception of orthodoxy became imbued in a similar way with the sociological pattern of the national Church as it gathered in the masses, and with the political actuality of an existing State Church. It is obvious that in such a climate the problem of schism could no longer be of any practical significance, or become the object of theological concern.

4. Nevertheless, although separatist churches of some size did, in spite of everything, come into existence, this only happened either beyond the boundaries of the Empire, or in those border provinces where the Empire was not able to control the centrifugal tendencies of national Churches. Thus the doctrinal separation became at the same time a political, ethnic, and geographical one. The consequence of this was that the actually existing church divisions, sheltered as they were behind geographical, ethnic, and political boundaries, no longer constituted a pressing ecclesiastical and theological problem, and an intensive confrontation became superfluous

II

It is this result of the development of the ancient Church which gives its character to the situation in the Middle Ages. This is why the history of the medieval Church, at least in its first half, is surprisingly free from the problem of schism. There are various reasons why this legacy of the ecclesiastical policy of the Christianized Roman Empire survived, even through the disastrous break away caused by the movements of peoples, the dissolution of the western Roman Empire, and the shift of the political centre of gravity to the Germanic north. It will suffice to recall the unrivalled position of Rome in the west; this, coupled with its cultural superiority over the young Germanic peoples, intellectually undistinguished, and devoted to the German idea of an exclusive national and State church, prevented the rise of fresh church divisions and even slighter heretical movements. Not until the peak of the medieval period was past did the threat of heretical movements become really serious; but from then onward it quickly became a rushing torrent, first with the Cathari and Waldenses, and finally with Wycliffe and Huss, to mention only the most familiar instances. These movements were part of the increasing diversity which accompanied the beginnings of the dissolution of medieval western unity; they were from the first stigmatized as illegal and politically suspect, a consequence of the ecclesiastical legislation of the late Roman Empire. It was due to the surprising tenacity of these medieval heresies that, in spite of the most atrocious measures directed to their extermination, their propagation continued as an uncontrollable underground movement. In one case, that of the Hussite movement, a limited measure of toleration and recognition was arrived at, entailing, however, an ethnic and geographical segregation. The national element implicit in the Hussite movement helps us to understand the otherwise incredible fact that the Church so far relented towards the heretic as to seek at least a *modus vivendi* by granting the Cup to the laity.

Thus towards the end of the Middle Ages there existed in the western Church something of the nature of a Confessional problem; its extent was however limited, and it was screened from observation partly by the proscription of sects as illegal, and partly by the geographical isolation of a separatist church of a definitely national character. Nevertheless, this had brought about no change in the absolute conception of the Church; on the contrary it had only been intensified in the meantime by the evolution of the centralized Papal system. It is indeed valuable to observe that its controversy with the medieval

heresies provided the Catholic Church with the occasion for a fundamental rethinking of its own conception of the Church. While it is
remarkable that the great theological compendiums of the Scholastics
contain no systematic treatment of the idea of the Church, it is noteworthy that the first work which deals fully and exclusively with the
nature of the Church is the *Summa de ecclesia* of the Spanish Thomist
Juan de Torquemada, which was directed against the Cathari and the
Waldenses.

Nevertheless, another set of circumstances which rent the unity of
the Church runs through the whole history of the medieval Church;
it must be reckoned as a subsidiary cause of the beginning of a separate
development of the western Church; it was intensified as the result of
this development, and has continued undiminished until the present
time as a Confessional schism: this was the opposition between the
Eastern Orthodox Church on the one side, and the Roman Catholic
Church on the other. While this historically unprecedented schism gave
rise to constantly repeated conflicts with changing fortunes, and to
various attempts at reunion on the part of the well-disposed, and even
to discussions of the theological questions involved, yet, purely from
the point of view of the history of theology, there is no indication here
of any trace of real Confessional study. The two churches were geo-
graphically separated, and, in spite of disputes concerning the imperial
boundaries, and numerous doctrinal and political causes of friction,
they managed to exist peaceably side by side. Although the unrest
caused by the division between the churches never wholly subsided,
and attempts to bring about a reunion were continually made, yet
people became accustomed to the situation, and did not feel deeply
disturbed by it.

III

It was through the Reformation that the full seriousness of the Confessional problem first made itself felt. This does not mean that it had
not existed before, and that only through the Reformation did the
disastrous consequences of schism become manifest. Our historical
retrospect has proved that the contrary was the case. In the history of

the Church in general the demonstrable, doctrinally and institutionally inviolable unity of the one holy Church had never existed. But the disturbing significance of the Reformation for the Confessional problem lay in the fact that it recognized this as being, in any case, not so much a historical as a fundamentally theological problem. It had in consequence recognized that no demonstrable, doctrinally and institutionally guaranteed and inviolable unity of the one holy Church either can or does exist in history. The one holy Church is rather to be regarded as an object of faith, and can therefore only be revealed in its unity and holiness at the final consummation. It was this revolutionizing of the Catholic conception of the Church, together with the central Reformation doctrine of justification by faith alone (*sola fide*), which enabled the full gravity of the Confessional problem to emerge, and not the mere circumstance that new separatist churches had asserted their right to exist alongside of the Roman Church and to challenge its claim to, and conception of, Catholicity. Admittedly, apart from the intensification of this problem, through the change in the conception of the Church, the Reformation had also brought into existence certain startling purely historical facts, which introduced an entirely new phase of the Confessional problem.

1. The adherents of a Confession which had renounced the Roman Catholic doctrines and had, in consequence, been excommunicated by the Roman Church, had succeeded in obtaining legal State recognition alongside of the Roman Church. The principle of the unity and sole authority of the Roman Church as the heir of the Constantinian settlement which had hitherto prevailed throughout the history of the West, was now breached by the Augsburg Peace of Religion. The Augsburg group of Confessional churches, although excluded from the communion of the Roman Church, did not sink into a sectarian form of existence, but succeeded in obtaining, at least in principle, if not actually in every respect, equal standing in State law. State ecclesiastical law had thus emancipated itself from the thousand-year-old tradition of canon law. The laws against heresy, where they should certainly have applied, were suspended. State action was now governed by a different conception of the Church from that of the Roman Church. What kind of conception was it?

That no answer to this question could be found shows the perplexity which had now arisen. To accept the possibility of a cleavage in the Faith would be to surrender the traditional conception of the Church. Minds, however, were far too firmly rooted in this conception to accept the substitution of a purely legal notion of the Church, either by way of a different theological idea of the Church, or an untheological secular one. Hence people avoided speaking of two Churches, since it was felt that this was a contradiction in terms. People spoke instead of two 'religious parties', leaving open what that might imply for the conception of the Church. Yet at the same time, another contradiction was involved. In face of the great breach which had been caused by the legal recognition of the Augsburg group of Confessional churches, a fresh barrier was immediately erected to prevent further inroads. Legal protection had only been granted to the signatories of the Augsburg Confession; the Augsburg Peace of Religion did not apply to the Reformed churches. If the latter wished nevertheless to avail themselves of its provisions, they must come under the shelter of the Augsburg Confession. This legal position involved a contradiction in so far as it did not make clear how two, but not three, religious parties could exist side by side. If the unity principle were once breached, the division of the Church legally established, and the Roman conception of the one holy Catholic Church surrendered, there was no longer a foothold for any kind of theological doctrine of the Church. It was only possible to be guided by practical political considerations, keeping in mind the relations between the powers, and that meant being guided by reasons of State.

The renunciation of a theologically based conception of the Church, but not of a theological conception of a sect, involved, therefore, a still graver contradiction. Everything that was neither Roman nor Lutheran was, moreover, in principle, liable to be treated as a sect, and that meant that its right to exist was denied on the ostensible theological ground that it was heresy. How, then, was it still possible to make use of the idea of heresy, when two religious parties, each charging the other with heresy, both enjoyed state recognition? The one basis which alone could give meaning to the concept of heresy was absent. The idea of a sect now employed as the ground of State recognition had been reduced to a figment. The exclusive validity of the one Truth no longer existed as its opposing counterpart. Moreover, the right to deny recognition to other Confessions had become doubtful. Although at first there was a refusal to admit the fact, it was impossible, out of the desire to maintain the unity of the Church, to continue the Age of Constantine.

2. That the Age of Constantine actually persisted for a long time, and very effectively, was connected with the belief that the Confessional problem could be shelved by the old method of geographical and political segregation. The unity of the Church from the point of view of the State might at least be preserved in the individual territories on the principle of *cuius regio eius religio*. The absolute claim of the one Church, once supported by the State, was now split up into the absolute authority of regional and State churches. In this way, in spite of Confessional division, it became possible to ensure within the wide limits of Confessionally united regions the traditional connection between ecclesiastical and political unity, both positively by the development of a cultural pattern, and negatively by denying the validity of dissidents. Yet regional boundaries were an inadequate protection against the Confessional problem. The Confessionally divided territories lay side by side in a strange motley pattern. In view of this regionally chequered pattern the principle of *cuius regio eius religio* was poor consolation. For within the larger confederation of the Empire, in the western culture-complex composed of a myriad intertwined strands, the break-up of the unity of the Church stood revealed as a legal, political, and cultural fact.

3. When we consider the theological aspect of the Confessional problem, now rendered acute through the Reformation, it is instructive to see how the two so-called religious parties came to terms over the problem which had become such an incredibly burning issue. For the Roman Church it was a practical, but not a fundamental problem. It held fast to its absolute claim, in spite of a partial failure of State protection. Although the Roman Church might have to submit to being treated to some extent as a religious party, it firmly maintained its uncompromising claim to be the sole Church, and therefore treated all ecclesiastical bodies which deviated from it as heretical and sectarian, whether or not they had secured the legal recognition of the State as sects.

Protestantism was not in a condition to deal so simply with the Confessional problem. On the one hand it was obliged to guard against being erroneously regarded as a new foundation of the Church. It desired to be known in no other way than as the reformation of the existing Church. On the other hand, the difference between the Protestant and the Catholic conception of the Church went so deep that Protestantism, forced into separation, was, on theological grounds, in no position to make a claim to absolutism corresponding to the Roman Catholic position, borrowed from it, and now directed against it. It was not only the actual course of the Reformation which destroyed the possibility of replacing Roman Catholicism by an Evangelical Catholicism, that is to say, by establishing a similar centralized and absolutist church order. Much rather was this due to the fact that the Reformed conception of the Church already precluded the idea of any such church order by rendering impossible the organization of a universal Church as well as any institutionally guaranteed infallibility. While on the one hand Protestantism, in the territories where it was victorious, was quite prepared to assume the legacy of the Roman Church, on the other hand it was not actually in the position to take over that legacy in its full extent because it had a fundamentally different conception of the Church. The result was that Protestantism only attained an organized form in particular regional churches, and therefore did not, and could not, become a united Evangelical Church. A particular church is unable from its very nature to make a claim to absoluteness, even within its own domain. The Reformation was unable to abandon the dialectic of an invisible and a visible Church as a decisive constituent element in its conception of the Church. This not only involved the recognition of many territorially defined separate churches, but also the acceptance of the fact that the Church universal lay concealed in other Confessional churches.

Was not such a position bound to produce endless differences and divisions in the Church? In fact the history of Protestantism has made such a result disturbingly evident. The Reformed conception of the Church makes it impossible to establish any absolute barrier or any institutional and doctrinal guarantee against further differentiations within Protestantism. In any case, Protestantism, especially in its

Lutheran form, now attempted to avert this undesirable development by drawing up credal statements as a standard, with a view to establishing the unity of the Church exclusively on the basis of unity of doctrine. But, unless the principle of infallibility is transferred to the credal statements, they are just so unable to recover what had been lost through the surrender of the Roman Catholic conception of the Church, namely, freedom from the Confessional problem. In fact, since the Reformation had destroyed the defences behind which Church and theology had been protected from the Confessional problem, that problem now entered upon a new stage in its history. The essential nature of Protestantism entailed that it alone should assume the burden of the Confessional problem. Hence it was incumbent upon Protestantism to establish Confessional study as a branch of theology. The question certainly arises whether it was straightway in a position to recognize the full extent of the problem, and how long it was before Protestantism addressed itself to the task.

The historical reasons for the fact that the change in the Confessional problem brought about by the Reformation was not at once fully realized as a cause for action lie as much in the political as in the ecclesiastical field.

When it is clearly recognized that a necessary connection exists between the change in the Confessional problem caused by the Reformation and the close of the Constantinian period, it becomes possible to realize the full extent of the political, ecclesiastical, cultural, and ethical problems which now come into play. It is necessary to bear this in mind if we are to avoid a hasty condemnation of the attempts at compromise which sought to seal up the opening gap and to erect a barrier against the advancing flood. A historical approach to our subject is necessary if we are to avoid an uncritical admiration for the radical approach, and a fundamental aversion to compromise of any kind. There are situations in history where a compromise has been reached at a considerable sacrifice, involving no dishonour. Who, for instance, taking everything into account, would venture to condemn the Augsburg Peace of Religion?

How far Protestantism itself shrank from allowing free play to the consequences of the change in the Confessional problem, appears in its use of the concept of a sect. It has already been shown that the idea of a sect is a very complicated one, only to be understood from the history of the Confessional problem. In the first place, a doctrinal issue is involved; but it did not remain a purely theological matter. As the result of the link between Church and State it acquired a sociological significance, and definite political and cultural considerations came into play. A sect had by this time come to be regarded as a small illegal religious body, cut off from vital contact with civil and public life in general. This was the meaning of a sect which Protestantism found in existence and accepted. A radical reduction of the concept of a sect to a purely theological category would have had to end in Lutheranism describing the Roman Catholic Church as a sect. This possibility was clearly recognized at the Reformation; but it was not, however, fully carried through. For, in those regions where the Reformation prevailed, it entered upon the heritage of the Roman Church, that is to say, it there became, for all practical purposes, the sole recognized religious authority for the entire population; it became the established Church under the protection of the State, and upon it now devolved the task of controversy with heretical developments. The result of this was that the sociological element in the idea of a sect was taken over and predominated. Whether the religious community in question anywhere had acquired exclusive public legal recognition, became the decisive factor in determining whether it should be designated as a sect. Thus from the Lutheran point of view neither the Roman Church, nor the Eastern Church, nor the Reformed Church, were sects, because, although in many places they occupied the position of a persecuted minority, in specific territories they enjoyed exclusive State support. Thus, we may add, they bore in principle the aspect of a national church, and where, temporarily, this was not the case, they were in principle prepared to assume such a position in the public life of the nation and the State. Hence we certainly get the impression that for a religious community to be designated as a sect did not depend entirely on whether it lacked recognition as the legally constituted Church of a specific territory. A more important factor in the decision seems to have been whether the community in question was, in the main, striving towards such a recognition and regarded it as a theologically sound aim.

Here a distinct doctrinal element entered into the concept of a sect; it was connected with the Protestant position as heir to the historical legacy of the Age of Constantine, and in a wider sense with the relation between Church and the public, Church and the world, Church and history. The emerging Protestant conception of a sect was to that extent related to the Roman Catholic concept, but its consistency was lacking because Protestantism was not in a position to take over similarly the Roman Catholic concept of the Church. This defect in consistency had a theological cause, since the Reformed concept of the Church contained within itself an insoluble empirical antinomy. On the one hand, the distinction between the true and the false Church had always to be kept in mind, lest Confessional distinctions should become merely relative. But on the other hand, the perception of the relation between the visible and the invisible Church prevented Confessional distinctions from becoming absolute in such a manner as to identify the Lutheran Church, say, which was certainly considered to be a true Church, with the Church in general. According to its own understanding of its character the Lutheran Church remained an individual church, and was not in any way a manifestation of the Church universal, which, as such, remained invisible. This antinomy within the concept of the Church made it impossible to deny to the so-called sects what had to be conceded in regard to the other large Confessional churches, namely, that somehow in them also the Church universal was concealed. The question thus arose whether the usual distinction within Protestantism between Church and sect was tenable. That depended on how long the primacy of a Confessional church in a specific territory would continue to exist.

Two things are certain: one is that regarded from the point of view of the Reformed conception of the Church the principle *cuius regio eius religio* is of extremely doubtful validity; the other is that in some respects that principle is firmly rooted historically in the Reformed concept of the Church. During the early stages of the Reformation the free choice of the individual prevailed, and through the emergence of opposing Confessions, the nature of Christian faith as a matter of individual choice, long unrecognized, became apparent. But the situation rapidly changed, and the Reformed church order likewise assumed a compulsory character; the individual's decision was removed from him by the religion which had come to prevail in the land and become the new tradition, and the early movement of Confessional change became stagnant. The Age of Orthodoxy was thenceforward wholly intent on preserving the situation thus reached, and therefore defended the principle *cuius regio eius religio*. The result was that the full force of the Confessional problem was not felt. On the side of the sects, their illegality to some extent served as a protection, and controversy with the other large Confessional churches was in general conducted under the protection of territorial boundaries. Thus a situation of static warfare intervened, and nothing actually happened except the continual strengthening of the established frontier and drawing more strictly the lines of demarcation. But this static warfare was, nevertheless, sufficiently bitter to engage the energies of those who were waging it, so that no leisure was left for a critical assessment of the situation, nor of the Confessional problem in which they were involved.

IV

The great intellectual transition to the modern age which, through the victorious upsurge of the modern spirit, brought the Age of Orthodoxy to an end, is closely linked with the Confessional problem. The sanguinary wars of religion during the period of the Counter-reformation had proved that the lost unity of western Christendom could not be restored by political means. The attempt to establish a Confessionalist policy failed. Necessity created a demand for religious toleration. Although partially, reluctantly, and incompletely, religious toleration gradually prevailed as a fundamental political necessity in nearly all the modern States. Similarly, in the domain of culture and the sciences, there was a tendency to rebel against the tutelage of a dogmatic system, which, apart from all other objections, no longer provided a common ground for union because of religious disagreements. The too self-confident claim to the possession of absolute truth, and the mutual accusations of heresy on the part of the Confessional churches played an indirect but important part in the emancipation of the modern spirit. The truth of Christianity in its Confessional form had ceased to be the unchallenged basis of a common spiritual life. But even in the Church and theology itself a reaction developed against the manner in which the Confessional problem was treated in the Age of Orthodoxy. Gottfried Arnold's book, *Unparteiische Kirchen- und Ketzerhistorie* throws a startling light on the changed attitude towards the Confessional problem. Confessional differences were completely minimized and treated as purely relative by the theology of the Enlightenment, in view of a so-called natural religion which they more or less clearly displayed. I shall deal with the complex of problems here involved only so far as they affect the Confessional problem:

1. The result of the principle of toleration was that State boundaries in general ceased to be Confessional boundaries. The adherents of the various Confessions now lived together and enjoyed free intercourse with one another in all spheres of life. This frequent intermingling brought the Confessional problem right into the smallest social group, the family.

2. This bringing together of the Confessions resulted in a demand for the deconfessionalization of public life, by which politics, culture, educational methods, legislation, science, and so forth, could not to any extent remain unaffected; indeed, some of the more thoughtful representatives of these activities emphasized the urgency of this demand. The question arises whether this demand for deconfessionalization does not thereby involve the dechristianization of public life. In any case, the secularization of all these departments of life could not be checked. The only debatable point is whether this process of secularization is necessarily to be regarded as anti-christian, and what limit can be set to it. However strong the attempted Confessional recovery may have been since the beginning of the nineteenth century, it is nevertheless very doubtful whether it has succeeded to any extent in altering the fundamental tendency of the development in the modern age. It might indeed be asked whether on the whole that might be desirable, either for public life as such, or for the task of the Church in the modern world.

3. A further effect of the transition to the modern age on the development of the Confessional problem concerns the legal status of the

Church. The termination of the Constantinian era which resulted in the acceptance of the principle of religious toleration and in the secularization of public life, did not leave untouched the legal status which the Church had hitherto enjoyed. The strength of tradition is to be seen in the survival of a situation which had come into existence under totally different conditions. The old Confessional churches which, in earlier times, exercised supreme authority in their own territories, retained in various ways a certain privileged status. The present ecclesiastical partition of German Protestantism, with its absolute preponderance of the territorial churches, shows this clearly. In principle, however, the so-called sects have emerged from their earlier legally unrecognized status, and now stand on an equal legalized footing with the old territorial churches. Thus the whole extent of the problem created by the distinction between Church and sect has been revealed; more completely, perhaps, in a country like North America, where no church has ever enjoyed the privileged position of State recognition. But even in Germany, where the opposition between the territorial and national churches (which are identical) and the rest of the numerous smaller church communities is the result of historical development, it has become necessary to introduce, in view of the actual state of affairs, the other idea of 'Free Churches'—which means the breaking down of the too simple alternative of Church or sect. Since the idea of 'sect' cannot simply be abandoned, it becomes necessary to arrive at a new theological definition of the idea of a sect. The difficulty which this task creates is sufficient proof that the old Confessional certainty within Protestantism has disappeared. It would be folly to close one's eyes to this.

4. This brings us to the ecclesiastical and theological consequences of the Confessional problem in the form which it has assumed in modern times. For the Roman Catholic Church there has been here no change in principle. After some merely marginal onsets of weakness during the period of the Enlightenment, from the beginning of the nineteenth century she has re-affirmed more clearly than ever her old absolute claim with some success, in spite of the fact that she has at first been swimming against the modern tide. The disaster in which the history of modern times has been overwhelmed has given birth to a

need for authority, of which Catholicism has availed itself in an attractive way, so that, unless all the signs are deceptive, a great future lies open before it. For Protestantism the situation is entirely different. In the first place the consequences of religious toleration had been realized, namely, the headlong course, especially in Anglo-Saxon Protestantism, of the process of differentiation which had been held in check during the Age of Reformation and of Orthodoxy. The other aspect of this Confessional situation in modern Protestantism is the inevitable rise of a movement towards an interconfessional meeting and rapprochement. The history of Protestantism in modern times has been characterized by the widest variations and varying degrees of success in the problem of union. Although the word 'union' may have a sinister sound on account of attempts to iron out Confessional differences, yet it cannot be ignored that something has taken place in the history of the modern Church, namely, that the Christian Confessions have increasingly been brought, by closer contact with their mutual problems, to feel the need of a real understanding of other Confessions. Moreover, Christians have been forced to face afresh the problem of the rights and limits of their own Confessions, so that a naïve self-complacent acquiescence in the fact of the existence in Christendom of a vast multiplicity of Confessions has become impossible. In the Ecumenical movement of the twentieth century this tendency has found a strong and promising development.

4

Russia and the West: a Study in Confessional History

A. Russia and the Roman Catholic Church

I

When light from the history of the Confessions is shed upon the subject of Russia and the West, the following fundamental patterns emerge :

1. The landscape is to some extent divided. The West appears as a Confessionally divided partner. The division of the subject into two lectures is not due to the acknowledged superabundance of material, but to the fact that Russia falls apart into two wholly different partnerships: to the Roman Catholic Church on the one hand, and to Protestantism on the other. But in this division of subject resulting from the division of the Confessions, it should at once be remarked, to prevent misapprehension, that we shall only be dealing with variations of the same subject, Russia and the West. The importance of the theme derives from the fact that the division into Catholicism and Protestantism is a specifically western development; this can only be understood if we recognize its origin in a joint participation for centuries in an undivided western Christendom; it must also be recognized that the separated Confessions were jointly involved in the fate of the West. Accordingly, the relation between Russia and the West passed at first through a long period unaffected by the internal western schism, but did not, however, in spite of this division, lose the characteristic polarity embracing the whole of the West. Russia, long ago stamped with a different Confessional character, remained, to all intents and purposes, unaffected by western Confessional controversies.

The question might also be raised whether the situation in Russia does not also call for a division of the theme. Mention might be made of the great cleavage running through Russian Christendom since the separation of the so-called 'Old Believers' in the seventeenth century; or of the complete loss of any identity of Russia with Russian Christendom since the eighteenth century. But the rise of internal Russian sects hardly constitutes an independent factor in considering the relations of Russia with the West; it is only an indication of the specific character of Russian Christianity as a whole. Moreover, secularist and atheist Russia, in spite of its deadly enmity towards Orthodox Russia, is remarkably at one with the latter so far as the relation with the Christian Church of the West is concerned.

2. The range of our selected theme 'Russia and the West' is not restricted by considering it from the point of view of Confessional history. On the contrary, it makes it necessary to overstep the admittedly wide limits of our subject, and makes it clear that this is both the universal and the essential approach to the whole problem. Russia's entry upon the stage of history coincides practically with its acceptance of Christianity. Since this originated from Byzantium and not from Rome, Russian history owes its origin to the historical legacy concealed in its connection with Byzantium. Together with this particular form of Christianity Russia also inherited its long-matured opposition to Rome. In order to understand Russia it is necessary to understand the nature of this legacy. To do so it is therefore essential to discover the hidden roots of the separation between eastern and western Christianity which go back almost as far as the beginnings of Russian Christianity. The West, too, has its own distinctive debt to Christianity, although in this case the link between antiquity, Christianity, and Germanity, is very different from that which unites the Slav world with Christianity and with antiquity—if antiquity may be regarded at all as a separate factor. In any case, when we consider the whole field of interacting forces which the encounter of Russia and the West presents, it becomes clear that Christianity is, in a measure, a determining factor, being at the same time both a uniting and a divisive influence. Here we may see fully developed the three great Confessional types of Christianity, the Eastern, the Roman, and the Protestant, predominant, but not tending towards harmonious relations between Russia and the West.

The so-called 'Holy Alliance' between the Tsar of Russia, the Austrian Emperor, and the King of Prussia, was an exception, and by no means an admirable one.

3. The part played by Christianity in the extraordinarily complicated pattern exhibited by Russia and the West, both individually and in relation to one another, makes the study of the history of the Confessions the means of penetrating to the heart of the development of the problem and of its significance, namely, the problem of the relation between Church and State, religion and culture, piety and morality, and above all the relation between faith and history which is involved in the tensions set up by all the above-mentioned relations. In this exceedingly complex situation, the greatest care is required in interpretation. In considering the active participation of Christianity in it, we must not overlook the regrettable effect of its influence in so many ways towards estrangement and separation. The fundamental divergences must not be attributed either to a difference in national character, or to opposing beliefs. In view of the multiplicity of the interwoven historical strands, we shall do well to deal carefully with the pattern of origins and consequences; above all we must be on our guard against a tendentious interpretation and evaluation arising from neglect of the obvious, and especially against misunderstanding a foreign language.

II

1. One of the remote causes of the cleavage in the Ecumenical order of the early Church is the linguistic difference underlying Greco-Roman antiquity. This is not to say that the distinction between Greek and Latin should be held responsible for the cleavage. The early Church participated in the rich linguistic community of the ancient culture and shared in its diversities and transformations. The spread of Christianity in the western Mediterranean area was entirely transmitted in Greek. The transition to Latin began with the general recovery of Latin about the turn of the third century in north Africa, and in the middle of that century in Rome in ecclesiastical usage. Moreover, mediated by the same difference of language, a difference in the conception and development of Christianity begins to appear to some

extent as between the letters of the Antiochene bishop Ignatius, and the so-called First Epistle of Clement of Rome; it appears more clearly as between the Greek Clement of Alexandria and Origen, and the Latin writers Tertullian and Cyprian. This difference is undoubtedly related to the fundamental tendencies of the Greek–Hellenistic, and the Roman–Latin spirit, namely, to put it broadly, the tendency to metaphysical mystery on the one hand, and juridical clarity on the other.

Nevertheless this did not split the Church, any more than the growing problem of the unity of the Empire. This element of political tension became relevant for the Church from the time when, as the result of the Constantinian conversion, she became involved in the preservation of the unity of the Empire; this forced the unity of the Church itself in a political sense, but was also a cause of embarrassment and doubt. The final partition of the Empire and the complete dis-appearance of the western Roman Empire did not at first cause any breach in the unity of the imperial Church; nevertheless it brought about a gradual estrangement between the two ecclesiastical realms. Their subsequent history was determined by a totally different political destiny, and their culture developed under widely different conditions.

The West experienced the migration of the Germanic peoples. In spite of the breach in its political continuity and the deterioration of its cultural life, this event proved the starting-point for the vigorous development of the legacy of a joint Christian and late classical culture in the newly expanding field of Romano–Germanic history. The adoption of Catholic Christianity by the Kingdom of the Franks, leading to the conversion of the Arian Germanic tribal churches to Catholicism; the great liberating victory of Charles Martel over the Arabs; and the *translatio imperii* symbolized in the assumption of the Imperial crown by Charlemagne; these are the principal landmarks along the road which revealed the initial disaster of the West to have been the starting-point of an undreamed-of future.

The eastern half of the Empire had skilfully diverted to the West that element of the Germanic threat which came from the north-east, and had astonishingly survived for a thousand years the final political col-lapse of the West. It continued to exist as the unbroken continuation of the Roman Empire until the fifteenth century, facing the West in proud consciousness of the legitimate possession of the Imperial title, and of a richly-stored cultural superiority. The remarkable persistence of Byzantium was, nevertheless, marked by misfortune and steady diminution; at first by Slavonic inroads from the north, and Persian attacks in the east; then by a complete transformation of the geo-political map through the Islamic invasion, resulting in the loss of the most important of the Byzantine provinces; finally by the Turks, who completely overran the remnant of the Empire which had been reduced to the condition of a Hellenic petty State. The fact that Byzantium so long withstood the inroads of Islam proves her to have possessed a strength and a wealth of historical achievement to which the western medieval period owed its possibility of development; in view of this fact we should be careful to avoid a depreciatory estimate of Byzantium as apparently petrified in the rigidity of tradition. Certainly we have here a situation wholly different from that which existed in the West; under the pressure of circumstances the East was compelled to concentrate all its efforts towards the preservation and intensive circumscription of its own distinctive character. In contrast with the Germanic, the Islamic migration did not invite the Church's missionary activity and attempts at intercourse. The political loss of the Syrian and Egyptian provinces practically coincided with the death of the Orthodox Church in these regions, while the heretical national churches which had resulted from the Christological controversies, and whose existence had so impaired Byzantium's stand against heresy, presented at most the appearance of a ghetto-enclosed Christian remnant in the Islamic world. This loss was not, however, adequately balanced by missionary expansion in the Slavonic area; this was of great significance for the future of the Eastern Church, but, compared with the analogous course of events in the West, took place in a much more advanced stage of development and had no effect on the tradition of Byzantine culture.

2. Closely connected with this profound divergence in the historical development of East and West was the intensification of the ecclesiastical differences. It is not accidental that their earliest effect was seen in the sphere of canon law and in the interlocked relation between

Church and State. Even in their initial missionary activities the eastern and western regions of the Church exhibit an entirely different pattern. In the east, as a result of the greater degree of differentiation, a number of church centres came into existence: Alexandria, Antioch, Jerusalem, mainly for religious reasons, and for political reasons, the new capital, Constantinople, the new Rome. The rivalry between these great bishoprics was a vital factor in the course of the doctrinal disputes in the early Church. In the western half of the Empire, on the other hand, Rome acquired an unchallenged pre-eminence as the original missionary centre, as the only church whose origins went back to an apostolic foundation, and, of course, as the church of the old capital of the Empire.

The consequences of this double development can be clearly seen. On the one hand, in the East a plurality of great Patriarchates developed, among which Constantinople was *primus inter pares*, but without jurisdictional primacy; on the other hand, the West tended towards an ever-increasing insistence on the primacy of the Bishop of Rome, with a view to legislative and juridical authority over the Church as a whole. A long period of time was needed for the full realization of this aim. It was first formally promulgated at the Vatican Council of 1870; but the trend of affairs was already clear in the early Church. This appeared from the fact that in principle the Roman claim to primacy was not confined to the western half of the Empire. The *de facto* authority of Rome was recognized in the East to the extent that an honorary precedence in the hierarchy was conceded to it, involving, however, no acknowledgement of any legal claim. Hence, while to all appearance the eastern half of the Church had no ambition to make the West dependent on it, Rome pursued this aim towards the East in respect of its own doctrinal claims; this was to prove an essential factor in the later schism.

These divergent conceptions concerning the hierarchical manifestation of the unity of the Church were favoured by the underlying differences in the political circumstances. The abolition of the central authority of the Empire in the West, in favour of separate states with a foreign, non-Catholic ruling class, presented the Roman bishop, as the highest representative of an established Catholic Christendom, with an ample opportunity of developing his position, not only from an ecclesiastical, but also from a political point of view. Trained in imperial methods of government, the Papacy, as it developed, because lacking an imperial partner, was able to invest itself with a relatively independent character as far as the relations between Church and State were concerned, and thus established the character of its relations with a newly created western Empire. Hence, for the history of the West, such phenomena as the creation of an ecclesiastical State, the foundation of spiritual principalities, and finally the conflict between the Empire and the Papacy with all its associated events and results, took on a certain inevitable character.

The course of events was totally different in Byzantium. The Bishop of Constantinople owed his position, not to Church Tradition, but to the Empire, and his authority was consequently subject to a double limitation: in relation to the other patriarchates he enjoyed no spiritual precedence, and in his relations with the Emperor he did not have sufficient distance. In the interests of his own authority the Emperor was obliged to keep the highest position in the Church vacant. He regarded himself, especially since Justinian's time, as invested with a double official character, spiritual and secular, after the analogy of Christ as a priestly King. This Byzantine type of State-Church, from the concept of which the West was later to borrow certain features, gave the Patriarch of Byzantium little scope for independent activity, so that his ecclesiastical position in principle remained unchanged even when under the infidel regime the maintenance and occupation of the other ancient patriarchates became largely fictional. It is a very revealing fact that, as the result of continual State interference, we find far more occupants of the bishopric, and disproportionately fewer significant personalities in the list of Byzantine patriarchs than in the Papal lists during the same period.

3. No justification for a separation in the Church can be found in broken relations or human traditions. It can only be based on a fundamental doctrinal difference. In this respect, however, the situation is surprising. In spite of all divisive factors, in matters of doctrine East and West remain united to an astonishing degree. The great fundamental formulations of the pre-Constantinian period are clearly common

ground. There are the twofold canon of Holy Scripture, the anti-Gnostic interpretation of the rule of faith, the monarchic episcopate based on the apostolic succession as the essential bond of unity between identically patterned local churches, the elaboration of a mystery-cult as the central element in divine worship, all these are fundamental doctrines which Protestantism, not, however, without exception, made its own. But, even in the post-Constantinian period, when the doctrinal controversies raged fiercely for centuries, and whose decisions led to the great schisms of the Arian, Monophysite, and Dyophysite Churches, the growing tension between East and West, in spite of a variety of disputes between the Greek and Latin halves of the Imperial Church, was unable to cause a doctrinal split. East and West were united in the final decisions on the Trinitarian and Christological controversy, and even in the Iconoclastic controversy which only affected Byzantium. Similarly, both sides were agreed in the recognition and enumeration of seven Ecumenical Councils in the early Church between the fourth and the eighth centuries, the only unimportant difference being the refusal of the East to accept the inclusion of an addition to the fifth and sixth Ecumenical Councils, the so-called Quinisextum, which was only concerned with disciplinary matters.

When, nevertheless, in the ninth century a temporary, and in the eleventh century the final breach between the Church of Rome and Constantinople took place, its apparently scanty grounds are very instructive. If we disregard the incidental causes due to church politics, and the very important differences in canon law, as well as the contributory claims to jurisdiction over their intersecting spheres of influence, the following picture emerges: Rome had brought no doctrinal charges against the Eastern Church, and hence only regarded her as schismatic, not as heretical. Byzantium, on the other hand, had declared a number of Roman deviations from ritual orthodoxy (for example, the use of unleavened bread in the Eucharist) to be heretical; but above all the gravamen of its accusation was the doctrinal sacrilege committed by the West in its insertion of the *filioque* clause in the third article of the Creed. That nuance of Trinitarian theology, going back to Augustine, which taught that the procession of the Holy Spirit from within the Trinity took place not only *ex patre*, but *ex patre filioque*, has, taken by itself, only a limited meaning; it should not, as easily happens, be applied speculatively to explain the greater freedom of charismatic activity in the Eastern Church. It was not the theological content of the *filioque*, but the fact of a subsequent alteration in the inviolable text of the Creed, which in the judgement of the Eastern Church constituted the real heresy. An additional cause of offence was the fact of its being first accepted by the Frankish Church, as well as the foundation of a new Empire, which made the relations between Byzantium and the West extremely difficult.

The Rome of the East, completely hedged in by tradition, regarded the West as having broken with tradition, and therefore as doubly heretical, both from a political and an ecclesiastical point of view. It definitely shut itself off from the evolutionary policy of the West. When, in the year 843, the aftermath of the Iconoclastic controversy reached its conclusion with the institution of the annual Festival of Orthodoxy, even before the breach with Rome, the full consciousness of the distinctive character of the Eastern Church found expression: it was an Orthodoxy which was not far from agreement with Rome in explicit doctrine, but at the same time implied a specific eastern interpretation, along with the specific forms of the Eastern Church; thus the tradition of the Eastern Church presented the appearance of flexibility within an indivisible living totality.

III

It was not a matter of course from its geographical situation, that, with the baptism of Vladimir of Kiev, at the end of the tenth century, and the consequent mass-baptism of his people, Russia received Christianity in this Orthodox Byzantine form. The Christian infiltration which preceded the official adoption of Christianity as the State religion also showed Roman Catholic influence. The old imperial ecclesiastical unity still existed formally, since the schism of the ninth century was only a brief episode. The question of the choice between Byzantium or Rome had thus not yet the full force of a Confessional alternative, although the mission to the Slavs could lead to a special development of a rivalry between the two centres of ecclesiastical authority. The

two Slav missionaries, Constantine and Methodius, who were working
in the Moravian area in the ninth century, were actually at the meeting-
point of the two spheres of influence: they came from and were commissioned by Byzantium, but were linked with Rome, and were
finally competing with the Frankish mission as a third independent
factor. Their outstanding achievement, the translation of the liturgy
and other works into a dialect which became through their efforts so-
called church-Slavic, was credited to the Eastern Church, the pattern
of whose organization allowed more latitude to national peculiarities
than did the Western Church which despite many concessions insisted
on the Church's linguistic unity, and was therefore called by the Eastern
Church the 'Latin' church. Together with political considerations, this
introduction of church-Slavic from Bulgaria may have been the
impulse which caused the Kingdom of Kiev to turn to the Orthodox
Church, when perhaps the ecclesiastical influence of Bulgaria was
stronger at first than the direct influence of Byzantium.

In view of the fact that the boundary between the Eastern and the
Roman Churches ran through the middle of Slavic territory, and up
to the present time has been a serious hindrance to good relations between Russia and Poland, it is a mistake to indulge in fantasies about a
special Slavic mentality to which Christianity in its eastern form was
more acceptable. Even if it were limited to the very varied types of east
Slavs living in Russia, such an assumption would be unfounded. Dis-
regarding all the important related problems, we only know the
Russian people as their character has been developed under the influence of eastern Christianity. Thus it is not in some supposedly
'natural' but only in their historical character, which has more or less
become their nature, that we really know them. It is an open question
whether national character, historical fate and the special form of
Christianity can be measured in their importance against one another.

Nevertheless, there are still some observations to be made about the
effects of an eastern Christianity of Byzantine origin upon the history
and formation of the Russian character, and the consequent transformation of the specific form of Russian Christianity. In general we may say
that certain peculiarities of eastern Christianity were intensified by their
working out in Russian history. This statement must be qualified by

the reservation that it should not be allowed to obscure the variety of aspects underlying a comparison between Russian Christianity, and Byzantine on the one hand, and Roman Catholic on the other.

1. The fusion of national character and religion, which, of course, also exists in the West, is specially close in the Eastern Church, as may be seen from the formation of national churches and the liturgical use of the vernacular; in Russia it is even slightly closer. The introduction of so mature and exclusive a form of Christianity as the Byzantine into a nation at the earliest stage of its historical development encouraged the highest degree of reciprocal assimilation. All the more so, since this reception from the religious point of view was not balanced by a corresponding cultural development of a different kind. The reception of the spiritual legacy of non-Christian antiquity in a slightly different tradition by the young Germanic peoples produced in them an increasingly eager appropriation and an independent version of the Christian heritage; but in Russia for a long time the legacy of antiquity was only merged in Church traditions, and hence provided no practical help towards spiritual independence in relation to these traditions.

2. Together with this extensive identity of Church religiosity with the spiritual contents active in the life of the nation, stress should be laid on a fundamental feature of the character of the Eastern Church, traditionalism; this was not dead as such, but was, within its limits, a living force. This tendency was, moreover, greatly strengthened by the isolation caused by the Tartar conquest, which not merely reduced to a minimum the relatively meagre contacts with the West, but also for a time those with Byzantium. During this time the tradition to some extent taken over from the Church by the Russian people compensated for their own isolated maintenance of their national self-consciousness by their own scanty historical tradition, and provided a heightened unsophisticated sense of tradition which gave them in turn a capacity for endurance, in which nation and Church were united as Holy Russia, and every foreigner was forthwith stigmatized as irreligious.

3. It is a very strange thing that, when in its revival in the late period the genius of Greece with its far-reaching and bold outlook had roused men's minds to deal with the challenge which the Christian faith

presents, it should finally have drifted into a phase of almost timid self-containment, in which the adventure of the spirit lay hidden, so to speak, in the taking seriously of symbolic rituals. It is much easier to understand how the transmission of this legacy to the Russian people, on their unsophisticated level, should have produced a massive ritualism, possessing perhaps an even more powerful emotional stimulus. Striking examples of this occur in the Russian internal controversies in the seventeenth century, about such matters as whether the sign of the Cross should be made with two or three fingers, or whether the name of Jesus should be pronounced 'Jissus' or 'Issus', and so on.

4. We recognized as a feature of the history of the Orthodox Church, as contrasted with that of the Western, the almost unremitting pressure, on the one side, of the heroically resisted inroads of Islam, and on the other, of the continual encroachment of the authority of the State on the affairs of the Church, sometimes accepted, sometimes merely endured. We find in Christian Russia this curious double aspect, standing out with the sharpness of a woodcut; we see her sorely tried and accepting suffering, yet unmoved and even grimly triumphant under hardship.

5. We have seen how Byzantium, conscious of her possession of the legitimate tradition, felt herself vastly superior to the West. It might have been expected that Russia, in view of Byzantium's origin and ecclesiastical eminence, would only have regarded her with an awestruck feeling of inferiority. But, just at the time of her segregation under Tartar domination, Russia was seized, in the life of the Church, by an urge to independence. In the middle of the fifteenth century she put forward a claim to choose the Moscow Metropolitan herself. Yet, in the strictly graded hierarchy of the whole Orthodox Church, this highest position in the Russian Church only occupied the one hundred and eighty-first place. However, one hundred years later, with a mighty leap, she attained the supreme position of the Patriarchate, creating the first alteration in the allotment of the Patriarchate for over a thousand years since the Council of Chalcedon. Moscow owed this promotion not least to the end of the political predominance of Byzantium. The tendency to seek pre-eminence was also operative here, and the example of Byzantium was a spur to emulation. From the political and ideological

point of view the conception of a new and final *translatio imperii* found expression in Moscow as a third Rome; a contributory factor also to be considered was that after the fall of Constantinople Moscow was the only political centre in the Eastern Church free from foreign rule. From this situation it was only a short step for Moscow to outstrip the ecclesiastical predominance of the Patriarchate of Constantinople.

6. This urge to the leadership of Orthodoxy was further expressed in the fact that Moscow not only took over the legacy of opposition to Rome, but also sought to surpass Constantinople in this respect. The Eastern Church was always opposed to the idea of union with Rome to the same extent that the latter was interested in it and anxious to bring it about. But, while the state of political relations in the thirteenth century, and now more forcibly in the fifteenth, compelled official Byzantium to make an approach towards union with Rome, Moscow saw in the subsequent fall of Constantinople the just punishment of a betrayal of Orthodoxy bordering on heresy. In our own time we have witnessed various attempts on the part of the Moscow Patriarchate to assume the leadership of the whole of Orthodoxy: for example, the experiment of summoning a conference of the Orthodox Churches; the polemic directed against Rome; the overruling of the Patriarch of Constantinople in the matter of sending Orthodox observers to the Second Vatican Council, in accordance with the wish of the Papacy to promote the union of the Orthodox Churches with Rome.

Here we must break off. A partial treatment of this theme is unavoidable. Many things which might rightly have been expected to be dealt with will be touched on in connection with the next subject. It was through Protestantism that the Catholic Church became Catholicized, and it is through the study of this double aspect that we may acquire a general picture of the special characteristics of Russian Christianity.

B. Russia and Protestantism

I

It is hardly possible to over-estimate the importance of the whole Confessional situation for the relation between Russia and the West. The interrelations between Eastern Orthodoxy and Catholicism on the one hand, and Protestantism on the other, present a vast and complicated collection of resemblances and contrasts, attraction and repulsion, mutual interactions and hopeless estrangement. When we consider their development as a whole up to the present, both fields of study are of equal importance from the historical point of view; but the nature and manner of their 'contact-history', if I may so describe it, is fundamentally different in each case.

1. The connection between the Eastern Church and the Roman Church is the result of a long common history. They stand together on a broad and deep common foundation. Each was directly and mutually responsible for their separation. Their relation resembled that existing between the separated partners of a marriage. The destiny of the one is inseparable from that of the other. Without Rome Constantinople and Moscow would not be Constantinople and Moscow, and without them Rome would not be Rome—at any rate not from the point of view of Confessional history; but that involves a far wider horizon. The subject of Russia and the Roman Catholic Church requires and allows a far-reaching historical retrospect; a survey of the great historical arches of the years which, resting on a few main piers, span the centuries. Thus the critical point of our study lies in the origin and transformation of the Confessional opposition; hence it is necessary to distinguish the nature of the legacy whose reception determined the character of the whole of Russian history, and, in the process of its assimilation, altered in certain respects the relations between the Eastern and the Roman Churches. It is necessary to understand the underlying previous history in order to have the key to the sequel, the various contacts and influences, the conflicts and rapprochements, which de-

veloped on the basis of a common Confessional relationship, but hardly succeeded in altering it. Certainly the later history of the encounters which took place between these sharply distinguished partners contains a number of remarkable occurrences. To recall only the best-known examples, we have the mad creation of a Western empire and a Latin hierarchy in Byzantium during the fourth Crusade, or the shocking treatment of the Confessional minority in the east European border territory either on the Polish or the Russian side at the time of the Union of Brest-Litovsk in the Polish-Lithuanian Kingdom at the end of the sixteenth century, and no less in their compulsory annexation by the Soviet Union at the end of the Second World War. We may also recall the story of the diplomatic relations between Moscow and the Vatican, and the doctrinal influences of a positive and negative kind; for instance, the reception of the Roman doctrine of the Seven Sacraments by eastern theology, in spite of the broader conception there entertained of the nature of a Mystery, avoiding sharp definitions; or the decided rejection by the East, understandably, of the dogma of papal infallibility, although according to Eastern teaching the Church is infallible; or the opposition to the latest Mariological dogma, although reverence for Mary is deeply rooted in Eastern piety.

2. The historical connection between the Eastern Church and Protestantism is, on the other hand, of a very different kind. This Confessional difference is not derived from a common history, and was not the result of a direct controversy. Just as the Eastern Church is not characterized by any out and out opposition to Protestantism, so the latter has not taken up a position antithetically opposed to the Eastern Church. The Reformation is an internal Western event, and, it would appear, so entirely unconnected with Eastern Orthodoxy that, at least at first, any invasion of its territory was never considered. Although the Reformation tide broke strongly over the eastern Catholic provinces of Poland or Hungary, the limit of its advance was unmistakably established at the point where the Eastern Church's sphere of influence began. The full extent of the divergence between East and West now became clearly visible. It might be said that the nature of the West is indicated by the fact that here and here only could the Reformation have taken place. Compare, for instance, the western Reformation and

a parallel reform movement in Russian Christendom which led to a similar schism, namely, the liturgical reform of the Patriarch Nikon in the seventeenth century. Certain ritual changes, unimportant from our point of view, in favour of the ancient Byzantine pattern, roused the passionate opposition of the Old Believers, for whom the habitual was the ancient. The impression of something immoderate and even grotesque in this controversy only emphasizes the difference in the ecclesiastical and general spiritual situation, and demonstrates the fact that within the domain of the Eastern Church there were no presuppositions for understanding what the Reformation was about. Thus the two Confessions existed side by side, at first independent and mutually alien in character, and subsequently, as two established powers, entering into relations with one another, although without any essential change in the nature of either. Their actual historical contacts are of secondary importance, however they may have seemed at the time. The picture of their relation threatens to dissolve into unrelated details. Instead of the broad fresco-like sweep of the world-embracing pattern which the theme of the relation between Byzantium, Moscow, and Rome presents, we find here a passion for things on a miniature scale, for the particular, the anecdotal; for the discovery of events which in general have remained unnoticed, and contribute nothing to the grand dramatic scene.

3. Now this description of the general pattern of the subject calls for some closer definition. Although contact between the Eastern Church and Protestantism, at first gradual and apparently marginal, developed into direct historical encounters, yet it would seem that from an early date there was a real historical relation between them, although hardly noticeable because of its indirect nature. In this connection it is of course natural to mention their mutual opposition to Rome, which represents a relation, although of a different nature, to a common adversary. This point of view has, in fact, up to the present, had an important influence on the Ecumenical relations between Orthodoxy and Protestantism, it is, however, too purely negative to promote progress. It looks back to the common history from which the three great Confessions derive their origin, and to the very same tradition which, in their different traditions, is a cause of dispute. They all go back to the basis and essential

nature of the *one* Church, the common Creed, whose different interpretations have separated them. Thus, to put the matter in a nutshell, that very unity of the Church, assumed by all, but differently interpreted, is the cause of their separation. The very nature of the Christian faith involves both contact and conflict in relation to the tradition. Protestantism, in its definite historical form, originated in the sixteenth century, but regards itself as the Church of Jesus Christ, and not in any way as a new foundation of the Church. It therefore considers itself as having rediscovered the true ground of the Church, and as having a valid claim to be the true continuation of the Church's tradition. Protestantism does not regard the first fifteen hundred years of the Church's history as simply non-existent, but rightly understood as its own history. That is especially true of the period of the early Church, so that from here a considerable amount of common tradition unites Protestantism to the Eastern Church. It is possible to recognize the relation thus established, without needing a closer acquaintance with the situation of the Eastern Church at that time, or a direct contact with it. Thus for Luther a comparison with the Greek Church played an important part in the controversy about the primacy of the Pope at the time of the Leipzig disputation, and equally important for the Reformation as a whole was the agreement with the doctrine of the early Church, and the appeal to patristic theology for which the later Melanchthon especially was responsible. Nevertheless we must not blink the fact that, in spite of a general agreement with the Eastern Church in opposition to Rome, that which separated the Reformation from the Roman Church, also separated it to a great extent from the Eastern Church.

II

1. Against the background of the above-mentioned inner relations between the Eastern Church and Protestantism, a further interest attaches to the beginnings of contact, leading to an extensive range of connections. In the first place a theological aspect is apparent; the question arises whether, in regard to the exclusive attitude of the

Eastern Church towards the Roman Church, the former might experience a new readiness for self-examination, a movement directed towards the breaking-down of stagnation, by meeting with those who have come out of the Roman Church, and have freed themselves from it by a critical Reformed return to the Gospel. The further question arises, whether, conversely, Protestantism, deeply engaged with the Roman Church, though very differently from the Eastern Church, might experience an increasing freedom of recognition, and a protection from the danger of becoming cramped in a rigid attitude of protest, by coming into contact with a form of the Church which can trace its historical continuity back to the beginnings of church history, but is not encumbered with certain distortions such as may be seen in the Roman Church and have evoked protest.

With this observation concerning the theological aspect of the situation another point of view is connected which has a special bearing on its cultural and political aspect. Here the question arises whether Russia, taking into account the fact that her contact with Protestantism has been chiefly through the Eastern Church, may see that her relations with the West have taken on an altered character, in that the latter has lost its exclusively Roman Catholic aspect; one example of this change may be seen in the fact that the numerous dynastic alliances between Russia and the West have been almost exclusively with the Protestant nobility. A further question arises, whether the West whose specifically western character has possibly been radically changed by Protestantism, may not, in the encounter with Russia, find an antidote against dangerous ingrowing tendencies.

2. After the first period of complete lack of contact, many causes contributed to meetings between the Eastern Church's sphere of influence, especially Russia, and Protestantism. These were partly of a purely religious and ecclesiastical nature and mainly from the side of Protestantism; partly on the cultural level, chiefly as a result of Russia's turning towards the West; and partly in the narrower sense of a political nature, through Protestant immigration into Russia, or Russian Orthodox migration into the West, or through the events of war which threw East and West together in the experiences of occupations and prison camps. Finally there is the fact, not yet completely

realized, that the homeland of the Reformation and the main centres of Protestant culture, the places where Luther and Bach, Kant and Hegel, Schiller and Goethe, lived and worked, now lie within the sphere of Russian influence.

3. During the last decade the study of Confessional history has devoted greater attention to the very varied and scattered details of this history of the contacts between the Confessions and has recovered much from the forgotten past. We cannot now dilate on this subject, but must be content with a kind of topographical outline.

During the sixteenth century only scanty and confused rumours about the Reformation reached the East. The Turks took some political interest in it, and the Patriarch of Constantinople found occasion to seek for fuller information. By his orders in 1559 a deacon spent six months in Wittenberg. Melanchthon gave this man a letter to the Patriarch together with a Greek translation of the Augsburg Confession. Of this, however, we have nothing but a rumour. It was not until the seventies that this clue received an addition. A Tübingen theological tutor officiated as a mission-preacher in Constantinople, and established links between the Patriarchate and the Tübingen Faculty of Theology, leading to a very instructive correspondence about the Greek translation of the Augsburg Confession, which was now sent a second time from Tübingen. This exchange was carried on with humanistic enthusiasm and naïve Confessional motives on the part of the Tübingen Faculty, and was finally broken off by the Patriarch in disillusionment.

About the same time, but on a less modest level, a Confessional dispute arose in Moscow between the Tsar Ivan IV, not entirely without justice named 'the Terrible', and a pastor of the Moravian Brothers at the head of a Polish mission. The Tsar, who had at least a lively interest in theology, denounced the new heresy, and at their second encounter produced his refutation in the form of an expensively bound book in which, forsooth, his name appeared as the author; in reality, however, it was plagiarized from a contemporary polemical treatise against the liberal teaching of a renegade monk which provided a prototype for the Russian conception of Protestantism. Ivan did not use literary means in the instruction of his own subjects, as is exemplified in the conquest of Livonia by the fate of a certain evangelical pastor whom the

Tsar thrashed with his own hands and had thrown under the ice in the Dvina.

There was more serious Protestant influence during the seventeenth century, in Constantinople, where even the Patriarch, Cyrillos Lukaris, made use of Calvinist ideas, obviously in order to rebut Jesuit activity. The Jesuits for their part exploited this Protestant influence in their propaganda, although there can be no doubt of the basic orthodoxy of the Patriarch, who thereafter died so tragically. His *Confessio Fidei*, which was first published in Geneva, produced counter-confessions, so that even in the appearance of this form of so-called symbolic writings, which was quite foreign to the Eastern Church, there was an indirect influence of the Reformation.

The events had an effect in Russia, where the Metropolitan of Kiev, Peter Mogila, not in connivance with Rome, but, on the contrary, in order to guard against the tendency to union, and to increase the controversial ability of his clergy, attempted to provide a more thorough theological training for them after the Roman Catholic pattern. In pursuit of this policy he stood out as the decided opponent of Cyrillos Lukaris, and as the champion of Latin studies, a significant indication of the increasing westernization of Russia, and of the initial poverty of theological studies in Russia. How great was the ignorance underlying the intensified polemic against Protestantism at that time is shown by the fact that in the anathemas which, since 1639, were required from a Protestant who wished to join the Russian Orthodox Church, Zwingli had mistakenly become two persons—'Cvik' and 'Glijan'.

About the beginning of the eighteenth century Protestant influences in Russia were suddenly intensified. When this is considered from the historical point of view it is not so strange as it appears to us today. It was the result of the activity of two such fundamentally different men as Peter the Great and August Hermann Francke of Halle, an activity in which the influences of the Enlightenment and Pietism were combined. We shall not be doing Peter the Great an injustice if we regard his religious policy, the proclamation of tolerance, admittedly only for foreigners, his interference in ecclesiastical organization, and his restrictive measures against monasticism, as not primarily dictated by religious motives.

But his adviser, the Ukrainian Prokopovič, was a theologian who was genuinely interested in Protestantism; he was anti-Roman, and, under the influence of Wolffian philosophy, anti-Scholastic; at the same time in contact with the Pietism of Halle, which, in a literary form, was permeating Russia. Above all, the four books of Johann Arndt concerning true Christianity, had a wide circulation in Russian. The thought-forms of Lutheran mysticism, especially Boehme's, also found an entrance into Russian spiritual life in the work of the Frenchman Saint-Martin. The printing was mostly done in Halle, the first German university to establish a faculty of Slavonic studies, and whence pietistic envoys journeyed into Russia, with not much better success than Zinzendorf's somewhat later visit to Russia, which ended in his arrest in Riga. Among the most successful of the activities of Prokopovič may undoubtedly be reckoned the promotion of preaching and instruction; less satisfactory was the substitution, for which he was responsible, of the Holy Synod by Peter the Great for the Patriarchate which had been in abeyance since 1700; the Lutheran Consistory may have provided the model for this institution, which, as is well known, came to an end in 1917.

The nineteenth century saw a great increase of various forms of Protestant influence: there was the revival movement, especially in connection with Jung-Stilling and Johannes Evangelista Gossner, with which was linked the activity of the *Bibelgesellschaft*, soon proscribed; then there was the spread of idealist and romantic philosophy: in professorial rooms of the Moscow theological academy there still stood in the twentieth century busts of Fichte, Schelling, and Hegel; this influence was extremely active in the various types of Russian philosophy of religion during the nineteenth and twentieth centuries, and towards the end of the nineteenth century mingled with the influence of liberal theology; this is evident, to mention only the best-known names, in the work both of Tolstoy and of Dostoievski.

About the same time, nourished by various Free Churches, especially Baptist, appeared the movement known as 'Stundism', from the name 'Stunde' given by its members to their devotional gatherings, or 'Hours'. The movement later took the name Gospel Christians and in modern times the Pentecostal movement seems to play an important part among them. All these Protestant influences have a disintegrating tendency in relation to the structure of the Church, both with regard to its tradition and its worship. Hence the Orthodox Church, threatened at the same time by increasing religious indifference and by atheism, regards Protestantism, even in its neo-pietistic form, in spite of the latter's fundamental opposition to such tendencies, as the ally of modern secularism. On the other hand, it has to deal with the fact that this form of Protestantism has for the first time gained an extensive hold on the Russian population.

The history of the growth of evangelical communities is marked by the following features: scattered foreign communities existing in segregated groups, political assimilation of Protestant German Balts, and evangelical immigrants whose communities, at least in the country-side, began to spread out into the Russian population. In consequence of the events of the last half-century, the relatively small evangelical Lutheran Church in Russia, composed mainly of Christians of non-Russian extraction, which had come into existence as the result of the above-mentioned conditions, was almost entirely obliterated. On the other hand the Gospel Christian movement spread extensively, being favoured among other things by the abuses due to the low spiritual level of the Russian Orthodox Church.

The appearance in Russia itself of Protestant missionary activity, in conjunction with a, to say the least, one-sided conception of the nature of Protestantism, still further intensified the always prevailing hostility of Russian Orthodoxy towards Protestantism. Some moderation of this was possible in the attitude adopted towards the Ecumenical movement, in line with the current political trend, when, as the result of the conference in New Delhi, the possibility of joining the World Council of Churches was envisaged, although, in 1948, anti-Protestant animosity provided an argument for the brusque rejection of Ecumenism. In striking contrast, Protestantism, during recent decades, in connection with internal changes which it experienced, has evinced an extraordinary growth of interest in, and understanding of, the Russian Orthodox Church; this may be welcomed as a happy sign, so long as it does not lapse into sentimentality, but remains sober.

III

This historical outline brings us back once more from the confused details to the essential problems. The most perplexing feature in the history of the meeting between Russia and Protestantism is the question whether Russia has ever really come into contact with Protestantism. This involves three important and closely connected considerations.

1. We are confronted with two situations, historically utterly different, and with little direct contact. We see Russia so firmly attached to the Eastern tradition, and Protestantism equally firmly attached to the Western, that it is questionable whether any contact is possible which is not distorted by a difference in the very means of understanding. The view that for evangelical Christians dialogue with the Eastern Church may be easier than with the Roman Catholic Church because of a closer actual connection from the first, runs the risk of being based on a superficial impression. The fact that Catholicism and Protestantism, having developed in the same cultural area, share a common language and thought-forms, makes it much easier to come quickly to grips with the issues involved; while in order to arrive at a dialogue with Russian Orthodox Christians a great effort is needed to understand even to a small degree their distinctive characteristics, apart from the irritating influence of totally different surroundings.

2. What really does 'Protestantism' mean? The Russian picture of Protestantism has two characteristic features: on the one hand, it displays the influence of the Enlightenment, and on the other, of a pietism of very varied types; in this picture, however, the rationalistic and subjective element so far predominates as to affect the interpretation of the biblicistic element or that characterized by the doctrine of justification. There can be no doubt that these are manifestations of Protestantism. It would be too superficial an explanation of their existence to claim that they were merely incidental manifestations of Protestantism. In view of the history of Protestantism, its nature raises an extraordinarily difficult problem, not merely for outsiders, but for Protestants themselves; a much more difficult problem than that raised by the nature of Eastern Orthodoxy. Nevertheless the fact remains that

members of the Eastern Church have hardly encountered, still less understood, the real nature of the Reformed movement; at any rate to a much slighter degree than Protestants have encountered and comprehended the nature of the Eastern Church. This ignorance of the nature of the Reformed movement, however, involves the inability to form a correct estimate of rationalistic or pietistic aspects of Protestantism. The Eastern Church is not merely unable to judge such aspects by the standard of the Reformation, but not even to form a correct estimate of their position in relation to the whole history of Protestantism; a further result, moreover, is an inability to understand why and how far these different forms of Protestantism, once they are established in the Russian environment, are immediately changed by it, and inevitably change themselves.

3. The problem of Russia and the modern world is very closely bound up with the relation between Russia and Protestantism, as distinct from its relation with the Roman Church. It is not merely because, historically, this Confessional relation belongs entirely to the modern world, but for weighty reasons which intensify the difficulty of the problem. However little the Reformation is the cause of the modern world, and however little Protestantism is merely the specific modern form of Christianity, it is nevertheless undeniable, and more clearly recognizable when based on comparisons drawn from Confessional history, that there is a close inner relation between the Reformation and the modern world. While Protestantism, clearly with more energy than Catholicism, has assumed responsibility for, and addressed itself to, the tasks presented by the modern world, the Russian Orthodox Church has completely ignored these problems. It is not the case that the responsibility has not similarly made its demands upon her. The historical fact that Russia received the form of Christianity as something complete in itself, independent of the course of time, was destined, by a secret inner connection, to be repeated in the way in which the modern world presented itself, if not to the Russian people in general, at least to Russian Orthodoxy, as something essentially ready-made, coming from outside. Perhaps the encounter between Russia and the modern world has been so shattering because the spiritual element in Protestantism, with reserve be it said, has been

inadequately represented. And perhaps that is why only that form of Protestantism has found expression in Russia, which on the one hand shows clear traces of the modern world, as is the case with the extreme form of Neo-Pietism, and on the other hand avoids all real contact with the tasks which the modern world demands, as is likewise the case with this type of religiosity.

Since the mere satisfaction of historical interest is not the contribution to the subject of Russia and the West which we expect from Confessional history, but an aid to our understanding of the contemporary scene, we find ourselves, at the close of this introduction, only at the beginning of what is needed for a real grasp of the situation. What is needed is not fashionable slogans, but, by means of a searching analysis, to set that going which has hitherto been lacking—namely: a meeting between the Eastern Church and Protestantism, a meeting whose success depends on the inclusion of the Roman Church. An understanding can only be attained when the three great Confessions arrive at a mutual comprehension of their distinctive characteristics. When this takes place, something will be liberated which has been congealed in their differences and even in their antagonisms, and which is seeking to recover the vitality of their origin. When those who are responsible for the present state of affairs—and who is not to some extent?—are at least prepared to tackle the actual grounds upon which the Eastern Church, Protestantism, and Catholicism, rest, then it will be possible to achieve a contribution to the theme 'Russia and the West' which will involve not merely an understanding of the oppressive weight of the situation, but also some hope of changing it.

5

Has the Opposition of the Confessions a Philosophical Side?

The more one tries to understand the basic Confessional opposition, the difference between Catholicism and Protestantism, and to grasp each of these complex historical entities, both in their manifold outward forms and also in what divides them, from the standpoint of the unity of one internal basis, the more clearly does one recognize that the very attempt to understand is affected by the Confessional difference. Underneath the diversities and doctrinal differences we encounter extraordinarily deep-rooted and active differences in modes of thought, in the understanding of reality, and in speech, whose existence seems to militate against any possibility of understanding. In recent Catholic controversial literature the Confessional difference has been approached as an ontological problem.[1] In this connection it is interesting to recall an early treatment of this problem in a late work of the Ritschlian school.

The last major publication by Julius Kaftan bears the title '*Philosophy of Protestantism*' with the sub-title *An Apologia for the Evangelical Faith*. The book appeared at the time of the anniversary celebration of the Reformation, in 1917, Not only did it appear under the unfavourable conditions of the last years of the war and the first post-war years, but it was also then completely overwhelmed by the flood of dialectical theological writing. The statistics of the publishing firm of J. C. B. Mohr (Paul Siebeck) show that the demand for the book ceased suddenly in 1923, the result, of course, of the inflation. To the best of my knowledge, in the works of the leading theologians during the next decade the book is never mentioned, a characteristic symptom of the break in that generation. The catch-words of the title, '*Philosophy of Protestantism*', and '*An Apologia for the Evangelical Faith*', already betray

89

the fact that, set against the prevailing mode of expression characteristic of the new theology, the work was doomed to be a hopelessly antiquated undertaking. Although the book represents what is for us a mode of thought belonging to the distant past, nevertheless the work of this cautious dogmatic theologian deserves attention as a serious contribution to the Confessional problem. It may stir us up to further reflection, and is more closely related to the modern changed state of the problem than might appear from the first impression.

In a short review, somewhat too effusive, but touching the main problem, Wilhelm Herrmann has in the following words set the book in its historical theological perspective: 'It has been unfortunate for Protestant theology that Luther absolutely rejected Thomism and its master, Aristotle, but at the same time failed to meet the spiritual need which Thomism had supplied for the Middle Ages. This lack has now fortunately been met by Kaftan's work.' According to Herrmann, Kaftan has 'provided the completion which the work of Luther required'.[2]

I shall only touch on a few points:

1. Although Catholicism is not Kaftan's immediate subject, nevertheless his whole statement of the problem is directed towards the opposition of the two Confessions. The object of his undertaking is precisely to throw light on the specific underlying difference between Catholicism and Protestantism. Merely to treat them as separate Confessions and separate Churches leaves the actual situation insufficiently revealed. 'The contrasting difference does not merely lie in the religious and ecclesiastical sphere, but extends over the whole pattern of life.'[3] The universal character of the Christian faith entails the necessity that a methodical Confessional study should embrace as wide a horizon as possible. Christianity was 'more than merely a new religion; it was, indeed, a great new pattern of life, which, in the life of nations or individuals, left nothing untouched for those who were apprehended by it. The same truth holds good for both Catholicism and Protestantism: they are historical manifestations of life, each in its own way a characteristic expression of the Christian form of life'.[4] In these forms of life we have to do with 'organic unities'. 'A unity is constituted by the fact that everything which appertains to it is linked together as the

limbs are to the body, making the *one* body.'[5] 'For this reason the Christian Confessions differ completely from one another.'[6] The unities and the differences are not merely incidental parts of the whole. 'What they have in common is absorbed into the whole. This entails that they all, each in its own way, represent Christianity. In no less a degree do the things which distinguish them belong to the whole. Even the minutest differences extend to the whole.'[7]

What then is the key to the understanding of the Catholic-Protestant opposition? Obviously the differences become apparent throughout the whole range of the *regula fidei*, as well as in every department of life, especially in so far as the difference has found expression institutionally. The opposition, however, does not merely affect the content of the faith, but even the faith itself. 'For the preaching of the Reformers the word of faith had become a liberating word, and it continues to be such up to the present day, in so far as practical piety is concerned, in spite of the distortion and infection of its dogmatic system by Scholasticism. The opposition between Catholicism and Protestantism can be clearly seen in the way faith is understood, and the place it is given in the whole.'[8]

With these words the Confessional opposition is extended to the nature and manner of the spiritual appropriation of faith. It is at this point in the matter of faith that the problem of philosophy becomes acute. Religion and faith, as such, are not dependent on philosophy. Their position is guaranteed for and by themselves. 'Conviction and acceptance in this sphere are in the first instance independent of any philosophical basis.' Moreover the religious person is 'not merely a subject of religion, but is also a subject of the intellectual life of his time'.[9] 'Hence arises the imperative need to relate the Christian faith to the whole of intellectual life in such a way as to establish an inner connection between them.'[10] This point of view is not only relevant for Christianity, although it concerns the latter in a very special degree. For 'Christianity, being a spiritual religion, must be apprehended in an *inward* spiritual way. Only when this takes place does it become a subjective reality.'[11]

This inward spiritual appropriation is 'dependent on the spiritual means by which it is achieved', and these in their turn are 'conditioned by the predominant pattern of spiritual life in its totality, that is, they are historically conditioned'.[12] According to Kaftan the explicit indication of the place of faith in the life of the spirit as a whole is, alongside dogmatics which is concerned with the rule of faith, a task of special importance. Its designation as 'apologetic' should not be misunderstood to mean a specific defence against opponents. The apologetic which Kaftan has in mind is one which we employ 'not for the sake of others but for our own sake'.[13] As each Confession has its own dogmatics, each has similarly its own apologetic, that is to say, a definite 'conception and ordering of its own spiritual life in its totality'.[14] Hence apologetic to some extent precedes dogmatics, in so far as each Confession 'in its own way and in the form of its doctrine, receives its distinctive character from the way in which it inserts Christianity into the rest of its spiritual life; that is, from the source whence it derives its apologetic, and from the basis on which its apologetic rests'.[15] In other words, apologetic is therefore concerned with that which, to use Aristotelian terms, determines the internal form of dogmatics. We might say, developing Kaftan's thought still further, that apologetic consists in the reflection of a Confession upon its own ultimate spiritual principles; it is the self-consciousness of a particular Confession. Since then Kaftan considers philosophy to be the self-consciousness of the spirit, it is easier to understand why he regards the task of apologetic to be a philosophic one, and hence can formulate his fundamental thesis in the following terms: 'The difference between what is Protestant and what is Catholic . . . is also observable in their philosophy.'[16] 'On either side the basic fabric of the spirit takes on a different shape and character.'[17]

2. This basic problem of Kaftan's book raises a question concerning the spiritual means by which the inner spiritual appropriation of the revelation is brought about, and upon which it depends. Here Kaftan seems to have a double consideration in mind, involving both a connection and a distinction. On the one hand he calls to mind the influence which the spiritual character of an age exerts upon its thought-forms, and hence upon its appropriation of the revelation. In this respect, the task of the apologetic of the Christian faith continually changes with every change in the historical and spiritual situation, bringing the faith into relation with the spiritual life of the age as a

whole. This particular aspect of the problem is not necessarily connected with the Confessional opposition. Here, however, the other aspect, with which Kaftan is specially occupied, comes to the fore. Since Christianity exists in Confessional forms, the permanent distinctive task of apologetic is determined by the historical fact that every Confession already possesses a definite form of appropriation, a definite way of relating the faith to spiritual life as a whole, a way which is independent of any historical spiritual change and persists throughout as something specifically characteristic of the Confession in question. In this respect it would appear that the fulfilment of the task of apologetic is determined once for all, whatever subsequent change may take place.

These two aspects of the problem of apologetic can of course be joined together. The two Confessional types of apologetic, that is the philosophy of Catholicism and the philosophy of Protestantism, stand fast as established facts. In dealing with new historical and spiritual situations which have presented a similar challenge to each of them, the Confessions react in their philosophy in fundamentally different ways. It might, indeed, be asked whether the connection is not to be understood somewhat differently: whether the philosophy of Catholicism, or of Protestantism, in a given historical and spiritual situation, although its basic characteristics are established, yet has to be thought through afresh in each situation. Moreover, in this connection, there is a double aspect of the active relation between faith and spiritual life as a whole to be considered. On the one hand, given spiritual factors, independent of the Christian faith, can exert an influence upon the nature and manner of the appropriation of revelation. On the other hand, the fact must be taken into account that the faith, or a particular interpretation of the faith, can create spiritual factors and the resulting thought-forms and modes of spiritual appropriation.

Can these two possibilities be assigned to the two different aspects of the apologetic task which we have already distinguished? In the origin of a Confession, and in the subsequent development of its basic philosophic trend, is faith the ultimate active factor, creating its specific thought-forms, while in the further historical development of the Confession is the relation reversed? Or is there a double movement in process as the Confessions assume their characteristic form: a formative energy proceeding from faith, as well as the effect of outside spiritual factors upon the appropriation of faith? Or must a distinction be made in the case of the individual Confessions, to the effect that, in one case the philosophy of a Confession owes its origin to the influence of external spiritual factors, as for example, through the 'Hellenization' of Christianity; while in the other case the philosophy of a Confession owes its origin to faith itself, entirely independently of any outside influences?

Even if it proves impossible to include all the details of the intricate historical reality of the Confessions in a systematic pattern, it still remains possible to recognize in the history of the Confessions certain definite basic situations. There are two conclusions which are of special importance for Kaftan's position: in the spiritual development of the two Confessions he attaches the greatest importance to the fact that, in the Western culture area, as any new spiritual historical situations arise, they are drawn into the stream of the two great basic alternatives, namely, Catholic and Protestant philosophy. He also maintains that with regard to the relation between faith and reason, Catholicism, in its origin and character, exhibits a fundamentally different pattern from that of Protestantism.

3. A further question is raised by Kaftan's distinction between dogmatics and apologetics. He repeatedly emphasizes the closeness of the link between them; they must always correspond to one another in theology. 'As apologetics is responsible for bringing Christianity (i.e., religion) into relation with the totality of spiritual life, that is, in the basic conception of spirit, so dogmatics is responsible for the definite pattern of the rule of faith, since they both originate from the same root, from the inward appropriation of the revelation, in a definite concrete pattern of spiritual life as a whole.'[18] This does not indeed exclude the possibility of irrelevant discrepancies. However, since, according to Kaftan, 'this kind of apologetics' is 'a component element of the task of theology',[19] why is it a task to be distinguished at all from dogmatics? Since in fact its task is one which must be decisively affirmed, namely, to grasp the relation of the Christian faith to spiritual life as a whole, then this is simply a radical conception of the task of understanding. Is not this the very task of dogmatics? That task

does not consist in tending and glorifying the traditional rule of faith in a realm sheltered from contact with spiritual life in its totality, but rather in the interpretation of faith in an unceasing encounter with the whole of reality. Thus the function of dogmatics is accomplished in an 'apologetic' sense; it must also engage in the study of the relevant thought-forms, not merely as a preparation for authoritative prolegomena, but as an indispensable part of the whole work of dogmatics.

In his separation of the tasks, Kaftan is impelled by a valuable insight. 'This kind of apologetics is a component element of the task of theology. It is the philosophic task of theology, implicit therein. It must, however, be achieved independently of theology, that is to say, without any admixture of theological presuppositions. All that it involves is a philosophic outline, claiming no validity but that which rests on philosophic grounds. Only thus can it acquire universal significance, and only thus can it meet the *real need* of the Christian.'[20] At first sight this seems to involve a contradiction: 'a component element of the task of theology', 'independently of theology'; a 'Catholic or a Protestant philosophy', yet 'without any admixture of theological presuppositions'? It is evident that the reason why Kaftan attaches such importance to the philosophic character of this task, and why he will not hear of any admixture of theological presuppositions, is because he claims for the so-called apologetics a universal intelligibility and binding force. Its claim for validity should rest on no other grounds than those which have validity for philosophy.

The bringing of the Christian faith into relation with the whole pattern of spiritual life should therefore follow a line which is intelligible to everyone and can enlighten everyone; its accomplishment must be independent of the Christian Confession. In order that theology may not allow the Christian faith in its relation to spiritual life as a whole to enter an isolation foreign to its essential nature, it must as a definite part of its work, in its reflection on this totality of spiritual life, make such statements as are independent of the faith for their truth, and can carry the conviction of reality. They should not, however, aim at proving the truth of the faith itself. It may, perhaps, be the duty of theology to make statements about reality whose meaning may be disclosed in the Christian faith, but is not inseparable from it. In my opinion Kaftan is justified in insisting that in theology also there should be statements of a philosophic character possessing universal validity, which serve a theological purpose by the connection in which they stand. I cannot, however, help doubting whether Kaftan's distinction between dogmatics and apologetics is tenable. It seems to me that this philosophic task of theology has its immediate place in the actual work of dogmatics. At any rate, this has far-reaching consequences in relation to the understanding of dogmatics which cannot be developed now.

4. We turn now to Kaftan's conception of philosophy. Here we have to do with the fundamental question of Confessional decision, or, to put it more correctly, here the fundamental oppositions between the Confessions are revealed. For in the definition of the concept of philosophy one's own standpoint is revealed. Kaftan is not making use of a suppositious neutral conception of philosophy, but from the outset is working with the conception of philosophy which accords with the position of Protestant theology. Kaftan can follow this line because he is convinced that the position of Protestant theology agrees with the modern understanding of philosophy which is becoming more and more established.

This, in turn, agrees with the accompanying conception of science. Kaftan emphatically affirms the empirical character of modern science,[21] and the 'narrower and more specialized meaning' which the word 'science' has acquired in the modern age.[22] 'It is my opinion', he says, 'that unless we hold fast to the fundamental datum implicit in all knowledge and science, namely, that it is wholly based on experience, we lose everything.'[23] Certainly the opposition between empirical and deductive methods is not absolute. But here, however, we have to ask where the criterion of truth is to be sought.[24] Experience is the real criterion of truth.[25] This does not only concern the natural sciences, but also exposes the fallacy of a conception of science which regards thought, as such, as the source of knowledge, with the implication that 'what must be capable of being thought is also real'.[26] Accordingly logic can be described as 'creative, that is, truth-producing'.[27]

Philosophy is thus science, and from science we are carried directly into philosophy. 'The great thinkers, Plato and Aristotle, especially the latter, forged this bond, or rather, this union, between philosophy and science. It was Aristotle who brought those studies which were merely occupied with details into connection with philosophy, and thus became the founder of the union between the two disciplines. Under his auspices philosophy as a science has come down through the centuries up to and beyond Kant.'[28] To this type of philosophy which regards itself as science Kaftan has attached the epithet 'Intellectualism'. Its underlying conception of truth is theoretical knowledge, objective truth.[29] A philosophy which regards itself as a science is a dogmatic philosophy.

This conception of philosophy has now, however, had the ground cut from under its feet. If a particular point of time is to be assigned to the change, Kant is indicated. He has 'dug the grave of intellectualism.'[30] This is true in a double sense: first, through the idea put forward in his critical philosophy of the distinction between 'the thing-in-itself' and 'phenomena', or better, between 'reality in itself' and 'reality for us';[31] secondly, through the point of view of the primacy of the practical reason. Thus it has become impossible to understand philosophy in the strict sense as science, although, as Kaftan, following Kant's usage, puts it, 'reason aspires to attain to science'.[32] It is not enough, however, to refer to Kant in answer to the question concerning the real cause of this great historical and spiritual change. In addition to Kant two events call for consideration. One is the acquisition by science of an empirical character, freeing it from philosophy (i.e., from a philosophy which falsely regards itself as science), and disputing the claim of philosophy to be regarded as science in the strict sense. The other still more important event occurred in the religious sphere, and its significance for philosophy can only be understood when certain considerations concerning the relation between philosophy and religion are taken into account.

Kaftan regards philosophy as the self-consciousness of the spirit. This involves three considerations. First, Kaftan eliminates materialism and naturalism as serious claimants to be called philosophy. Only an idealist philosophy can be regarded as such. Next, his attention is specially directed towards history, and in it specially to science, ethics, and religion as the principal factors in the life of the spirit. Finally, it is the task of philosophy to enquire concerning the unity of this spiritual reality, concerning the connection between everything which we recognize as truth, and concerning the solution of the problem of the world and the meaning of existence. In these questions about the ultimate, philosophy turns out to be 'something that is related to religion',[33] religion for Kaftan not being reducible to the metaphysical instinct, the latter being rather a variation of religion.[34]

Philosophy itself is committed to take account of religion in that 'the growth of religion is bound up with the growth of spirit'.[35] This contact between religion and philosophy explains why an ultimate difference in the sphere of religion has its parallel in philosophy. As in philosophy idealism is the ultimate, so in religion the spiritual element is the ultimate consideration. There are, however, two types of spiritual religion, each of which arises from a different relation to ethics. The one represents pure spirituality, where the moral element is not taken up into the idea of the highest good, or of God. Historically this type of mystical and ascetic redemption religion is to be found in Brahmanism, Neo-platonism, or Sufiism. Over against this, Christianity represents the type of spiritual religion in which spirituality and morality are united. In the first case knowledge predominates, in the second, moral obedience. Correspondingly, there are also two types of idealist philosophy which differ on the question whether the primacy belongs to theoretical or practical reason, whether logic or ethics constitutes the essence of spirit.[36]

5. The circle closes when we return once more to the Confessional problem. The philosophy of Catholicism is of the intellectualist type of idealist philosophy. It is hardly necessary to apologize for speaking of *the* philosophy of Catholicism in the light of the position which is assigned to the philosophy of Aquinas in the Encyclical of Leo XIII, Aug. 4, 1879.[37] 'Behind Thomas Aquinas stands Aristotle and the intellectualism of Greek idealist philosophy'.[38] Catholicism, however, does not embody the purely intellectualist type. Its philosophy is a hybrid form, in so far as it represents a form of Christianity which came into existence as a result of the appropriation of the revelation through the medium of Greco–Roman civilization. Nevertheless, the intellectualist unity of the spirit constitutes the predominant element in Catholicism.[39] This is manifested most of all in an intellectualist distortion of the concept of faith into an acceptance of authority.

The essential opposition between the Confessions, deeper than any differences in individual matters of faith, lies in a different conception of faith itself. From the Protestant point of view, faith is 'a knowledge based on a personal relation to its object, i.e., to God'.[40] 'The opposition between Catholicism and Protestantism is clearly shown in the way in which faith is understood, and by the place which it occupies in the whole. That the idea of faith has once for all been actually carried to its conclusion, and established in the face of everything in the surrounding circumstances tending to obscure it, is the condition for a complete accomplishment of what we owe to the Reformation, and of the meaning of Protestantism.'[41] The last sentence opens up an extraordinarily important perspective in relation to the consequences of the Reformed concept of faith. It implies 'a different conception of knowledge from that which alone was universally accepted up to the time of the Reformation'. 'The Protestant idea of faith indirectly implies a new philosophic principle.'[42]

Nevertheless, for the recognition and full achievement of this a struggle is still necessary. In contrast with Catholicism which, as Kaftan maintains, is a complete and self-contained body, Protestantism is still in process of development.[43] Here Kaftan makes a very pertinent observation: the difference between the two Churches has been most completely achieved where institutions are concerned. 'With regard to them it is a straight question of alternatives; a Church either possesses them, or it does not. The situation is settled in either sense. Where, on the other hand, the freer forms of spiritual life are concerned, whose whole development necessarily plays a determinative part, it has long been maintained, even to some extent up to the present time, that Protestantism and Catholicism stand together on the same footing.'[44] The concept of faith, it is true, was altered by the Reformation. We may 'confidently maintain that this concept of faith is one for which we have the authority of the New Testament'.[45] But the spiritual context in which its validity was established remains unchanged. At first there was a tendency to refashion theology completely, since the Protestant concept of faith was by no means simply a change in one doctrinal detail, but a new theological principle, indeed a new standpoint in the field of knowledge, But the time was not yet ripe for such a change. 'Protestant theology was at first faced with the necessity of coming to terms with the philosophic presuppositions of Catholicism.'[46] 'Owing to the situation in which it found itself, the Reformation was not immediately in a position to overcome the philosophy of Catholicism. The assault on the sphere of personal piety, the breach with the old system in the more intimate recesses of life, was not powerful enough to loosen the grip of that unity of the spirit which prevailed in every sphere of the spiritual life. Hence Protestant Christianity was at first obliged, under the continuing predominance of the philosophy of Catholicism, to appear as a new form of Christian *religion*'.[47] Hence the apologetics of the old Protestant theologians was 'no different from that of Catholicism, an apologetics which was out of keeping with the real position of Protestant faith, and entangled with the intellectualism of the Romish system. The effects of this are seen to this day. Neither in the field of apologetics or of dogmatics have we really succeeded in overcoming the old connection with Scholasticism.'[48]

Certainly the decisive break-through has already taken place. 'It was Kant, with his doctrine of the primacy of practical reason, who rightly understood and demonstrated the Protestant concept of faith as being a new philosophic principle.'[49] Whereas Catholicism was formed by a philosophy coming from without, philosophic thought, conversely, formed the view of faith held by the Reformers. Kaftan says of Kant: 'He did not draw this out of pure reason, but it grew out of the great historical context of his time.'[50] 'It was first due to Kant that the unity of the spirit, corresponding to the Christian religious type which was renewed by the Reformation, received a philosophical vindication.'[51] The emergence of empirical science and the Reformed conception of faith are here seen working together in a remarkable consensus towards the overcoming of intellectualism. Kaftan speaks expressly of a parallel, but adds that, in the fundamental basis of spirit, both are closely connected.[52]

Kaftan was no blind follower of Kant. He shows himself to be a philosophic thinker when, criticizing Kant, he seeks to prove that 'the great critic of Intellectualism, who laid the axe to its root, appears from every angle to be dependent on Intellectualism'.[53] That philosophy is never something finished, from which scholarly conclusions can be drawn, is also true of the philosophy of Protestantism. It does not rest 'upon the dependence of theology on an outside authority, but on the result of theological work as such'.[54]

In Kaftan's 'philosophy of Protestantism' we find, in a mature form, a presentation whose essential features are in accordance with the main stream of the Protestant theology of the nineteenth century. According to him the contrast between Catholicism and Protestantism resolves itself into a total difference in modes of thought, a difference which, to put it bluntly, is that between medieval and modern modes of thought. According to this point of view Reformation and the Moderns stand together ultimately in a united front against Catholicism, while the latter is expressly committed to an anti-Modernist attitude. This view has basically determined the cultural, spiritual, and to a large extent the political aspect of the West in the modern world up to the First World War. Although for us the simplicity of such a conception has been destroyed, and the connection between the Confessional opposition and the basic forms of thought must be reconsidered, yet, for this very undertaking the discussion with Kaftan can be profitable. To bring about such a discussion has been the purpose of this revival of a forgotten writer.

6

' Sola Scriptura ' and Tradition

A. *Their involvement with one another*

Any discussion of the problem of Tradition from the theological point of view necessarily involves a discussion of the difference between 'Tradition' and 'Traditions'. Here the question of a standard by which the authority of tradition may be measured becomes the burning issue in the theological problem of Tradition. The Reformers' answer to the question found expression in the formula *sola scriptura*.[1] Hence, in the discussion of the problem of Tradition, the phrase *sola scriptura* must be our subject.

Although this is the Reformers' answer, it has nevertheless been recently called in question from the Protestant side. The remark, credibly reported, from the Protestant side, in Ecumenical conversations, '*sola scriptura* has become obsolete', reveals a judgement based on insufficient grounds. One should be just as little swayed by this tendency as by the earlier animosity towards the concept of Tradition. It would seem, however, that the formula *sola scriptura* is in need of re-interpretation. Its genuine Reformation sense needs to be clarified in view of current misinterpretations, and an altered situation calls for a new response.

The connection between the so-called Reformation principle of Scripture and the problem of Tradition confronts us in various ways.

1. *The common antithesis between* '*sola scriptura*' *and* '*Scripture and Tradition*'. In the traditional terminology of theological controversy, '*sola scriptura*' represents the battle-cry raised in answer to the Catholic formula 'Scripture and Tradition'. The exclusive adjective '*sola*' would thus seem to exclude, subject to closer definition, any autonomous theological authority for Tradition side by side with Scripture. From

its negative attitude towards the Catholic principle of Tradition the Reformed principle of Scripture seems to lead towards a general rejection of the phenomenon of tradition. Superficial consideration of the term 'Tradition' has caused, and still causes, it to be regarded as non-Protestant. This current estimate of the situation is, nevertheless, inaccurate and confused; but it exercises a powerful influence, and actually determines the starting-point of every discussion of the problem of Tradition in modern theology, especially in Ecumenical conversations. Hence it is necessary to take into consideration whether corrections are needed, and if they are, of what kind they should be.

2. *The significance of 'sola scriptura' for the history of the concept of Tradition.* The rise in theological controversy of the antithesis between *sola scriptura* and Scripture and Tradition during the Reformation caused a decisive break in the history of the concept of Tradition,[2] and led to a keener awareness, a deeper comprehension, and a broader discussion of the problems involved. Important material certainly exists in the early Church concerning the relation between the apostolic tradition in Holy Scripture and its existence in oral tradition. But actual discussion of the subject, especially in Irenaeus, Tertullian, Basil the Great, and Vincent of Lérins, is in general relatively scanty. As its patristic legacy the Mediaeval Church and its theology inherited what may be designated 'Scripture and Tradition' as an indivisible whole whose authority was accepted without question. Nevertheless the word *Tradition* hardly occurs in Scholastic theology, and not as a subject of study.[3] It was not felt necessary to define the relation between oral Tradition and Holy Scripture more exactly, since the possibility of a tension between them was not raised. Holy doctrine was so obviously identical with Holy Scripture that 'sacred Scripture' and the 'sacred page' could be interchangeable terms for theology.[4] Scholasticism offers much more scope for the study of its principle of Scripture than for that of its doctrine of Tradition.[5]

Thus, up to the beginning of the sixteenth century, the history of theology provides us with fundamental statements about the problem of Tradition, but, surprisingly, shows little evidence of any attempt to clarify them. From the historical point of view Humanism brought to light a significant distinction between Scripture and Tradition.[6] But it was the Reformation which, by the depth and intensity of its theological protest, first made a fresh discussion of the concept of Tradition necessary, and forced the Council of Trent at its fourth session to formulate a first, very incomplete, definition of the relation between Scripture and Tradition.[7] This resulted in a closer attention being devoted by post-Tridentine theology to the problems raised by the concept of tradition. In the nineteenth century this attention received a further stimulus especially from the historical studies of J. A. Möhler. There was a renewed interest in the twentieth century partly through the Bible movement and the Catholic Reform movement, and partly through the discussion of the dogma of the Assumption of the Virgin which began in 1950. Since the Reformation principle of *sola scriptura* now came to be recognized as touching upon a problem of decisive importance, which had hitherto not been clearly understood, it released for the first time the comprehensive exposition of Roman Catholic doctrine from Tradition. The *sola scriptura* principle therefore continues to be a fundamental objection for this doctrine, which plays a constitutive part. For the same reason the subject of *sola scriptura* may not be separated from the treatment of the theological problem of Tradition.

3. *The urgency of the problem of Tradition in Protestant theology.* The phenomenon of Tradition has now become relevant in various ways within Protestantism itself. It had already become apparent in the theology of the Reformers in their acceptance of early church dogma, as well as in the crystallization of their own doctrinal Tradition in written creeds. Interest in Tradition occupied an important place in the theological thought of Melanchthon, and had a decisive influence on the shaping of early Protestant orthodoxy.[8] For the Reformers the conservative value of Tradition was an essential factor in their attitude towards Confessional controversy. Agreement with the early Church was to be the proof of true catholicity and of the legitimacy of the Reformation.[9] Nevertheless, the necessity of vindicating the principle of *sola scriptura* against the Roman Catholic interpretation of Tradition militated against an impartial study of the theological importance of

the problem of Tradition. This appears, even in the exhaustive analysis of the Tradition-complex undertaken by M. Chemnitz in his *Examen Concilii Tridentini*. In this work he contrasted with the polychromatic Tridentine concept of Tradition, which permitted the entry of unscriptural views, seven *genera traditionum*, in part identical with Scripture, in part in factual agreement with it, and in part not contradicting it.

Certainly Catholic theologians were just as little inclined to deal with the problem of Tradition, evident in the Tridentine use of the plural (*sine scripto traditiones*), so long as Tradition was thought of as derived from a single *Traditum*. Only with the modern insight into historicity did theology become aware of the extent and difficulty of the problem of Tradition. This came about as the result of the historical approach, and was largely independent of the questions raised in theological controversy. The effect upon the spirit was that of a liberation from the limitation of Confessional prejudice. Nevertheless it reacted upon the controversial situation, and raised fresh problems for the theological understanding of the Confessional opposition. The chief characteristic of the historical approach is its emancipation from the unproved assumption of the authority of Tradition. It is only when criticism enables us to see the process of transmission in its true perspective that we become aware of the powerful influence exerted by Tradition, and can realize more clearly the part which historically conditioned traditions have played in history. This has produced a greatly enhanced ability to understand the situation with regard to Tradition in detail, as well as a basic insight into the historical function of Tradition. At the same time, however, the phenomenon of Tradition has been historicized and its validity called into question, quite independently of whether, among individual scholars, the critical or the conservative tendency happened to prevail. For Tradition to be recognized as historical does not strengthen its authority, but rather constitutes a threat to its validity as such. The historical study of Tradition, and the responsible appropriation and realization of Tradition, are in tension with one another.[10]

The influence of historical thinking upon theology is variously reflected in the wide range of problems opened up by the theme 'Scripture and Tradition'. Special mention should be made of biblical historical criticism. The study of the origin of Holy Scripture threw into relief the phenomenon of Tradition in hitherto unsuspected ways. The science of Church history recognized the differences between the Confessions as historically conditioned, and produced, within certain limits, an acceptance of their relativity. The revived attention to the phenonemon of Tradition, brought about by the historical approach, assumed an importance which varied according to the ecclesiastical tasks and interests with which it was connected. Hence the problem of Tradition involved the question of the language which was appropriate for preaching in the changed historical circumstances, and particularly that of translation in missionary work; then there was the question of the possibility of the confirmation or the revival of the form of the Church in the face of a tendency to dissolution or to petrifaction; there was the question of the causes of Confessional divisions and estrangement, as well as of the conditions needed to arrive at an Ecumenical understanding. In every case, however, the historical problem involved in the key-word 'Tradition' had to be seriously considered from the dogmatic point of view and thoroughly worked out. This represents the basic theological task of the new Protestant theology; for it was through the historical approach that the distinctive doctrine of old Protestant orthodoxy was finished. What should have served to secure the Reformers' principle of Scripture, namely, the doctrine of verbal inspiration, now turned out to be a danger to the principle of *sola scriptura*. At any rate, the traditional interpretation of the authority of Scripture was called in question. Moreover, the impression could arise that the attention being paid to the problem of Tradition means a weakening or surrender of the principle of *sola scriptura*. But the reduction of Scripture to 'mere' tradition by regarding it as history is not the only threat to the principle of *sola scriptura*. In addition, a heightened appreciation of the idea of Tradition has resulted from two causes: on the one hand from the recognition by biblical scholarship of the historical character of Tradition; and on the other hand, as the result of a general intellectual change, producing a fresh understanding of Tradition, and a dawning belief that the basic meaning of Tradition involves a real mastery of the problem of historicity. Thus the questionable nature of the principle of *sola scriptura* would only seem to have been enhanced.

It would, however, be a mistake to suppose that the problem of Tradition in the form in which it is presented by the historical approach of the new age, represents any confirmation of the Catholic conception of Tradition. The Catholic interpretation expressed in broad outline at the Councils of Trent and Vatican I is quite incapable of meeting the changed situation of the problem in the modern world. As the result of the new insight into the problem of historicity, both the Catholic doctrine of Scripture and Tradition, and the Reformers' principle of *sola scriptura*, need fresh interpretation and clarification. The difficulties which the task involves have become apparent in the first phase of Vatican II.

There is no justification whatever for speaking of a reconciliation between the Confessional positions, at least in view of the example of the official interpretation of Scripture and Tradition provided by the decree on the Assumption of the Virgin, which has not only been a shock to Protestants.[12] On the contrary, it has given a fresh impulse to the protest embodied in the Reformers' principle of *sola scriptura*, and a confirmation surpassing all previous occasions. Other symptoms, however, seem to suggest that the controversial situation is no longer acute. It can at least be said that there is a distinct trend in contemporary Catholic theology towards a 'Scripture' principle involving in itself the point of view of Tradition,[13] while, conversely, it appears that Protestant theology is learning to accept a form of 'Tradition' principle as a corrective of the too narrowly conceived 'Scripture' principle of the Reformers. It is in fact remarkable to see Catholic theologians enthusiastically supporting the claim of *sola scriptura* while Protestant theologians are writing it off as obsolete. These counter-trends should make us hesitate to assume that the Confessional understanding of the problem of Scripture and Tradition is appreciably nearer. Careful testing is needed to show whether on the Catholic side the modern interpretation of the relation between Scripture and Tradition in the sense of *sola scriptura*, really represents a movement towards the Protestant conception; or whether it should not be regarded as a subtle intensification of the Confessional opposition. Similarly the question might be raised whether on the Protestant side the serious attention being paid to the problem of Tradition really involves the surrender of the Reformers' *sola scriptura*, or whether, on the contrary, rightly understood, the Reformers' *sola scriptura* does not imply the principle of Tradition, although in a different sense from the Catholic interpretation of the Scripture principle. In order to clarify a situation giving rise to so much perplexity, it is only by a thoroughgoing exposition of the meaning of *sola scriptura* that Protestant theology can arrive at the much-needed interpretation of the problem of Tradition.

B. *Objections and misunderstandings*

In setting up a mere antithesis between *sola scriptura* and the Roman Catholic juxtaposition of Scripture and Tradition, there is a danger of narrowing and contracting the meaning of *sola scriptura*. Hence it is first of all necessary to remove some widespread misunderstandings.

1. *'Sola scriptura' accused of hostility to Tradition.* Far from being hostile to Tradition, it is itself a specific form of Tradition. This statement only seems strange because in controversial usage the idea of Tradition has long been limited to unwritten Tradition (*Traditio non scripta*), and therefore distinguished from Holy Scripture. Admittedly, this does not explain why the Reformers did not oppose to this usage the claim that Holy Scripture alone, as 'apostolic', is genuinely Tradition. Moreover, apart from the actual narrowing of the usage, Protestant interpretation has evidently been reluctant to designate as 'Tradition' the real concern of Holy Scripture in its ultimate significance. For this concern the Reformers preferred to use the expression 'the Word of God'. Although it cannot be denied that in the strict sense the Word of God, as in the concern of the Gospel, only reaches us in the form of Tradition, it is questionable whether the concept of Tradition should be raised to the pre-eminent theological position. The attempt has indeed been made, in dependence on the varied use of the term, to derive παραδι-δόναι, the apostolic 'Tradition', along with the opposed 'Tradition' in Jude, from a divine 'Tradition' identical with revelation itself, and in this

way to bring the whole content of the Gospel within the concept of Tradition.[14] Even if exegetical qualms about this clever, biblicist, lexical approach are discounted, in any case the explanatory use of such a comprehensive concept of Tradition does not involve its elevation to a theological technical term, to be played off against the Roman Catholic interpretation of Tradition, as though it represented the essential meaning of the Reformers' *sola scriptura*. For this purpose it would be better to adhere to the obvious meaning of Tradition, and to emphasize the exclusive validity of the original Tradition: namely, that the Gospel has reached us in the definite form of a history of which Jesus is the centre. Hence, since Jesus is its subject, the body of Tradition contained in both the New and the Old Testament, constituting the subject-matter of the Gospel as the original Tradition, is of unique and irreplaceable significance. Thus *sola scriptura* clearly implies an adherence to the original Tradition, unmixed with foreign elements, permitting the force of the biblical Tradition to be transmitted to the modern world.

This involves questions which need further discussion. Why has the Gospel reached us at all in the form of history, and why from this particular history? Why is its presentation expressly related to this history? What, moreover, is the significance of originality; how is it to be defined, and by what criteria? How is the continuation of this original witness secured, involving the transmission of this Tradition? Under what conditions is its purity preserved in spite of, or directly by means of, its perpetuation? If *sola scriptura* succeeds in answering these questions, a double problem arises. *Sola scriptura* may represent the struggle for the genuine Tradition; but the concept of Tradition hardly suffices to indicate the peculiar content of the *sola scriptura* principle. It has to be conceded that the term 'Scripture', taken by itself, is just a little, perhaps, even less an accurate description of the subject-matter under discussion in its entirety. The claim, then, of *sola scriptura* to interpret correctly the duality of Scripture and Tradition, can only be justified if it describes unambiguously the way in which the Gospel has been transmitted, that is, if it actually embraces and remains within the ambit of the transmission of the Gospel.

2. *The Priority and Vitality of Tradition as an Objection against the 'Sola scriptura' principle.* The objection has been made to *'sola scriptura'* that by its limitation to the written word it ignores both the historical priority of oral transmission and the obvious fact that transmission must have taken place through living witnesses. But both these points of view are essentially implied in the Reformers' *sola scriptura*. Their inner connection was, in fact, only understood for the first time in the Reformers' understanding of the Gospel. This important fact should not be obscured by the circumstance, for which Protestant theology was partly to blame, that later Catholic polemic made use of both these points of view as arguments against the misunderstood Reformed principle of Scripture.

It has, of course, always been recognized that Christianity did not begin with the New Testament. The fundamental fact of revelation is not a book. The New Testament writings should rather be regarded as the deposit of the previous preaching, or of its fulfilment in the genuine epistles; in any case, as the *result* of the revelation. In reality the canon came into existence as the outcome of a long process. The very pattern of the New Testament demonstrates its origin from oral transmission, the more so in that Jesus himself, and to a large extent the apostles as well, left nothing written. Moreover, the reports given by Eusebius of Caesarea concerning the history of the canon keep alive at least a faint idea of the historically secondary role of the written form of the revelation. The idea, too, that oral propagation is the appropriate method of transmitting doctrine is a very ancient one. It can be traced both in Judaism and in ancient philosophy.[15] In early Christianity there was a tendency to avoid it, on account of the Gnostic appeal to secret oral Tradition.[16] The basic aspect of that preference for the oral form of transmission is almost exclusively confined to Clement of Alexandria.[17] But even here the special connection between the Gospel and its oral transmission is not fully understood.

It can indeed be shown that both in the case of the early Church and of medieval Scholasticism, the understanding of the *matter* of the Christian faith was an understanding of the *Word* in its concrete spoken form, implying its written form. The nature of the Word was conceived of as bound up with letters and their descriptive function, and this constituted its strength as the firmly established prototype. But at the same time, however, the weakness and limitation of the spoken word becomes apparent. It could be the vehicle of instruction or orders, but the fundamental issue, the thing itself, the power of the Holy Spirit, grace, cannot be imparted by the mere word, but only through the sacramental operation of the Church. Thus, for example, the problem for Thomas Aquinas was,[18] whether the *lex nova*, given in the heart, not spoken, but an active, living, law, namely the grace of the Holy Spirit, could nevertheless be given in words. It is equally characteristic that for Thomas the question of the *lex nova* being given in spoken form was a question of its written form, and that he regarded this aspect of the *lex nova* as entirely secondary. For him it only meant instruction, serving as preparation for, and proper dealing with, grace, whereas the real beneficial experience of grace itself was the effect of the sacrament. Hence the written form is not here seen in rivalry with the spoken form, but rather as giving expression to the real nature of the spoken word.[19] In view of the dominant presuppositions of ecclesiastical doctrinal Tradition, the Reformers' *sola scriptura*, especially in its connection with '*solo verbo*'–'*sola fide*', was bound to be misunderstood as setting up the primacy of the written form of the Gospel, not, however, in distinction from its oral form, but in opposition to the living activity of grace operating through the sacraments of the Church.

The true meaning of the Reformers' *sola scriptura* can however only be understood in connection with their interpretation of the *matter* of the Christian faith and of the *Word* corresponding to it, with its implications of oral transmission. Hence, according to the Reformed point of view, the exclusive authority of Holy Scripture rests, paradoxically, on the Gospel, which, in essence, is not the written, but the *spoken word*. The Old Testament 'alone has the right to be called Holy Scripture, and Gospel should not be Scripture but the spoken Word which explains the Scripture, as did Christ and the Apostles. Hence also, Christ himself wrote nothing, but only spoke; and his teaching was not called Scripture, but Gospel, that is, good news, or preaching, that should not be propagated with the pen, but with the mouth.'[20] 'For in the New Testament sermons were wont to take place orally with living words, bringing into speech and hearing what was formerly concealed in letters and secret vision. Since the New Testament is nothing else but the exposition and revelation of the Old Testament . . . Hence it is not the New Testament way, to write books about Christian doctrine, but there should be everywhere, without books, good, learned, spiritual, zealous preachers, who should draw out the living word from the ancient Scriptures, and unceasingly exhort the people as the Apostles did. For before they wrote they had first preached to the people with actual words and converted them, and this was their real Apostolic and New Testament work . . . But that it should be necessary to write books was a great loss and failure of the Spirit; it was the result of compulsion, and not the manner of the New Testament. . . .'[21]

How remarkably deep was the Reformers' understanding of the Gospel is shown by the existence of this necessary connection between the content of this Tradition and its essential oral character. If, nevertheless, *sola scriptura* became the Reformers' watchword, this can only be understood in a sense that does not contradict the fact that the Word of God was imparted by verbal preaching, and was therefore oral Tradition. The exact value of *sola scriptura* is that it contributes to a right understanding of the essentially oral character of 'transmission'. Hence it is only rightly understood when it is referred back to the event of preaching, and when the origin of Scripture is seen to lie in the act of preaching.

Even the old Protestant orthodoxy which laid such stress on the *verbum Dei scriptum*, was conscious of the historical priority of the *verbum Dei non scriptum*. Luther's view of the oral character of the Gospel was more clearly defined by the work of Lessing, Semler, Herder[22] and others with regard to the secondary character of the reduction of the tradition to writing; then in detail the preceding course of the development of Tradition was revealed by historical and critical study;[23] Catholic criticism of *sola scriptura* could have had the effect of broadening and defining it; the same might be said about the discoveries of Orthodoxy concerning the origin of the Bible, although that had a revolutionary effect upon the dominant view of the origin of the Bible. For the rest, this historical aspect of the origin of the Bible need not serve as an argument against the necessity of its assuming a written form. On the contrary, as Luther in the above quotations has already shown the positive significance of the reduction of the New Testament to writing,[24] so an insight into the history of early Christianity reveals the irreplaceable value of the written transmission. It is only necessary to consider what would have become of the Synoptic tradition if it had only been preserved in oral form; or what the course of Church history would have been without the transmission of the Pauline correspondence, although Paul's own letters bear witness to long periods of misunderstanding and neglect of Paul himself. It is certainly true that old Protestant orthodoxy did not make extensive use of the historical priority of *verbum Dei non scriptum* as an aid to understanding *verbum Dei scriptum*. But its representatives were of course aware that the *verbum Dei* takes place as *viva vox*, and that to concentrate attention on *verbum Dei scriptum* should be of value for oral preaching. Nevertheless, in defence of Confessional interests, there is a tendency to avoid discussion of the meaning of *sola scriptura* too closely with regard to the tension that exists between the written and the spoken character of the Word of God, of which the importance appears in oral proclamation. It is very significant that Johann Gerhard opposes as the utterance of a controversial opponent the statement that the written form does not really suit the nature of the Gospel message,[25] instead of appealing to Luther in support of *sola scriptura*.

3. *The Formation of the Canon and its Authority as an Argument against sola scriptura*. What appears to be the strongest objection, and one which, up to the present, Catholics advance with a triumphant assumption of its irrefutability, runs as follows: *sola scriptura* is a contradiction in terms, since it presupposes the Catholic principle of Tradition; it bases itself upon the Church's decision about Scripture as it found expression in the events which led up to the formation of the canon, and likewise in the Church's teaching about Scripture, before and after. The following is an example of one of the most recent utterances of this kind: 'Ever since there has been a Catholic–Protestant controversy about the principle of *sola scriptura* enunciated by the Reformers, the biblical canon of Scripture has always been one of the strongest arguments on the Catholic side. The more closely the history of the origin of the books of the Bible and of the Canon is studied, the stronger does the

argument become. How, during the vicissitudes of many centuries, the various contingencies, special occasions, and historical situations, affecting the canonical or non-canonical books, have finally combined to produce a canon of Scripture everywhere recognized as normative, is something which can never be explained without the assumption of a normative tradition of faith, accepted as the guiding power of the Spirit of God, bringing the canon into existence . . . Canon and Church are inseparable, and that implies that Scripture and Tradition are inseparable . . . In practice, almost every Protestant theologian in his doctrinal formulation, and every preacher in his pulpit, reasons in this way, as though the canon were something whose limits were fixed, and which claimed acceptance of its contents . . . The *de facto* acceptance of the tradition extends far more widely than conscious reasoning (reference is here made to H. Diem's designation of the canon as "an accepted dogma") would allow.'[26]

The fact is that the fixing of the canon is the work of the post-apostolic Church. Such a comprehensive statement should not, indeed, be allowed to obscure the variety of events which led to the emergence of the canon. Alongside of and before the official ecclesiastical decision which fixed the canon for the sake of unity and to bring about agreement over the developments taking place in the various provinces of the Church, the important thing that was happening was simply that the use of certain books in church had become obligatory, and that these subsequently acquired their undisputed authority through the idea of the canon, and in agreement with the Old Testament came to be regarded as 'Holy Scripture'. As the complexity of the history of the canon comes to be increasingly recognized, both of the following attitudes become untenable: it is neither permissible to deduce directly from the New Testament writings themselves the idea and limits of the canon, nor to infer the existence of an independent principle of Tradition with regard to Scripture from the process of the formation of the canon. It is not only a fact that none of the New Testament writings accepted as canonical (with the exception of the Revelation of St. John) expressly claim to be such, or supply information about their assembling or its completion; it would be equally meaningless to attempt to deduce directly from Scripture a proof of the *sola scriptura* principle, since such a proof, if it is to be convincing, must take for granted the very thing which has to be proved, namely, the canonical authority of Scripture. The following reasons compel the rejection of the claim that, owing to the insufficiency of Scripture, Tradition must be accepted as a second source of revelation: first, the limitation of the canon seems to consist merely in the actual existence of the New Testament writings in the canon; it is not a formally revealed element of the canon; secondly, the declaration that this collection of writings is 'the sole rule and plumb-line', meaning *sola scriptura* in its usually accepted sense, is not in the canon itself, but only implied by its designation as the canon; lastly, although the strict sense of the Scripture principle is Scripture as a *principium*, its acceptance as a principle is then declared to be a dogma. If *sola scriptura*, since it is proclaimed as such by the Church, is to be regarded as a contradiction in terms, by the same reasoning the canon, since it is established by the decree of the Church, must be a contradiction in terms. Conversely, moreover, it would be a contradiction in terms to understand the judgement of the Church, that the New Testament writings are alone canonical, as the affirmation of a Tradition-principle side by side with the canon; while in that 'judgement' the sole recognition of Scripture as constituting the canon is subordinated to the judgement of Scripture. Only in contradiction to what is expressly declared in the acceptance of the New Testament writings as canonical, can this be put forward as evidence against *sola scriptura*. In view of the history of the canon, it is a double-edged undertaking to make use of the argument of *contradictio in adiecto*, since, just as it has been used by Catholics against the *sola scriptura* principle, so it can be used against the Catholic attempt to justify, from the formation of the canon, the assumption of a special Tradition-principle side by side with Scripture. But more is involved here than the mere contradiction of the Confessional position. The problem posed by the existence of a canon of New Testament writings, indisputably closed, collected and promulgated by the Church itself, helps—through the fact that the Church breaks out in the way we have described—towards a clearer understanding of the canon.

The Church's decision concerning the canonicity of the New Testament writings is not to be taken as an affirmation of the position of

Scripture *extra usum scripturae*, any more than should the emphasis of *sola scriptura* on this point of view of the canonicity be so regarded. So far as Scripture is concerned it is the answer to the matter that finds utterance in it. Just as the Creed does not give authority to that which it confesses, but rather acknowledges and proclaims that authority which it actually experiences in the act of confession—in this connection the old Protestant doctrine rightly spoke of an *auctoritas causativa*—so the affirmation of canonicity, and correspondingly that of *sola scriptura*, is a credal utterance. In the last resort it relates to the *testimonium spiritus sancti internum* as the manner in which validity is imparted to the content of Scripture. Just as Scripture may not be separated from its use in preaching, so also it is obvious that the *testimonium spiritus sancti internum* may not be separated from the witness of the Church in its continuing activity of preaching, constituting the actual encounter with Scripture. If the inseparable connection between Scripture and Church, Scripture and Tradition is understood to mean that Scripture does not exist in isolation in the form of a book, but is transmitted in the activity of preaching, not in order that it may remain in written form as 'Holy Scripture', but to serve as an aid to preaching, and to constitute its subject as the preacher's text, then there need be no dispute about *sola scriptura*. But if the question of authority is detached from the subject of the connection of Scripture and Church, Scripture and Tradition, then the *testimonium ecclesiae* should not be treated in isolation, but only as the fulfilment of its preaching activity, which is related to the *testimonium scripturae*, and is directed towards the *testimonium spiritus sancti internum*, and thus towards the total validity of the matter of Scripture itself. Only thus is the *testimonium ecclesiae* the witness of *sola scriptura*. This is why Old Protestant orthodoxy, with reference to the Scripture-principle, distinguished between the *testimonium ecclesiae* as a mere aid (*testimonium ministeriale*), and the actual witness of the matter of the Scripture itself (*testimonium principale*). With regard to the content of *sola scriptura*, the witness of the Church is not an objection against the Scripture-principle, but, as a witness to Scripture, is the result of the content of Scripture.[27]

If the controversy about the relation between Scripture and Tradition becomes acute, in connection with the problem of the canon, it at any rate clarifies the matter that the *meaning* of the canon has to be discussed. As this very thing is a source of obscurity, it would be foolish to regard the meaning of the canon as obviously clear, or that it is clear in what sense the New Testament writings are canonical, or how they have become 'standard' or 'authoritative', or, the obviously related question, in what way the writings of the Old Testament canon are canonical. It should not be regarded as the sign of weakening of the meaning of the canon in certain Protestant writings, when the question of the authority of the canon is set off against the truth of its contents, and when it may seem that the strictness of its formal authority is relaxed through a rival criterion of factual truth.

It is a fact that the designation *'sola scriptura'* as a 'formal principle' is of Protestant origin.[28] Yet this description, which goes back to the beginning of the nineteenth century, brings to light the problem of the formal meaning of the authority of Scripture. It recalls the position of Holy Scripture as the *'principium'* of theology in old Protestant dogmatics,[29] but it treats the 'principle' concept in an entirely different way: not as a methodological scientific term, laying down the basis for a scientific method without discussion,[30] but as a historiographical term, which introduces into the concept that which underlines the complex and variable historical element as its real specific and unifying feature. While in the one case it is a question of the principle of *theology*, in the other it is a question of the principle of *Protestantism*. Now of course there is a relation between the historical phenomenological designation of Holy Scripture as the formal principle of Protestantism, and the dogmatic designation of Holy Scripture as the principle of theology. The orthodox position is definitely adopted, but with a critical reservation, accepting the designation of the 'Scripture principle', but in the limited sense of a 'formal principle'; this calls for completion by means of a 'material principle', as which the Reformers' doctrine of justification is usually presented. In spite of the apparent terminological and factual resemblance to orthodox doctrine, there is nevertheless a profound difference. Orthodox doctrine does not regard Holy Scripture in this sense as a 'formal principle' needing to be supplemented by a 'material principle'. Even there a distinction is made theologically between God as the ground of being (*principium essendi*)

and Holy Scripture as the ground of knowledge (*principium cognoscendi*)
From the scientific and methodological point of view, however, we
are only concerned with the latter, so that Holy Scripture can be
designated as *unicum et proprium theologiae principium*.[31] With the
Scripture-principle thus conceived, on the basis of modern hermeneutical experience, through the critical use of the term 'formal principle',
the fundamental meaning of *sola scriptura* was recognized as the essential characteristic of Protestantism, but with the reservation that the
attribution of exclusive authority to Scripture did not guarantee that it
was understood in the Reformers' sense. Hence Holy Scripture is not
unconditionally relied upon to guarantee its own correct interpretation, and an attempt is made to avoid risks in interpretation by introducing a 'material principle' to assume the function of a factual hermeneutical principle. The mode of thought characteristic of the modern
world is here apparent in the way in which a distinction is made between
the bare empty 'form', and the essential 'content'. In Aristotelian
terminology the converse formulation would be required, namely, the
classification of Scripture under the category of 'material principle', in
relation to the doctrine of justification as the 'formal principle', or
more precisely, as *ratio formalis* of the right understanding of Scripture.[32]
From the modern point of view the Scripture principle, taken by itself,
appears as formal in the sense of factually undefined, as ambiguous; so
that it only becomes unambiguous in the Reformers' sense through the
introduction of a material principle. Behind this Protestant duality of
'formal' and 'material' principle there lies the conviction that this
material principle is in accord with Scripture, and is really a canon
within the canon. Nevertheless the question arises whether the pattern
of these two principles does not bear a close relation to the Catholic
duality of Scripture and Tradition, in so far as Scripture, for its correct
interpretation, requires to be secured by a fixed tradition of interpretation, such as is provided by the Reformed Confession.

The fact that by the distinction between the formal and the material
principle, the problem of the canon takes on the form of a question of
the *understanding* of the canon, and that of *sola scriptura* as one of the
interpretation of Scripture, undoubtedly makes for clarification. Yet
this only reveals what is essentially implied in the judgement about

canonicity, and in the corresponding affirmation concerning *sola scriptura*. For it would be erroneous to suppose that the Scripture-principle, even in the orthodox sense, is purely formal. It means explicitly that Scripture is the Word of God. Even if the impression that here we have to do with a purely formal definition can be carried over to the conception of the Word of God, it will have to be admitted that by predicating Scripture as the Word of God *sola scriptura* is being interpreted, and that thus at least the direction is given towards the understanding of authority with which we are now concerned, and also towards the understanding of what is here actually involved. And even if the concept of the Word of God is brought into action, in however indeterminate a way, it gives a general indication of what the canonicity of Scripture actually means, and represents a certain criterion, perhaps very vaguely conceived, nevertheless capable of and needing explanation, of the canonicity of the canon. By its fundamental interpretation of Scripture as the Word of God, Old Protestant orthodoxy provided the factual meaning of canonicity and of *sola scriptura*, and intended perhaps a more precise meaning than was actually expressed.

What, however, holds good with regard to the orthodox Scripture-principle, is also basically true of every understanding of the canon, including the Catholic. It necessarily implies a factual criterion, however much it is concealed. A formal Scripture-principle is an impossibility. The double character of the writings designated as canonical on the one hand, and of the interpretation of their canonicity and authority on the other, has created a situation involving its own special tension; this is apparent in theology as the late distinction between the formal and the material principle, although its implications were not fully grasped. If they had been, then, instead of reasoning from two separate principles, scope would have been left for the movement of thought which would have enabled the canonical writings to establish their own canonicity and to make its meaning clear. What has happened is that the designation and acceptance of these writings as canonical, as Holy Scripture, has merely raised a claim which will have to be justified; or, to put it more accurately perhaps, has expressed a promise which has to be recognized; at any rate it has imposed a task which must be taken up in connection with the interpretation of Scripture.

The designation of the writings as a canon is, in the precise meaning of the word, a 'pre-judgement',[33] which calls for the testing and confirmation of Scripture itself.

When, however, the designation of Scripture as canon makes the task of interpretation imperative, in order that by means of the fulness of what the Scriptures say it may be made clear how far they are 'canonical', and what their canonicity means, then it cannot be denied that the task imposed by the canon as such, is a critical one, continually engaged in exposing any false use of the canon and any false interpretation of its meaning.[34] The work of purifying, clarifying, and validating the canon as such, can only be performed in the first place through preaching to that human reality for which both preaching and canon are necessary. This comprehensive process of arriving at clarifying decisions obviously involves an understanding of the canon as such and of its use against every kind of obscurity and error. This, moreover, necessarily includes an internal criticism of the canon, involving a critical study of the position of individual texts within the canon, in order to guard against any threat to the unity of the canon. The manner in which Luther used this internal criticism of the canon is well known, though perhaps not as well known as it should be; he placed the Epistle to the Hebrews and the Epistle of James after the Johannine epistles, and the unnumbered series of what now become the last four New Testament writings, namely, the Epistle to the Hebrews, the Epistle of James, the Epistle of Jude, and the Revelation of St. John outside the numbered sequence of the other twenty-three books of the New Testament;[35] he also made value judgements, 'which are the authentic and noblest books of the New Testament',[36] and corresponding negative utterances about other New Testament writings.[37]

What Luther here does—admittedly in a specially striking way—is done, either explicitly or implicitly, in every study of the canon, if it is regarded as a canon at all. It cannot be denied that a revision of the canon is thus made possible, but this can only be regarded as an objection if the tension in the pattern of the canon between the general assumption of canonicity and the concrete proof of canonicity is not recognized, and if the actual canonicity is shifted from the texts to be interpreted to a definitive decree, and thus in principle to an interpretation. To admit the possibility of a revision of the canon means the same thing, with regard to the Holy Scriptures, as undertaking to correct its interpretation and confession of the Christian faith. To exclude this from the outset would mean that the canonicity of Scripture was not taken seriously. It would betray a lack of understanding with regard to the nature of the Confession of faith, and also of the nature of interpretation, if the Confession were to be regarded as uncertain because it is dependent on Holy Scripture as 'the sole rule and plumb-line', or, to put it another way, if the interpretation were not to be taken seriously because its proof depends on the text and may never take the place of the text.

The Roman Catholic interpretation of the canon, which in the last analysis anchors the authority of the canon to an ecclesiastical decree, can therefore only admit the canonicity of Scripture as subject to a tradition of interpretation. The Reformers' interpretation of the canon, on the other hand, which allows its authority to depend on the collection of writings accepted as canonical, can only accept the ecclesiastical decree as canonical in the sense that, as interpretation, it is tested by Scripture itself, and thus is bound to the Word in its judgement about the canonicity of Scripture.

For the rest, too great a preoccupation with the extreme possibility of a revision of the canon—for which, as far as the New Testament is concerned, Luther thought there was no occasion, in spite of his internal criticism of the canon—diverts attention from the decisive question. The question whether individual writings or parts of them do not rightfully belong to the canon, easily suggests an erroneous understanding of the canon, according to which it is not really a collection of historically different testimonies, but a legally available manual of doctrine, and the necessity of interpretation is regarded as a basic contradiction of the conception of the canon. The central problem, implied by the watchword of internal criticism, is inseparable from the existence of the canon, whatever may be its extent, and therefore cannot be eliminated by any revision of the canon. It involves the obligation of using the canon as a canon, and of carrying out the principle of *sola scriptura*.

C. The Truth in 'sola scriptura'

Our discussion of the objections which have been levelled against *sola scriptura*, especially with reference to the phenomenon of the canon, has prepared the way for a positive exposition of the meaning of *sola scriptura*. We must now, by way of contrast, with the Catholic conjunction of 'Scripture and Tradition', make '*sola scriptura*' our theme, yet in such a way as to test its truth by as complete an understanding as possible of the opposite position.

1. *The hermeneutic meaning of the formula 'Scripture and Tradition'.* It is by no means self-evident how far the formula 'Scripture and Tradition' contradicts the principle of *sola scriptura*. The *particula exclusiva* is only valid in a specific reference, and therefore does not exclude a reference to other books and traditions; on the contrary, it requires them for the very reason that only by contact with the richness of everything that is in some way or other important for human existence can that which is attested in Holy Scripture be shown to be unique and valid. There can be no doubt that it is not the purpose of the formula 'Scripture and Tradition' to attack or diminish the unique character of Holy Scripture as it stands in the canon. If *sola scriptura*, as one would in the first instance suppose, simply emphasizes the special place of Holy Scripture in the canon, then it is clearly valid on the Catholic side as well. The Tridentine formula '*pari pietas affectu ac reverentia*',[38] in spite of its assertion of equal status for Scripture and Tradition, is not absolved from the obligation of giving such an account of this distinction as may establish the unchallenged position of the Bible as a canonical writing.[39] For neither the unique authority of Holy Scripture (its canonicity), nor its claim to reverence as revelation, inseparable from its canonicity (its inspiration,) are matters of controversy as between Catholicism and the Reformers. At the Reformation the point of view of canonicity was more strictly defined: hence the adherence to the narrower Hebrew canon and consequently the exclusion of the Apocryphal books; in the New Testament a distinction was made between proto- and deutero-

canonical writings, corresponding to the Antilegomena in the history of the canon; only the original text was regarded as authoritative. All this is symptomatic, not of a less, but of a more strict attitude towards the canon; correspondingly, in the orthodox doctrinal pattern the inspiration of Scripture assumed the highest possible importance. Nevertheless, in spite of such distinction of grades, the fundamental difference implied in *sola scriptura* as a controversial theological formula is not fully grasped. It is a mistake to see the situation as involving various circles of what is normative, Protestantism as limiting its norm to the biblical canon in its most restricted sense, and Catholicism as affirming the canonicity of oral tradition in addition to that of Scripture. This may serve as a rough description of the actual situation, and, perhaps, not only of the conception which the two Confessional partners have of one another, but also of their self-understanding at its trivial level. But from both the Catholic and the Protestant sides its inadequacy may be easily perceived.

As soon as one gives concrete shape to this idea of two neighbouring areas of differing standards, so that the division of Holy Scripture into Old and New Testaments is expanded by the domain of Tradition into a *Biblia tripartita*, Holy Scripture receives the addition of a third part, and the extent of the canon becomes virtually unlimited, the absurdity of the interpretation becomes apparent. This interpretation is not wholly without foundation, but results from the unclear nature of the Catholic conception of tradition, and from the always debated problem, which especially engages the attention of modern Catholicism, of how tradition is to be related to Holy Scripture. The impression of confusion caused by the Catholic conception of Tradition is first created by its limitation to unwritten tradition. Certainly the word 'Tradition' can also be used in the wider sense to include both written and unwritten Tradition.[40] In practice, however, the narrower usage prevailed, either explicitly preferred,[41] or tacitly implied, as is the case in the universal use of the singular 'Tradition' by modern Catholicism. Thus what is incontestably true in the idea of Tradition has been replaced by a theological conception of Tradition which has been ranged alongside Scripture, and claims the recognition of Tradition as the complement of Scripture. Yet Scripture, too, rightly understood, is Tradition, and

Tradition alongside Scripture always tends to become fixed in written form.

Here, increasing the difficulties, we are confronted by the ambivalence of *traditio* as *traditum*, and as *actus tradendi*. If, by the word 'Tradition', as the plural use *'sine scripto traditiones'* mainly implies, we might understand only those apostolic *tradita* which were not committed to writing, but were at first only orally transmitted in the form of specific usages or directions, it would be an obvious assumption that these *tradita* were finally, in some form or other, written down. It would be an indication of the real interest taken in the recognition, preservation, and pure form of those apostolic *tradita*, that consideration should be given to their setting down in written form. Moreover, the only possible evidence for the existence of a tradition is its survival in writing. In no other way could the claim of a tradition to Apostolicity be established and preserved from the imputation of fictitiousness. Furthermore it is by this means that an actual distinction can be made between Apostolic and Church traditions, and those of merely human origin.[42] Yet these considerations leave untouched the real concern in the Catholic concept of Tradition. It was not by accident that at the Council of Trent the proposal to define the meaning of *sine scripto traditiones* was allowed to disappear.[43] What are usually cited as examples of Apostolic traditions not found in Scripture, mostly concern ritual or disciplinary details, such as Infant Baptism, Auricular Confession, and such like; the question may well arise whether, in the last resort, the Apostolic origin of such things is important, and whether it has anything to do with 'the purity of the Gospel';[44] it may moreover be questioned whether such matters which can, by and large, be regarded as marginal complements to Scripture, are enough to justify the creation of a doctrine of Tradition. In the case, however, where essentially dogmatic *tradita* are in question, for which support must be sought in a tradition supplementing Scripture, such as the Mariological decrees, any strictly historical interpretation of Apostolicity, or even of a mere supplement to Scripture, is of doubtful validity.

The decisive emphasis laid on the unwritten character of the tradition shows that interest is far more attached to the continuing *actus tradendi* than to specific *tradita*. Looked at in this way the relation of tradition to

Scripture might not seem to present any problem: Scripture would be the *traditum tradendum*, which in *Tradition* as the *actus tradendi*, would be transmitted in the form of oral proclamation; not, of course, in mechanical repetition, but in translation and interpretation, so that the relation between Scripture and Tradition would be that of Text and Interpretation.[45] Undoubtedly this conception of a continuing transmission of what has been once for all revealed, is a definite element in the Catholic concept of Tradition.[46] Nevertheless, the problem involved in the Catholic statement of the formula 'Scripture and Tradition' cannot be simply reduced to an interpretation of 'Tradition' as merely the *actus tradendi*, and its distinction from Scripture not also considered in relation to the *traditum* itself. When we consider that the Church itself, on the one hand, is the Tradition in the sense of being the continuing process of the *traditio*, and on the other hand, that she is, in the form of the infallible doctrinal authority, both the standard and final court of appeal as to what is to be regarded as the *traditum* of the *divino-apostolica traditio*, and that this *traditum* is set forth and expounded in this process of the Tradition, it becomes clear that at this point the distinction between *traditum* and *actus tradendi* finally disappears, and both blend together into the reality of revelation transmitted as the Church. The Church, as the *corpus Christi mysticum*, is the Tradition in the unity of *traditum tradendum* and *actus tradendi*.

An instructive indication of the shape which the problem is assuming today is to be found in the current lively discussion in Roman Catholic circles of the question whether Scripture and Tradition should be regarded as two sources of revelation, or as two forms of the one revelation;[47] the parallel question is also under discussion, whether the relation of Tradition to Scripture is a supplementary one, or has merely an interpretational role. But, cautious as we need to be in the knowledge that the decisive answer demanded by Catholic doctrine can only be given in reality by the doctrinal authority of the Church itself, we can hardly maintain that the variety of standpoints within Catholicism are incompatible with one another; nor should the importance of the decision as to which position is preferable be over-emphasized. For anyone who maintains the view of two complementary sources of revelation will be obliged to take into account the connection between the doctrine of Tradition and the doctrine of the Church's authority in matters concerning the interpretation of Scripture,[48] and must also give an account of the nature and manner of the agreement between the contents of the two sources of revelation. On the other hand, the supporters of the view of the total sufficiency of Scripture, and of the purely interpretational function of Tradition, must explain how specific elements of Tradition can also be understood as interpretation of the content of Scripture, and how the purely interpretational function of tradition agrees with disputed aspects of exegesis.[49] For even here agreement exists between the opposed standpoints: one unique revelation is in question, hence, in the authoritative Tradition, *a priori*, nothing of the nature of a new or different revelation is to be found. In that case, however, the task remains of explaining the connection which is based on the revelation itself, that is, of interpreting Tradition, in its supplementary role, as ultimately identical with the content of Scripture, that is, of understanding it as interpretation. The supplementary function of Tradition would in fact be only a kind of interpretation in the broad sense of the term. Since the supplementary view of Tradition cannot exist by itself, but only in a certain attachment to the point of view of the interpretation, the conception of the interpretational function of Tradition is the more consistent in so far as the former is absorbed into the latter. This certainly strains the concept of interpretation to the utmost. But in the Catholic concept of the interpretation of Scripture[50] it is all the same whether, in a marginal context, one prefers to speak of 'supplementing' instead of 'interpreting'. Looking at the whole confused and many-sided phenomenon of the Catholic interpretation of Scripture, one thing stands out as certain: in the formula 'Scripture and Tradition' is comprised the Catholic response to the hermeneutic problem of theology: the revelation to which Scripture bears witness cannot be rightly understood apart from the Tradition represented in the Church. Indeed, the Church as the Tradition is the authoritative interpretation of the revelation to which Scripture bears witness.[51]

2. '*Sola scriptura*' *as the hermeneutic basis of the Reformation.* If the formula 'Scripture and Tradition' turns out to be a hermeneutic proposi-

tion, 'sola scriptura' must similarly be regarded as having the character of a hermeneutic basic thesis. The Reformers' principle of Scripture does not therefore need to be supplemented by a hermeneutic principle in the sense of a material principle guiding the interpretation of Scripture, but the Scripture principle itself, as such, is a hermeneutic principle. *Sola scriptura* in the Reformation sense is not adequately understood as reduction of all the 'sources' to Holy Scripture, with the exclusion of additional supplementary traditions alongside Holy Scripture. While this of course is also valid, its significance is only fully apprehended if the *particula exclusiva* excludes the hermeneutic function of Tradition, and therefore declares the sufficiency and independence of Holy Scripture in respect of its hermeneutic function. *Sola scriptura* is therefore the formal affirmation of the position that the Holy Scriptures are the sole source of their own interpretation. The fact that they are the sole source of revelation is only fully grasped when it is understood that they are the sole source of their interpretation, and that as such they do not need another source for it. In that case they would not be sources of the revelation. The statement that 'Holy Scripture is the sole judge, standard, and touchstone' applies in the strict sense to everything that claims to be interpretation of Scripture. Tradition does not determine the correct interpretation of Scripture, but only scripture itself, which is therefore the '*iudex, norma et regula*' of Tradition.

The idea of a mere juxtaposition of different areas of what is normative only superficially represents the controversial situation; this is shown by the fact that on the Protestant side the conception of *sola scriptura* as a mere reduction of authoritative sources fails to convey the specific meaning which *sola scriptura* had for the Reformers. This could only be done by making clear the Reformers' conception of the authority of Holy Scripture. Otherwise the Reformers' *sola scriptura* would not differ either from the medieval heretical interpretation of it, or from the traditional Catholic conception of it. The formula as such is not peculiar to the Reformers. The medieval movements which criticized the papacy, and not only those of heretical origin, but the genuine reforming movements within the Church, made extensive use of the Scripture principle as an appeal to the pure *lex divina*.[53] This took place, it is true, in connection with the traditional authority of the canon, and hence in keeping with a conception of *sola scriptura* recognized by the theology of the Church;[54] only the reservation of the Church's privilege to interpret more or less consistently disappeared. But little though this hermeneutic reservation was adequately reflected upon before the Reformation, the hermeneutic meaning of the heretical use of the *sola scriptura* principle was taken into account. Thus Luther himself could appeal to his Erfurt teacher, the Nominalist Trutfetter, for his *sola scriptura* principle,[55] without any suspicion arising that the Reformed conception of *sola scriptura* did not decisively differ from the conception of it previously held. But this difference would not be properly described by saying that there was agreement about *sola scriptura* as a 'formal' principle, and the difference lay only in the 'material' principle. The new feature of the Reformed conception of the *sola scriptura* principle lay rather in its application to hermeneutics. But this involves the task of coming to grips with the inner connection between the Reformed *sola scriptura* and the Reformed view of the Gospel. It would be only a superficial representation of this connection to say that the limitation to Scripture alone yields the Gospel which is contained in it. For its comprehension as hermeneutic instruction, *sola scriptura* must rather be regarded as originating from the fact of the Gospel. The study and exposition of the hermeneutic range of the disputed controversial theological formulas would have to prove that, just as the Catholic standpoint of Scripture and Tradition is not merely the cause, but also and in reality the consequence and expression of the Catholic understanding of the Christian faith, similarly the Reformers' *sola scriptura* is not merely the cause, but also and in reality the consequence and expression of the fundamental Protestant interpretation of the Christian faith. This may be clarified by means of Luther's statements about *sola scriptura*.

The first comprehensive discussion of the subject occurred relatively late, at the end of 1520 in the introduction to *Assertio omnium articulorum M. Lutheri per bullam Leonis X novissimam damnatorum*.[56] *Sola scriptura* does not appear at the beginning of the development of Luther's theology as its theoretical basis, although his theological thinking, was from the beginning—and as a matter of course, as was possible within the setting of traditional theology—orientated towards the study of Holy Scripture. An occasion for a fundamental consideration of his relation to Scripture first arose in the conflict with the ecclesiastical and theological authorities of his time. Not as though the Holy Scriptures were a kind of last surviving remnant of the great collapse of authorities which took place for Luther during 1517–1520, and were then used as a last ditch to legitimate what had happened. What actually happened was that he was so powerfully apprehended by Holy Scripture and given such freedom as to regard all other authorities as subordinate to this one *auctoritas*. But although the motive force was derived from his experience of the authority of Scripture itself, it was possible for him to let the full consequences of the question of doctrinal authority develop under external pressure. The realization of the meaning of *sola scriptura*, even as it already appears in the great attack on Roman sacramental doctrine in *De captivitate babylonica*, has the character of a final account of the implications of authority and responsibility in theology and Church.

Luther is fully aware that the question of the authority of Scripture is dependent on the question of the interpretation of Scripture. He is at once confronted by the difficulty which this view raises against his determination to accept no ecclesiastical authority unless sanctioned by Holy Scripture.[57] This brought him into conflict with the well-known hermeneutic principle, understood by few, that Holy Scripture may not be interpreted by the intelligence of the individual, and hence neither as the meaning may appear to a single person, nor at his own discretion, nor wilfully.[58] According to Luther's fundamental theological position *propria justitia* was the original sin against God, and the gift of the Gospel was the *justitia aliena extra nos in Christo*;[59] herein he far exceeded the traditional condemnation of the *proprius sensus* as the root of heresy, as well as the monastic renunciation of the *propria voluntas*. He was also fully aware that it was possible to make heretical use of *sola scriptura*.[60] He was not only prepared to treat the basic view which was held up against him as a subject for discussion, but was determined to find out what it really meant, what *sola scriptura* aimed at, and what arguments could be brought against the dominant ecclesiastical attitude towards the interpretation of Holy Scripture. The way in which Church Tradition had handled the fundamental thesis 'non esse scripturas sanctas proprio spiritu interpretandas' had produced the opposite effect. The attempt was made to guard against the danger by external means, namely, by creating a mass of interpretations which diverted attention from the text to themselves, and by the doctrine of the infallibility and finality of the Bishop of Rome's interpretation of Scripture.[61] The question arises whether the danger of *proprius spiritus* is avoided by accepting the authority of Augustine, and thereby incurring the danger of interpreting the Scripture according to the *proprius spiritus* of Augustine, unless, on the other hand, Augustine is interpreted according to Holy Scripture.[62] Moreover, what protection is there against interpreting Augustine in one's own sense? If the correctness of his interpretation must be guaranteed by that of someone else, then this interpretation must be guaranteed by that of another interpreter, and so on, *ad infinitum*.[63]

The dictum that Scripture must not be understood *proprio spiritu* is evidently misunderstood if it results in dependence on human commentaries instead of on the text of Holy Scripture, and thus causes an ever diminishing contact with the text itself. Its real meaning is that Holy Scripture can only be understood with the help of the Spirit through whom it was written, and with whom no more present and living contact can be established than in the biblical text itself.[64] The greater the danger of interpreting Scripture *proprio spiritu*, the greater is the need of turning from all human writings to Holy Scripture alone.[65] For there alone can the Spirit be drawn upon which enables us to judge both pagan and Christian writings.[66] The arguments which are usually adduced in support of the hermeneutic function of an authoritative tradition of interpretation, namely, that the holy Catholic Church is invested with the same Spirit of faith as at its beginning and that one is exposed to a conflict of opinions in the field of interpretation, are the very arguments used by Luther as a basis for the right and necessity of the study of Holy Scripture itself.[67]

For Scripture is its own interpreter, that is, it speaks for itself. It does not need to seek elsewhere for sources of understanding to throw light upon it, as though it were obscure, difficult, and unapproachable. On the contrary, it is itself the source of understanding, illumination and certainty in the very measure in which it brings everything into light.[68] Commenting on passages in Psalm 119 Luther illustrates the fact that with regard to Holy Scripture the real hermeneutic concern is not directed towards throwing light on the difficulty and obscurity of the text, but springs from the illuminating and dominating power of the contents of the Holy Scriptures, the Word of God.[69] Since the Word of God is the subject-matter of Holy Scripture, Scripture in the last resort does not require illumination, but is itself the source of enlightenment. But it must not therefore be assumed that it is an automatic source of enlightenment for everyone, since it is, on the contrary, an occasion of greater blindness for many.[70] Nor must it be supposed that the meaning of Scripture is so obviously clear as to render hard and devoted labour for its understanding unnecessary.[71] Nevertheless it must be realized that interpretation of Scripture means allowing full play for its own self-interpretation, and the surrender of the mind of the interpreter to the mind of Scripture.[72] That Scripture is 'sui ipsius interpres' is not to be taken as a declaration of the superfluousness of interpretation in general, but represents the fundamental principle of appropriate interpretation, and therefore makes explicit the hermeneutic meaning of sola scriptura.

We have, first of all, to do with an apparently purely formal and general rule of interpretation, namely, that interpretation is nothing else but allowing the text to speak for itself; it is the process of making clear and establishing what the text actually says, and thus enabling it, as it were, to interpret itself. Verbal utterance as such is a means of understanding.[73] This is why, in normal circumstances, the spoken word, arising out of a particular situation,[74] does not require interpretation; whereas that which is transmitted in written form raises a problem when it is applied to a situation which may differ in various respects. Interpretation should therefore have regard only to the interpretative function of the text itself and create regard for it. In its general application this principle also includes the traditional rule that obscure passages in the text are to be interpreted by those which are clear; although of course a question may arise as to the extent of the applicability of this rule, since the justification for its use depends on how the unity of Scripture is understood, and the necessity for its use depends on the conception whether, in what degree, and in what sense, individual passages may be regarded as incapable of interpretation. Here, however, Luther carries to its extreme limit the general principle of the self-interpretation of the text by relating it to the Word of God as the content of Holy Scripture; so that, by reason of this content, the Word of Scripture acquires hermeneutic relevance for all human words.[75] By this interpretation based on the content of Holy Scripture itself, the principle of *sui ipsius interpres* becomes a hermeneutic canon strictly limited to Holy Scripture, and expressing with similar exclusiveness the authority of *sola scriptura*. What we have here is not some kind of special hermeneutic rule designed to guard Scripture, which is otherwise unable to withstand any threat; it is rather an indication of the hermeneutic status of the Word of God, which should be observed for the sake of the correct interpretation of Holy Scripture.

Luther has further developed the hermeneutic significance of *sola scriptura* in his treatise *De Servo Arbitrio*, as an exposition of the double clarity of Scripture.[76] Erasmus, making use of the scholastic idea that some parts of Scripture were obscure,[77] taught that in the last resort the doctrinal decisions of the Church, even if not understood, must be accepted;[78] against this Luther set, as his '*primum principium*',[79] the clarity of Scripture which, in spite of individual obscurities, was the clarity of the content of Scripture,[80] and that in a double sense: namely, the 'external clarity' of the *verbum externum* of public proclamation, and the 'inward clarity' of the illumination of the heart through the Holy Spirit.[81] A detailed discussion is not now possible, but a final sketch may be given of the antithesis between *sola scriptura* as the central conception in the Reformers' understanding of Scripture, and the Catholic position.

The difference between the Reformers' principle of '*sola scriptura*' and the Catholic formula of 'Scripture and Tradition' makes that which they both have in common, namely, the revelational authority of Scripture, that is, its soteriological relevance, involving its relation to the contemporary scene, a matter of debate. Since Scripture is assumed to be 'Holy' Scripture, and therefore canonical, this contemporary relevance is part of, or, strictly speaking, is the subject-matter of Scripture, what Scripture is about, the opposition between *sola scriptura* and Scripture and Tradition makes the *subject* of Scripture a matter of debate. The central issue in this debate about the subject of Scripture is whether, to put it briefly, the very *object* of Scripture is to establish the authority of the content of Scripture.[82] This means, to define whether, and in what way, Scripture itself is the determining factor of its own content, and what Scripture as Scripture can do to establish its own validity. This is the implication of the question whether Scripture, in the Reformers' sense, previously indicated, in order to bring out the illuminating clarity of its subject-matter, and by means of it, interprets itself.

The bearing of the Catholic answer 'Scripture and Tradition' on this comprehensive range of problems will become clearer if it is understood in the light of that interpretation of 'Scripture and Tradition' which has already been given.[83] The various aspects of the extraordinarily elusive concept of Tradition are united in the assumption that the meaning of Holy Scripture can only be made clear through the Church, and that only thus in the duality of Scripture and Church does the correct understanding of Scripture, and the assertion of the authority of its contents become possible. From this it follows that we should not really possess Holy Scripture if we only possessed 'Scripture alone', and had not the Church as well. Hence the Church as the living *process of Tradition* in its continuing historical existence must be conjoined with Scripture: it must also be conjoined with Scripture in what we may now express as a partial completion or continuation of the interpretation of the *content of tradition*: and lastly the Church must be conjoined with Scripture in its purely preservative function as the guardian of the content of Tradition in its process, and the exponent of the *credenda*. In the exercise of this function the Church assumes the form of the unique and supreme teaching authority, and the visible *standard of Tradition*. If 'Scripture and Tradition' thus understood are regarded as an expression of the conflict about the subject of Scripture, then the Church must be regarded as the subject of Scripture, which, in respect of its basis and origin, is contained in Scripture itself, although, in respect of its continuing sacramental activity as the effective operation of divine grace, it has an independent position alongside Scripture as that to which Scripture in its teaching and ministry refers, and in which the vast variety of its utterances (*credenda* and *agenda*) has a common point of reference. Thus the subject of Scripture is not only *in*, but indeed primarily,[84] so far as our contact with it is concerned, *outside* Scripture. This is why the interpretation of Scripture is standardized by the Church, but at the same time made relative; since what the Church makes into the reality of grace is not, or at least not solely, dependent on and to be expected from the interpretation of Scripture, because it does not come from the Word of preaching. Hence the interpretation of Scripture escapes from hermeneutic responsibility, whatever freedom of activity it may still retain.[85] In other words, the final hermeneutic responsibility exists in the fundamental recognition of the justice of a claim that interpretation depends for its full achievement on a *laudabiliter se subicere*.

The presentation of *sola scriptura* in opposition to this should not entail the discarding of those problems into which it appears to be the strength of the Catholic position to enter. It is all the more necessary for *sola scriptura* to demonstrate that it likewise enters into those problems, and if the general theological position be taken into account, even more convincingly than is the case with the Catholic conception, in spite of the attraction of its rounded position.

It is obvious that the relation between Scripture and Church cannot be disputed, if it is understood to mean that the content of Scripture has not been transmitted by 'mere Scripture', but rather through the spoken word of preaching, addressed therefore to the Church and borne witness to by the Church. We have already seen that *sola scriptura* is only rightly understood as the carrying out, *solo verbo*, of the activity of preaching;[86] this includes, in the Reformers' meaning of the term, the sacraments as being in a specific sense a creative Word-event.

The relation between Scripture and Church is undoubtedly also at work in the fact that the transmission of the content of Holy Scripture does not consist in the preservation of the past, nor in a retreat into an imaginary timeless sphere, but in a language transformation which cannot be separated as a purely formal consideration from the problem of subject-matter itself. But it is precisely from the point of view of *sola scriptura* that the relevance of the problem of interpretation for that of the historicity of the Church comes into much sharper relief than it does from the Catholic position.[87]

Moreover, it is important to remember that the process of interpretation also involves the question of a court of appeal and a standard. There can be no interpretation without some kind of counterpart to the text, a specific point to which the text is directed; it must be addressed to an intelligence capable of understanding and accepting the interpretation as satisfying the purpose for which it was uttered. Nor can interpretation exist without some criterion by which to determine its correctness or the reverse. As a matter of fact, the Reformed understanding of *sola scriptura* supplies a decisive answer to both questions, as is shown by Luther's doctrine of the clarity of Scripture. The connection of his doctrine of double clarity with the important duality of the public *ministerium verbi* and the tribunal of conscience, shows how *sola scriptura* answers the question of a court of appeal,[88] and how, by affirming Christ to be the real subject of Scripture, it answers the question of a standard of interpretation. The inner unity of this affirmation is evident from the way in which the given instances resound with *'solo verbo'*, *'sola fide'*, and *'solus Christus'*.

According to the Catholic interpretation the Church as the present reality of grace is the subject of Scripture, and hence is only to be found in Scripture in a very restricted sense, because the clarity of Scripture is only to be attained in the conjunction of 'Scripture and Tradition', or 'Scripture and Church'. On the other hand, according to the Reformers' interpretation Jesus Christ is the substance of Scripture.[89] *Sola scriptura* is the necessary result of such an interpretation, since it is only in Scripture that Christ is to be found. But his presence in the Scriptures must not be thought of as competing with his presence in the Word as preached, in the sacraments, and in the Church. Both these aspects of Christ's presence are inseparable; but the direction is irreversible; only the Christ to whom Scripture bears witness is the present Christ, and the Word alone is the way of his presence, and only through faith. Thus Christ as the *verbum promissionis*, and therefore as the *verbum fidei*, is the substance of Scripture. Since this manner of making his presence known in the Word corresponds to his nature, the Church is and continues to be solely dependent on Scripture as the source[90] from which she can and must continually draw afresh the contemporary proclamation of the Word of God, Hence it is here that *sola scriptura* is shown to be most closely bound up with the Reformers' basic understanding of the Gospel. Since faith alone justifies, and faith alone apprehends the present Christ in the word of promise,[91] it is necessary, for the sake of the purity of the Gospel and of holding fast to the word of the faith, to turn to the place where the original witness to Christ is to be met with, and by this means to empower the contemporary witness to Christ.

This dependence on the biblical text makes the task of interpretation an extremely serious one. The resolute attention paid to the *sensus literalis* of the original text owes its inspiration to the Reformers' recognition of the importance of the subject-matter of Scripture, and may not be separated from *sola scriptura*. Nevertheless it must not be supposed that the task of interpretation is accomplished by the citation of individual passages of Scripture without critical study of their context. *Sola scriptura* will not tolerate a legally determined interpretation of Scripture which fails to present Christ as the subject of Scripture.[92] The *sui ipsius interpres* must be carried through to the ultimate findings of a Christ-centred critical study of individual passages of Scripture.[93]

Sola scriptura only fulfils its essential function in the following ways: it preserves intact the distinction between text and interpretation; while the Catholic conception is in danger of ascribing to an interpretation the value of an authoritative text. Next, *sola scriptura* maintains that the Word of God has absolute authority over the Church as brought into existence by the Word of God, and therefore that the Church itself is not the authoritative source of the Word of God, a view which blurs the distinction between the Word of God and the Church.[94] Lastly, *sola scriptura* maintains that Christ remains distinct from the Church as its Head, and that the Church is the result of and dependent on the event that constituted her a Church.

All this involves startling consequences for the doctrine of the Church. Along with juridical and institutional assumption of an infallible interpretation the unambiguous representation of the unity of the Church disappears. But the view that this results in uncertainty in relation to the Word of God fails to recognize the radical change that has taken place in the understanding of the content of the Christian faith. Directly connected with *sola scriptura* is the certainty of faith, which adheres to the Word of the Gospel that gives assurance to the conscience.[95] Where faith is concerned, there can be no appeal to any other authority on the question of certainty; on the contrary, it is faith that gives a man certainty through Christ before God.[96] Since we are concerned with another interpretation of the content of Scripture, we also find in *sola scriptura* a different understanding of the meaning of certainty from that which is offered by the Catholic doctrine of Scripture and Tradition: certainty does not rest on the decision of an ecclesiastical decree, but on the actual decision of faith in Christ.

The basis and activity of the Church's magisterium rests upon the formula 'Scripture and Tradition'.[97] Its significance for the individual believer is in the last analysis only that it admits him to participation in the Church's sacramental reality of grace,[98] and thus affords only an indirect expression of the meaning of the redemptive event itself. On the other hand we have in *sola scriptura* the confession of what is necessary for salvation. It focuses attention on the fact that Jesus Christ exists *pro nobis* in the Word, and on the reality of our being in Christ *extra nos* through faith. Moreover, it bases this Word-event on the text which alone makes it possible, holds it to its own concern, and so presents it as the fresh and unadulterated Gospel. For both witnesses and hearers must have free access to the text, which is the source whence both Word and Faith derive their power, and to which both Christian Word and Christian Faith appeal as the inexhaustible source of their existence in the Word of God. Here they meet themselves. However, in reality everyone is both witness and hearer: witness is the result of hearing, and hearing creates witnesses. Thus *sola scriptura* is intended to meet the simple case of the tempted, for whom there is no help save in the *verbum externum*, that assurance-giving Word which is Jesus Christ himself. Judged from this point of view, the formula 'Scripture and Tradition' is not concerned with interpreting the content of Scripture, but, irrespective of whether Tradition were held to be supplementary or merely interpretative, affects the purity and assurance-giving clarity of the content of Scripture by the creation of an additional independent entity alongside of Scripture.[99]

3. *'Sola scriptura' in the modern hermeneutic situation.* It has already been indicated in the introduction[100] that, in the present state of the hermeneutic and theological controversy, the account of the Reformers' principle of *sola scriptura* needs to be supplemented by an account of the changed conditions of interpretation which seem to threaten *sola scriptura* in an extraordinary way. This task far exceeds the scope of an essay whose primary object was to contrast an inadequate and crude conception of the Confessional differences with their real understanding of *sola scriptura* in its connection with the Reformers' understanding of the Christian faith as a whole. The attempt to pierce below the surface implicitly involves a discussion of the problems presented by the changed situation. But over and above this we must give some indication of this change in the situation, and of the resultant direction of theological thinking in the wake of the Reformation.

It would, at the outset, be a mistaken approach to this question to regard the Reformers' *sola scriptura* as a ready-made position, which is at the mercy of the subsequent cultural and theological development, so that it is only possible either to accept it unchanged, or to reject it in more or less concealed fashion. Although the Reformation so decisively affirmed the principle of *sola scriptura*, it is possible to raise the question whether the Reformers had fully considered its theological implications. Hence, if we admit that the fundamental hermeneutic basis of the Reformation is to be found in the character of *sola scriptura*, we have still to ask whether at the time of the Reformation the hermeneutic significance of *sola scriptura* together with its consequences had already been recognized. The fact that the hermeneutic significance of the formula 'Scripture and Tradition' is still, and in one respect even more today, a matter of dispute,[101] suggests that even in relation to *sola scriptura*, problems are still outstanding which in the sixteenth century had not been solved, or had not been recognized. Indeed, the history of the hermeneutic problem since the Reformation is a unique proof of the fact that, not in mere opposition to the Reformation, even if not in direct consequence and continuation of it, questions that are implicit in the Reformers' *sola scriptura* have pressed for clarification.[102] In particular, the following points may be adduced as symptomatic of an insufficient explanation of *sola scriptura* in the thinking of the Reformers themselves: the relation of the Word of God to individual passages of Scripture; the relation between the assumed unity of Scripture and the variety of aspects which it presents, as well as the meaning of *sola scriptura* for the method of theological study.

Old Protestant Orthodoxy has been accused, not without justice, of having misrepresented the Reformers' understanding of Scripture, and of being the cause of the later crisis in the understanding of Scripture which is still not entirely settled; it is, however, necessary to evaluate this accusation from the point of view of its positive intention. The doctrine of verbal inspiration, which embraced even the Massoretic pointing, was not so much an absurdly exaggerated claim to authority on behalf of *sola scriptura*, as the result of an anxiety to establish, in opposition to the authority of Tradition and Church, the hermeneutic significance of the *particula exclusiva* by demonstrating the complete absence of ambiguity in the substance and meaning of Scripture. Hence orthodox teaching about Scripture was specially concerned to maintain the *perspicuitas* of Scripture, and adopted the basic feature of the Reformers' *sola scriptura*, the doctrine of the *claritas* of Scripture. Nevertheless the emphasis shifted from the clarity of the subject-matter to the inviolability of the actual words and letters of Scripture which might not be called in question; the difficulties thus created had to be concealed by an occasional resort to the mysterious obscurity of the subject-matter.[108] Another result of this was that the unity of Scripture was determined not by concentration upon the unity of the subject-matter, but by the summation of its variety in a totality which was decreed to be indivisible. Furthermore, the unifying conception of the Word of God became to a great extent formalized, so that the inner connection between *sola scriptura* and the Reformers' fundamental insight of *solus Christus*, *solo verbo*, and *sola fide* was weakened, if not entirely lost, and at any rate no longer recognizable. Hence it now became necessary to safeguard the connection by treating the doctrinal tradition of the Reformers as, practically, a *regula* and *norma* for the interpretation of Scripture.

While it would be misleading, in this connection, to speak of a principle of Tradition supplementing the principle of Scripture, yet what is lacking here is both the hermeneutic consideration of this situation, and above all the risk of drawing the consequences of *sola scriptura* for theological methodology. It is extremely remarkable that a theological doctrine of principles which so emphatically declared Holy Scripture to be the *unicum principium cognoscendi*, should have laid the foundation of the primacy of a systematic theology which succeeded in protecting itself against excesses from the side of exegesis, and condemned exegetic theology to sterility. The Scripture principle should not by any means be played against systematic theology. This may be done in two ways: either by a formal exegesis of individual texts displaying an unconditional preference for a systematic method of exposition; or, from a purely biblical point of view, regarding the task of theology as consisting in acquiring biblical modes of expression. The result in both cases is a misunderstanding of the hermeneutic task, which cannot be rightly conceived of as an isolated treatment, or a harmonization, of biblical texts. The Reformers' exegesis still treated as a single hermeneutic process what was later to diverge into two separate streams: not into a mere difference in modes of approach, namely, the exegetic and the systematic; but into a keen rivalry between two different attitudes towards the problems to be dealt with, namely, the historical and the dogmatic. Old Protestant theology should not be reproached for what is really to its credit, that it worked out a dogmatic theology on the basis of the Reformers' *sola scriptura*. This was certainly intelligible on historical grounds, and unavoidable in that cultural and Confessional situation. Nevertheless it was a questionable proceeding to work the standpoint of *sola scriptura*, as well as the corresponding Reformed view of the nature of Christian faith, into a dogmatic conception[104] which was in the last resort (though not explicitly) determined by the standpoint of 'Scripture and Tradition' and the corresponding Catholic view of Christian faith. What should have been done was to attack the problem of a dogmatic theology *de novo* on the basis of the Reformed *sola scriptura*.

The revolution in Protestant theology, bringing to an end the age of Old Protestant Orthodoxy, introduced Pietism and the Enlightenment, and, however manifold the historical forces now at work, still drew its theological legitimation from *sola scriptura*. If we disregard, as contributory factors, the historical origin of Protestantism, and the opposition to Rome, what unites its manifold aspects is not so much a definite doctrinal content, as the firmly held *sola scriptura* principle. Although this was very variously understood and treated, and its connection with the Reformers' fundamental insight on the whole not properly pondered, nevertheless it included in itself specific consequences for the understanding of faith. The principle of orthodox dogmatic became the criterion by which to judge its orthodoxy. That revealed, on the one hand, the difference between the Reformers' *sola scriptura* and its orthodox interpretation; all subsequent Protestant movements appealed, on various points, and with varying degrees of justification, to the Reformation against the orthodox dogmatic pattern. On the other hand, it revealed the dilemma of the orthodox pattern itself, as between its declaration that Holy Scripture is the *unicum principium cognoscendi*, and the possibility, basically implied, but in intention denied, that it could be used against itself. If we consider Pietism with its urge to reduce the traditional dogmatic pattern to the simplicity of a bible theology; the Enlightenment with its demand for a scholarly explanation of the relation between Scriptural statements, reason, and moral experience; and lastly the rising historical criticism of the Bible, with its inexorable attentiveness to the text as representing a different time; we can see that each of these in its own way and within its own limits, adopts a relation to the points of view which were implicit in the principle of the orthodox dogmatic pattern itself. In this way they were committed to the hermeneutic problem contained in s*ola scriptura*, and thus abandoned the standpoint of orthodox dogmatic, of which the hermeneutic principle consists, in the last resort, in the avoidance of hermeneutic questioning, agreeing therein with its Catholic partner.

All this, however, raises the insistent question whether the result of bringing to light the problems implicit in *sola scriptura* is not the dissolution of the Scripture principle. The usual lament over the so-called destruction of the authority of Scripture overlooks the problem of the use of the orthodox understanding of the authority of Scripture as a criterion, as well as the fact that the historico-critical interpretation of Scripture throws open the whole problem of the authority of Scripture.

For the historico-critical method is not so much concerned with the hermeneutic problem as a whole, as with the explanation of its implications, and with the exposition of the facts which it discloses. Hence it is a process of hermeneutic radicalization which is distinct, but not separate from what is usually understood by the historico-critical method in the technical sense. Nevertheless the question still remains whether, on occasion, in relation to Scripture, the historico-critical method does not confront us with a situation which destroys the principle of *sola scriptura*. Closely connected with this is the further question how historico-critical interpretation of Scripture is justified in terms of the total hermeneutic question in theology.

Although the change in understanding due to the historical approach of the modern age has produced an immense variety of problems with regard to Scripture, their focal point, so far as *sola scriptura* is concerned, is the question of the unity of Holy Scripture. Upon this depends the significance of its validity as a Canon, as well as the question whether its treatment is sufficiently free from ambiguity to allow *sola scriptura* to be used in the Reformers' understanding of it. The question of the unity of Scripture therefore coincides with that of the illuminating power of its content. Now, the character of the historico-critical method of approach consists in bringing differences to light in order to destroy the mere semblance of unity and clarity. This involves, to put it briefly, the observation of time-difference (which is what 'historico-critical' really means) as for instance the difference between then and now, or between the date of the transmitted text and the time of the modern reader, or between the various chronological periods of the past. Then there may be contemporary differences, which, in so far as they are time-differences, make time itself a disputed issue. These various forms of time-difference which it is the business of the historico-critical method to work out, appear as linguistic differences, as well as factual differences, a more difficult problem.

In the biblical canon itself it is possible, to some extent, to observe the historical stages of its development, and the consequent linguistic and factual changes. Moreover, every reader in some way or other, as a result of linguistic and factual difficulties, finds himself confronted by the problem of his own time-distance from the text. Hence these matters have always been a factor in one way or another in dealing with Holy Scripture. Nevertheless the modern historico-critical method enables us to see the situation with a greater degree of precision, and to recognize that earlier methods of dealing with certain problems of this kind were wholly inadequate. The fact that the history of the historical criticism of the Scriptures shows many errors and failures in no way justifies our making cheap apologetic capital out of the matter, and refusing to consider the problem. In spite of inconsistencies in the 'findings' of scientific research, and the ceaseless change in the state of scholarship, certain fundamental positions in the field of biblical scholarship have been placed beyond question. There is also general agreement among biblical scholars that there are many questions which are bound to be in dispute, whether for a shorter or a longer time.

Instead of giving particular instances, it may be relevant to quote from Ernst Käsemann's essay, 'Begründet der neutestamentliche Kanon die Einheit der Kirche?'[105] ('Does the New Testament Canon establish the Unity of the Church?'). Basing his argument on a description of the variety and occasional contradictions in the various patterns of the early Christian kerygma, Käsemann maintains that: 'The age in which Scripture as a totality could be opposed to Catholicism has gone, never to return. Today Protestantism can no longer make use of the so-called formal principle without rendering itself untrustworthy in the face of historical analysis. The canon of the New Testament does not stand between Judaism and early Catholicism, but finds room in itself for both.' From this he draws the conclusion with regard to the canon: 'The canon of the New Testament as such is not the basis of the unity of the Church. It is, on the contrary, as such, the basis, acknowledged by historians, of the multiplicity of Confessions.' Already in primitive Christianity a number of various Confessions existed side by side. 'Hence it is understandable that contemporary Confessions all appeal to the New Testament canon. The expositor cannot dispute, either on methodological or factual grounds, their right to do so. On the contrary, he is fundamentally bound to acknowledge it.'[106]

I cannot now discuss in detail these provocative conclusions, which seem to me to be not incontestable, or at any rate open to misunderstanding.[107] They are directed against the legal view of the canon, widely prevalent also in Protestantism, which regards the unity of Scripture as the unity of a dogmatic doctrinal system. Such a view can only be carried through to its logical conclusion either by doing what the Catholic Church does, namely, falling back on the hermeneutic function of tradition, or, in an apparently arbitrary fashion, establishing a canon within the canon in the form of a specific body of writings or a specific doctrine as a standard of criticism. The supposition that the Reformers chose the second alternative does not hold good, since they do not hold its necessary presupposition, namely, the legal conception of the canon. Hence, in my opinion, Käsemann's thesis is completely lacking in a correct critical understanding of the Reformers' conception of the canon. For the unity, the real substance, of Scripture, does not consist in a dogmatic doctrinal structure, but in the Word-event, fully effective in the name of Jesus Christ, since it appeals to him and is based on him; this creates faith and is the event of the saving Gospel. The evidence for the event of this Word is found in the transmitted witness of the preaching of Christ which creates faith; but this is no mere report of a past event, but in virtue of liberating power bears its own witness in present responsibility.

If due attention is paid to the increased importance of the hermeneutic situation in the modern age, it will result in a keener apprehension of the Reformers' *sola scriptura*, in that the question of the unity of Scripture will lead on to the nature of its authority today; hence the historical criticism of the *traditum* summons us to fulfil the hermeneutic task by the responsible completion of the *traditio*.[108]

D. *Tradition*

Since the truth of *sola scriptura* depends on the reliable transmission of the Gospel, the Scripture-principle necessarily involves a doctrine of tradition.[109] Its exposition represents a comprehensive task, calling for the hermeneutic consideration of the content of the Christian faith with regard to historicity, and including the questions of canon law and responsible activity in the world. For the present we must leave this subject on one side, and turn our attention to the theological position.

The warnings implicit in the language and thought of the reformers against surrender to the concept of Tradition should not be disregarded. As is well known, the Reformation only described *traditio* in negative theological terms drawn from the New Testament polemic against the Jewish conception of 'Scripture and Tradition', since, in the New Testament itself the noun 'Tradition' occurs in a generally critical sense as applied to the *traditiones humanae* in opposition to the *verbum Dei*.[110] The Catholic use of the term *traditio*, which at that time was not yet fully developed—if we connect it with the correspondence, elsewhere pointed out, between the New Testament criticism of Judaism and the Reformers' criticism of Roman Catholicism—suggests that the Catholic concept of Tradition is derived from the late Jewish conception, both with regard to its supplementary character in relation to Scriptural Tradition, and to the character of these *traditiones* as single legal *tradita*. Against this view the biblical use of παραδιδόναι and παράδοσις in a positive sense was not able to get established, the more so since the prevailing use of the term *traditio* was limited to those individual traditions which were supplementary to Scripture. Hence, in the Reformers' thinking the danger developed of failing to recognize the theological importance of the problem of Tradition, although this was far from being a necessary consequence of the Reformation's understanding of the theological situation. In any case the negative emphasis was intensified through the unexampled historical break with a mass of traditions which had occurred in the Reformation, although the actual purpose of the Reformation was to guard or restore the authentic Tradition. Nevertheless it must at once be added that there was obviously no question of an archaizing restoration of specific early Christian traditions; on factual grounds, however, it is understandable that there should have been protests against the exaggerated theological importance attached to the concept of Tradition. For it was necessary to be constantly on guard against the danger that the Gospel might be confused with, or overlaid by, legal traditions, and that, coming to be regarded as law, or even as 'mere Tradition', it might consequently be abandoned.

If we wish to do justice from the theological point of view to the extraordinary ramifications of the problem of Tradition, we shall be justified in turning to those of its aspects which were neglected by the Reformation, and in pursuit of the Reformers' meaning of *sola scriptura*, enquire carefully into the nature of the *traditum tradendum*. When we consider Scripture from the point of view of historical criticism, it seems to add to our difficulties that the one *traditum tradendum* should have reached us only in the form of various oral and doctrinal traditions, from which no single one can be marked out as *the traditum tradendum*; but it is this that points to the decisive fact that the content of the *traditum tradendum* is not a doctrinal statement, nor a law, nor a book of Revelation, but the very Person of Jesus himself as the incarnate Word of God, giving its authority to the Gospel and to the event of the authoritative Word of faith; and correspondingly we have the Holy Spirit as God's Presence in the faith-creating Word of preaching. Theology can only speak of 'Tradition' in the true sense when it holds to this fundamental point of departure, and lets it have full play, in sharp contrast to all that is otherwise regarded as Tradition. In the Christian understanding of the term, the *traditum tradendum* is not law, but Gospel, hence contained in one Name, attested, not by the formation of a special tradition, but by the extension to all mankind of the saving eschatological message, not attained by works, but by faith alone. It is only the realization of the essential difference between the 'handing down' of the Gospel, and all historical traditions—which are both helpful and dangerous to mankind, and in spite of their universal claim always end in the formation of a particular tradition—that makes it possible to understand why the Gospel has and gives free access to a multiplicity of traditions, without having to be confused with any one of them. This unique situation, in which the *traditio* of that one *traditum tradendum* has only taken shape in the multiplicity of traditions, must and can fulfil its mission as Tradition wherever historical traditions exist; it is, in the last resort, identical with the essence of the Gospel itself as the eschatological fulfilment of what is necessarily still lacking in history.

From this point of view the Gospel is revealed not only as freedom *from* the false use of traditions, but also and especially as freedom *to* use them rightly. For the Gospel makes use of Tradition in many ways: the various forms of Christian witness and Christian preaching; the *verbum visibile* of sacramental ritual; the kerygmatic patterns; the orders and services of the ἐκκλησία; the authoritative texts; the tradition of theological interpretation; Christian ethics; it permeates the whole breadth of life in ethics, culture, and history. Nevertheless the real *traditio* of the Holy Spirit only finds its fulfilment in all these forms of tradition when they are brought into the service of the Word of faith, through which Jesus is transmitted to men, and men are committed to Jesus. The Christian Tradition is always in danger of becoming a legal tradition, and being false to the transmission of the Gospel. Doing justice to the Tradition does not consist in the preservation and handing on of its contents and forms, but in its rightful use as ways and means of the Gospel. And it is this correct use of traditions which *sola scriptura* serves, not as a legal prescription of traditions, but as the source of the one Tradition, the giving of free play to which is the standard by which all traditions must be judged.

Thus we have indicated the point of view from which, starting from *sola scriptura*, the problem of Tradition in its manifold concrete forms should be discussed: in its relation to the theological relevance of Church history; to the hermeneutic of the Confessional discussion and the ecumenical dialogue; to the problem of the language of preaching, of Church doctrine and canon law, as well as the responsibility of Christendom for the preservation, restoration, and creation of sound, world-regarding traditions in a world threatened with the loss of Tradition.

7

The New Testament and the Multiplicity of Confessions

The development of Protestantism in the modern world, seen from the point of view of the Scripture-principle, has followed a paradoxical course. On the one hand, the Reformers' Scripture-principle has empowered an intense and careful concentration on the interpretation of Scripture, making use of all available helps. The historical criticism of the Bible was not directly set on foot by the Scripture-principle. It is, however, undoubtedly due to the fact that the Scripture-principle implied an obligation to pursue the scientific study of Scripture, that in Protestantism this method has been taken up and fearlessly pursued. On the other hand, determined following out of the Scripture-principle seems to have led to its own undoing. For its underlying conception of the unity of Holy Scripture seems to have been called in question, if not destroyed, through the discovery of the historical and factual disagreements in Scripture.

Nevertheless, although the problems have been known for two hundred years, widespread perplexity still prevails in ecclesiastical, and even in theological circles. Outspoken discussions of the situation again and again have the effect, quite unjustifiably, of shocking people. In the following pages we discuss the situation in relation to an essay by Ernst Käsemann which has made some stir,[1] in which he has expounded the connection between the problem of the canon and that of the Confessions in a way which runs sharply counter to the usual understanding of it.

Käsemann starts from some of the examples of variations in New Testament preaching generally recognized in New Testament studies. The existence of four canonical Gospels is an expression and consequence of various tendencies. 'The Confession (common to all the Evangelists) that Jesus is the Son of God, is explained in various ways by means of

148

ideas taken from the environment.'[2] These variations can be an expression of the Evangelists' criticism of one another. This gives us only a quite fragmentary view of the differences which actually existed within primitive Christianity.[3] We must assume that there was a much greater degree of variation in the early Christian kerygma than the Gospels allow us to recognize. These differences should not be harmonized, representing in part, as they do, irreconcilable theological contrasts. We can observe, for example, how Jesus' logion in Mark 7:15 (about the origin of a man's defilement) was commented on in different ways in Palestinian and in Hellenistic Christianity, and in each case the radical character of the saying was lost. Even the earliest community was not only in continuity with Jesus, but in divergence from him; it was not merely an understanding community, but also a misunderstanding one.[4] Further examples are the criticism of the Pauline doctrine of justification in the Epistle of James, or the intrusion of early Catholic conceptions of the Spirit in the form of the official possession of the Spirit by the wielder of the Church's doctrinal authority.[5]

If we approach the subject from the point of view of *sola scriptura* the situation is less disturbing than the provocatively stated conclusions would suggest.[6] Käsemann's description of the varied character of the early Christian kerygma is one with which we can be in basic agreement. But it is only the basic insight into that variability which is of importance. The examples used to illustrate the differences might have been differently chosen, and are exposed to historical criticism in detail. The understanding of the individual historical situations may change. But that cannot upset the fundamental position arrived at from the historical study of early Christianity: the fact of this many-sidedness, Käsemann has formulated it in such a way as to imply that already in primitive Christianity a number of different Confessions existed side by side. This, of course, must be accepted with a grain of salt. We should not picture to ourselves well-defined organizations with established traditions, after the fashion of our modern Confessions, for everything in primitive Christianity was still in an extraordinary state of flux. But the conception of the beginnings of Christianity as a state of unbroken unity, which split up later as the result of a decline from the one unambiguously imparted Truth, and the unchallenged unity of the Church, is one which does not, at any rate, correspond with the facts. The movement of history followed rather the opposite course, namely, from a multiplicity of early Christian modes of expression to a unity resulting from a more or less systematic introduction of Catholicism. The canon of the New Testament reflects the differentiation, not merely indirectly by giving us a glimpse of the state of things in Corinth, Galatia, or Colossae, but also directly through divergent points of view, such as we find in Paul and the Epistle of James.

A right understanding of *sola scriptura* involved an entire awareness of this state of affairs, although the extent and seriousness of the problems involved only came to light through the application of historical criticism. When, nevertheless, it was possible to speak of *sola scriptura*, it was in a sense which was not belied by the existence of differences within the canon. And when *sola scriptura*, in spite of everything, presupposed the unity of the content of Holy Scripture, then this unity was clearly not understood as an agreement in every respect, and without any contradictions, of all the utterances of the New Testament with one another. The conception of the canon which is the subject of Käsemann's critical study is certainly not the authentic Reformers' conception. Käsemann himself knows and insists on the fact that the Reformers' understanding of Holy Scripture is not affected by his studies; on the contrary, it is confirmed by them, though by means of a critical presentation of the situation of a sharpness not generally known to Protestantism.

Nevertheless, Käsemann's conclusions are open to question. If we do not approach the question from the point of view of the Reformers' understanding of *sola scriptura*, according to which 'the canon is not simply identical with the Gospel, and is only the Word of God so far as it is and becomes Gospel';[7] but if, rather, we approach it from the point of view of a legal conception of the canon, according to which everything it contains is, on principle, of equal authority, so that each item can be considered in isolation, then there is nothing to prevent one person from appealing to statements of a Judaistic character, and another from appealing to other statements of an early Catholic character; on the other hand, the appeal to the authority of Paul loses some of its force through the realization that the Pauline corpus is only a part of the canon, and not the whole of Scripture. Käsemann therefore regards it as proved that the canon is not the source of the unity of the Church, but of the multiplicity of Confessions. This only appears convincing to the extent that the New Testament canon, being itself a witness to the Confessional multiplicity in primitive Christianity, is not in a position to overcome this multiplicity, but can only increase it when it is used as a court of appeal. The last statement must at once be limited by pointing out that the appeal in question is assumed to be made in an unreformed fashion, that is, in the assumption of the un-differentiated and isolated binding quality of all its statements. With such a presupposition an appeal to the authority of the New Testament can indeed be made in the most varied and completely contradictory ways; so that the expositor is not in a position to make a decision, and to prevent an appeal to the New Testament, so far as the appeal is in fact to opposed canonical texts. 'It is completely intelligible that con-temporary Confessions should make their common appeal to the New Testament canon. The expositor cannot contest this either on methodo-logical or factual grounds. He must, on the contrary, confirm it. If the canon as such is binding in its totality, then the various Confessions, with differing degrees of historical justification, may claim as their own larger or smaller portions of it, and better or less known New Testament writers. Their right to make such a claim is incontestable and capable of detailed proof.'[8]

In my opinion, however, this is too crude, and to some extent in-correct, a characterization of the situation. I shall leave aside the ques-tion in what sense and to what extent we may speak not only of dif-ferences, but of contradictions in the New Testament. In the last resort there has not been an indiscriminate acceptance of anything into the canon. The recognition of this need not cause any weakening of the now established fact of the variability of the primitive Christian kerygma in the New Testament canon. Yet we must still ask what, in this connection, variability, difference, or contradiction, really means, and what significance might be expected in unity. Käsemann has perhaps drawn too hasty an overall conclusion from examples of variability, which needed to be more carefully distinguished. This question, however, we leave aside.

In the first place doubts arise whether the connection which Käsemann has established between contemporary Confessions and the canon containing within itself 'Confessional' differences is not an oversimplification of the situation. This would make it seem that differences among the Confessions rest upon the fact that they each appeal to different New Testament texts or passages. This may play a certain role among other causes. Thus for Protestantism Rom 3:28 has a special significance, while for Catholicism, on the other hand, Matt 16:18ff. is of decisive importance. But the existence of a Confession is in itself far too complicated a structure of traditions to be derived simply from an appeal to specific passages of Scripture. Moreover, from the point of view of their relation to Scripture the difference between the Confessions can in no way be explained by the difference between the texts which they prefer. The real difference between the Confessions points rather to deep-seated hermeneutic differences. For even if one Confession prefers to appeal to this text, while another Confession appeals to that text, it does not simply mean that they reject the proof texts of the other. Each recognizes fundamentally all texts, and it is about the interpretation of these texts that the controversy rages, as is amply illustrated by the examples to which reference has been made. But the controversy is in no wise concerned merely with special Confessional proof texts, but essentially with all texts. Of course, so long as Catholic and Protestant exegesis remains within the limits of historical interpretation of individual texts there can be a considerable degree of mutual understanding. But as soon as exegesis, in attempting to understand the situation, becomes radical, it discovers that the interpretation of single texts has nothing further to give, since it has, so to speak, been outflanked by a hermeneutic change, that is, by ultimate differences in the presuppositions for understanding, and we may add, by ultimate linguistic differences, and different awareness of truth, and different experience of reality. The limits within which the Confessional dialogue can be carried on become apparent as soon as the dialogue turns to the exegesis of the New Testament. As soon as it becomes a question of what lies beneath the surface, the hermeneutic differences, which are so difficult to discuss, begin to make their appearance: either in the form of a different understanding of the canon, or as different linguistic and interpretative connections, on the basis of which the interpretation of individual texts is carried on.

This observation could certainly justify Käsemann's contention in this respect, that, in the Confessional controversy, the expositor is really helpless and even incompetent. But the reason would be different. In Käsemann's view the possibility of reaching a decision on exegetic grounds is slight because each Confession can find texts in the canon to which it can appeal, and because on the traditionally accepted understanding of the canon all texts are of equal authority. Hence he can say that the claim of the Confessions is fundamentally incontestable and capable of proof in detail. We, on the contrary, maintain that the difference in hermeneutic presuppositions does not merely make the exegetic controversy about details impossible of decision, but indeed leaves it questionable whether exegesis can decide anything.

Nevertheless, in spite of Käsemann's assumption of the equal exegetical standing of the various Confessions, I must interpose a question. The reference to the deeper hermeneutic differences to be met with in modern exegesis of individual texts, seems to make all exegesis relatively indifferent and unauthoritative. But such a judgement can only be arrived at by regarding the phenomenon of basic hermeneutic differences as an arbitrary difference, due to prejudices which make dialogue impossible, and these hermeneutic presuppositions as entirely independent of the actual interpretation. In reality, however, we are faced with a very intricate situation, such as we find wherever there are differences of understanding, and not just Confessional differences. However much one comes up against limits to understanding, it would be foolish, merely because of such limits, to abandon all attempts at understanding, and to appeal to the ultimate depths of the hermeneutic problem as an excuse for regarding all the detailed work of exegesis as superfluous labour. Hence, although it may involve so many hidden hermeneutic presuppositions, the controversy over the exegesis of specific passages should not be stigmatized out of hand as incapable of decision, even in the field of individual exegesis. Between Catholic and Protestant interpretation of Scripture questions exist, partly relating to the interpretation of single texts, partly concerned with deeper connections and interpretations of facts, and partly concerned with hermeneutic presuppositions, which are not simply to be regarded with resignation as beyond discussion, because each side alleges, with equal right, that it represents them.

Käsemann, however, is not thinking about the controversy over the interpretation of the same text, but only about that which concerns the appeal to different texts. There he touches on a situation which should be strongly emphasized in view of a naïve, over-complacent Protestant appeal to *sola scriptura* in the Confessional controversy. *Sola scriptura* was not only used by the Reformation as the weapon which was clearly directed against Roman Catholicism. In the modern world the historical criticism of the Bible has long continued to believe that the results of its findings on Holy Scripture would be a threat to Catholicism, and favourable to Protestantism. Actually, however, exegetical and historical Bible study during recent decades has taken a surprising turn, and in many respects has proved to support the Catholic point of view. For example, it has demonstrated the presence of early Catholic elements in later strata of the canon, and has also shown that certain theological motives which had generally been regarded as Catholic were already to be found in Paul and others. Käsemann is therefore justified in pointing out that Protestant theology can no longer use the naïve understanding of *sola scriptura* in the sense of a canon whose parts are all of equal authority, as a weapon against Catholicism. Nevertheless he is making too hasty a general conclusion when he assumes that the exegete cannot, either on methodological or factual grounds, contest the right of a modern Confession to appeal to the New Testament canon.

Käsemann himself acknowledges that his provocative thesis is by no means the last word on the subject. One hint to this effect unintentionally creeps in. His assertion that the claim of contemporary Confessions to appeal to the authority of the New Testament canon is incontestable and can be demonstrated implies as a dialectical antithesis the other affirmation that 'the unity of the Church ... from such a point of view, is fundamentally indemonstrable, and the absolute claim of every Confession is open to challenge.'[9] Käsemann joins both statements together in one sentence. And indeed they both spring from the same root. Since the New Testament canon contains Confessional differences within itself, the various Confessions have, on the one hand, the right to appeal to the canon; but, on the other hand, their right of appeal is not absolute. In that case there is at least one ground for recognizing that a case may arise in which the exegete must reject the Confessional appeal to the canon; if, for example, such a claim consists of the assertion that the unity of the Church can be shown and demonstrated from the canon, and if this exegetical claim is a Confessionally absolute one. The conclusion, not explicitly drawn by Käsemann, must follow, namely, that the manifold character of the Canon renders so many Confessional appeals to it possible; but it also renders certain of rejection one particular kind of appeal, namely, a Confessionally absolute appeal, since that is identical with the assumption that the unity of the Church can be shown in the New Testament canon. In this respect the exegete is also in a position to reject the Confessionally absolute claim of the Roman Church, that is, he can show that it contradicts the presupposed canon. This does not mean the rejection of the presupposed understanding of the canon. It is rather the case that the contradiction to which Käsemann refers already exists between the canon itself and the traditional understanding of the canon. The canon is regarded as an undisputed unity, which it certainly is not.

The Roman Church, indeed, has been protected from this controversy by the fact that she has long ago refused to enter into it, since this would mean the recognition of *sola scriptura*. She has only admitted the authority of Scripture in conjunction with the hermeneutic function of Tradition. Thus the Roman Church could paradoxically agree with Käsemann, since the only result of his arguments is what she has always maintained, namely, that *sola scriptura* is an internal impossibility, and that the canonical authority of Scripture is only available through the hermeneutic assistance of Tradition, which is in the last resort administered in the institution of an infallible doctrinal authority. If, on the other hand, the infallible doctrinal authority is rejected, controversy arises over the various ways in which the appeal to Scripture may be made, and Scripture itself leaves us in the lurch. Hence from the Catholic point of view, Käsemann's arguments will seem to be only concerned with Protestantism, as the logical self-dissolution, so to speak, of *sola scriptura*.

This would, in fact, be the case if Protestantism were based on the understanding of the canon presupposed by Käsemann and then rightly reduced by him *ad absurdum*. For when he reaches the conclusion that, from the point of view of a canon whose authority is equally binding in every part, every absolute Confessional claim is contestable, this sounds at first like an objection against the Roman Catholic position, but, in fact, it affects every Confessional position. Here it is necessary to discriminate in order to make it clear how far, on the one hand, the absolute Confessional claim is something specifically Catholic, with which Protestantism does not compete; but on the other hand can mean something that belongs to Christian faith and cannot be surrendered, as expressed in Luther's dictum in his *De servo arbitrio*, 'Take away affirmations and you have taken away Christianity.'[10] Thus it would ill accord with Protestant faith to advance an absolute ecclesiastical claim corresponding to the Roman Catholic position, and in direct rivalry with it; yet it would not be fitting if the Protestant faith did not affirm with indubitable certainty that which its creed contains, and appeal to Scripture with confidence in the clarity of its content. Actually, however, this certainty characteristic of the Protestant faith is not affected by Käsemann's criticism. For this criticism is directed against an unreformed conception of the canon, and its aim is the clarification of the true Protestant understanding of Scripture. Just as Catholicism will not rest content with that naïve, to put it briefly, legalistic egalitarian, conception of the canon, but corrects it by the doctrine of the hermeneutic significance of Tradition, so the genuine Reformed principle of *sola scriptura* will not rest content with that conception of the canon, but understands *sola scriptura* solely in relation to the Gospel. Yet a distinction exists between Catholicism and Protestantism in relation to the underlying conception of the canon. The Catholic principle of Tradition presupposes that legalistic egalitarian conception of the canon. Accordingly it admits that Scripture, by itself, is not clear, and needs the hermeneutic assistance of Tradition. On the other hand, the Reformed principle of Scripture correctly understood is not affected by Käsemann's demonstration of the obscurity of the New Testament canon, since the recognition of the clarity of Scripture underlying *sola scriptura* is not intended to assert the clarity of all texts, and therewith the absence of any contradictions in the literary material, but to assert the clarity of the content of Scripture, namely, the Gospel.

It is extremely instructive to observe how Käsemann, at the end of his essay, having reached a dead end, points the way to the Reformed view; here I am in complete agreement with him. The dead end is reached when, in view of the conflicting appeals of the Confessions to the New Testament canon, appeals which cannot however be refuted, the exegete finds himself unable to reach any decision; his last word must be in the terms of Lessing's parable of the rings in *Nathan the Wise*, 'Where one is obliged to fall back for support simply on "It is written", it is my conviction and belief that critical study of the New Testament ends in the confession of Lessing's fable'.[11] But Käsemann does not feel himself under any obligation to stop at this point. A starting-point for a further discussion of the problem is presented to him by the observation that, beside the words of the canon, the New Testament itself regards the task of theology as the discerning of spirits (διάκρισις πνευμάτων). This clearly means that the transmitted sayings do not as such decide everything, but rather introduce an ever new task to be mastered. He compares the problem thus initiated with the question of the relation between the letter and the spirit, as it is raised in 2 Cor 3 with regard to the Old Testament, but is equally valid for the New Testament canon. The 'letter' here refers to the divine claim as misused by man; misused in such a way as to make God the prisoner of his own claim. Thus this claim, only observed as it stands, actually puts the Law in the place of God. But this strikes a blow at God's own existence. 'Man can never possess God as an object to be grasped, since God would then cease to be God and our Lord. Man only possesses God if and so long as God possesses him.'[12] It is equally true that 'We do not find God as an object to be possessed in the New Testament canon.' 'In its bare existence the canon cannot be regarded as the Word of God.'[13] It is by no means Käsemann's intention to play off 'Spirit' against 'Tradition'. But Spirit and Tradition should not simply be identified. 'The tension between Spirit and Scripture is an essential element in the situation. This means that the canon is not simply identical with the Gospel, and is only God's Word so long as it is and continues to be Gospel. To that extent then it is the foundation of the unity of the Church; for it is the Gospel alone which is the foundation of a church at all times and in all places.'[14]

In these conclusions we have evidently an outline of the authentic Reformed position. They are directed against that legalistic conception of the canon which the whole argument presupposed and reduced to absurdity. Such a conception is inappropriate because it tries to make God disposable, does not let God be God, and contradicts the Holy Spirit and faith. Incontestably true as this final statement is as the beginning of a positive solution of the problem of the canon, nevertheless difficult questions remain. I find it unconvincing for the argument to be concentrated on the inappropriateness of the legalistic conception of the canon as opposed to its mere existence. Käsemann certainly does not intend his statement to be merely a negative one. But his positive intention must be to ensure that the clarity of the content of Scripture and the certainty of faith should appear as the evident expression of a right understanding of Scripture. That is doubtless intended by the reference to the Holy Spirit. Nevertheless what spirit really is should be discussed from this side in relation to the problem of the canon. Käsemann does not make it entirely clear how this view of spirit (which according to his interpretation means that God is not an object to be grasped, even in the New Testament canon) is to be linked up with the subject of Scripture, on the one hand, that is, with the Gospel, as Käsemann himself says, and with the actual material of the New Testament canon, on the other hand. For if, as Käsemann quite rightly sees, the correct use of the canon depends on the continuing activity of the Spirit, then the following question must be more precisely answered: What is really the essential element for Christian faith, and what is really the continuing *traditio tradenda*, if this is, on the one hand, preaching, spoken word, Gospel, and on the other hand, Holy Spirit and not 'the letter', although no Holy Spirit without 'the letter'? This connection between Gospel and Spirit must be considered in relation to the question of what is the real purpose, the authoritative element in the canon. Moreover, this question must not be separated from a clarification of the question of what is the real significance of the variability of the kerygma. Käsemann would occasionally seem to think that the variations are an unfortunate distortion. But is not the variability of the kerygma a legitimate, and even a necessary, process? This question goes back to the previous one about the essential element in the situation. What is the unity which manifests itself as capable of variation? What is this so-called kerygma if there are not merely illegitimate, but legitimate variations of the kerygma? This is where a beginning would have to be made, in order to clarify the question of what is the actual canonical element in the New Testament canon.[15]

8

The Word of God and Church Doctrine

I

Underlying the discussion of the theme 'The Word of God and Church Doctrine' are certain conditions of a general nature which we wish to make known by way of introduction. It is not a matter of partisan claims, but of insights whose obviousness has led to their being either overlooked or undervalued. They are basically relevant to any theological theme, but stand in particularly close relation to the problems raised by our theme. They are not by any means confined to the situation of the interconfessional dialogue, although they have special significance in relation to it.

1. *Theological discussion, as such, is exposed to Confessional differences.* The encounter of theologians of different Confessions only makes explicit what even without this determines theological work. We theologize either as Catholic or as Protestant theologians, to name only the most outstanding difference. It is doubtful whether the attempt to avoid either of these alternatives, and to find a position outside of, or beyond the Confessional differences, can be called theology. We are so accustomed to this situation that its significance escapes us. Let us for the present leave the question open whether Christian theology has not always, and essentially, been involved in Confessional decisions. Even if we limit our enquiry to the situation since the sixteenth century, a purely pragmatic explanation will be found insufficient: as the result of unfortunate occurrences in the course of Church history, there arose two main theological types, which, thanks to the prevailing interest of the Churches in theology, practically dominate the situation; this is demonstrated from the institutional point of view by the exclusive existence, side by side, of Protestant and Catholic faculties of theology. The relevant point here is rather that theology is essentially Church theology. The significance of this statement is less clear than it might

appear from its unanimous use in Catholic and Protestant dogmatics of all varieties. In any case this ecclesiastical character of theology is not a matter of heteronomous influence, but of what is given in the content of theology itself. But if, as we shall assume, the content of theology is the Word of God, then it is certainly determinative for theology that the event of the Word of God, its proclamation, its acceptance by faith, gratitude for it, and confession of it, is the totality which makes the Church what it is, and can neither be understood nor accounted for apart from the actual course of the history of the Church.

What we see as a division in the Church gives us a glimpse into such profound cleavages in relation to the content of theology, as to make us realize that it is the continuing task of theology to plumb the depths of these cleavages, that they may not be left behind us as settled. Emancipation from the Confessional controversy would mean that theology would lose its depth. It is not any prospect of success in reaching a Confessional understanding that makes encounters such as ours of first-rate importance, but the necessity of reaching the greatest possible degree of theological honesty. Our aim is not to iron out and trivialize the differences in Church doctrine, in order to produce a semblance of unity on the bare Word of God; but to make such an intensive study of the Confessional disputed issues in Church doctrine, that it may be vindicated as a witness to the Word of God. When, therefore, we endeavour to establish, on both sides, the validity of the most inward purity of Church doctrine, we must also remember the fact that even the apparently abstract and formal question of defining the relation between the Word of God and Church doctrine involves Confessional differences in that, not only the content—if a distinction can be made—but also the concept, of the Word of God, as well as the problematic link-word 'and', may be differently understood. The only hope of overcoming Confessional differences lies in taking them seriously.

2. *Theological discussion takes place on its own responsibility.* It may be urged that this contradicts the first statement that theological discussion depends on Church doctrine, and that the latter is fundamentally the Catholic conception, while, with the sole responsibility of the theologian we are introducing the Protestant contention. Against this super-

ficial impression lies the fact that both statements are inseparable; they belong together, and hence are obviously to be understood as referring to both Confessions. They are differently interpreted by each. But, just as Protestant theology cannot allow itself to be deprived of the point of view of Church doctrine, although many questions are connected with it, so Catholic theology cannot renounce the personal responsibility of the theologian, although, similarly, various problems are bound up with that. These considerations concern both the conduct of our dialogue and the subject-matter of our discussion. On neither side would we wish to limit ourselves to an exposition of Church doctrine, as though the task of dogmatics could be settled historically. A responsible theological statement can never dispense with some kind of personal note since that is characteristic of responsibility. Although we meet as Protestant and as Catholic theologians, we should not expect a double unison while holding back our own view because of partisan pressure. We must so act that the dialogue may be either rendered more difficult, or enriched, according to the point of view, through the theological differences within one's own Confession. In any case, when one is engaged in a dialogue with a member of another Confession, there should be no suppression of problems for tactical and therefore non-theological reasons, which are reserved for discussion in one's own Confession.

This brings us to the subject of our theme and to the realization that we cannot discuss what Church doctrine is without raising the question of how Church doctrine and theology are related to one another. There is doubtless some truth in the obvious view, on the one hand, that Church doctrine, as its name implies, is co-ordinated with a community or institution, and to that extent is superior (with whatever qualifications) to differences in men and times; and on the other hand that theology is an individual matter, and allows the characteristics of the individual to appear; this is not a regrettable defect, but an indispensable condition for the existence of theology. This confrontation of Church doctrine and theology should not, however, be caricatured, so as to give the picture of an objective and authoritative Church doctrine, contrasted with a theology stigmatized as an arbitrary and unauthoritative private opinion, or, conversely, contrasted with responsible theology, Church doctrine is regarded as the enslavement of a legalistic faith. The relation cannot therefore be an external addition, with the implication that to Church doctrine belongs the field of what is established and withdrawn from theological discussion; while the field of theology came in by the way to deal with less important matters, not strictly belonging to Church doctrine. Even if, from a certain point of view, the definitiveness and finality of theological discussion should be bound up with the concept of Church doctrine, this can hardly mean that theology is not responsible for Church doctrine in respect of the way in which it carries out interpretation, including its establishment and development. Rightly understood they cannot be thought of as merely existing side by side. For clearly responsibility for Church doctrine can only be a matter of theological perception. But if individual responsibility is a matter of the individual conscience, then the question arises whether the relation to the Word of God does not constitute the relevant subject for theology in respect to Church doctrine, namely, to think out the implications of the Word of God for Church doctrine, and of Church doctrine for the Word of God.

3. *Theological discussion should serve the cause of thorough understanding.* It is the business of theology to protect the Church from the positivism which appears in religious guise as a claim upon God in disregard of his divinity, and a claim upon man in disregard of man's nature. It can appear in various forms: as superstition, morality, legalism, or perversion of the truth. Positivist theology would therefore be self-contradictory, which does not unfortunately exclude the fact of its existence. Theology is fulfilling its true task when it interprets as the Word of God that which has been transmitted to it as the Word of God, that is, with reference to that Word-event through which conscience encounters full authority. This direction of attention to the fundamental event in which the subject of theology as the Word of God is apprehended by faith, determines the thoroughness of theology as a hermeneutic activity. Because of that thoroughness, theology cannot be conserved, and its task is inexhaustible. For, so long as there is time for that basic event, time imposes upon theology the responsibility of making known that the time has come for that basic event.

Hence, in discussing a theme such as ours, we should not leave out of discussion its basic elements such as 'God' and 'Church', 'Word' and 'Doctrine', and their implications, as presumably obvious, in order to devote ourselves to some extent to some specially insistent problem arising out of some definite aspect of those basic words. We must, on the contrary, if there is to be any genuine theological discussion, so explore the constituent elements of the apparently specialized problem, that the basis of theology itself is questioned as that which, in the last resort, has to be understood in every theological theme. For the Word of God does not elude understanding, but makes understanding possible. Moreover, Church doctrine does not forbid the attempt of theology to understand, but requires it and promotes it. A Word of God which is not understood cannot be accepted as the Word of God. Church doctrine which does not set theology in motion, would not be a witness to the Word of God, but an obscuration of it. Thus the distinction between the Word of God and Church doctrine which we have been discussing reveals a tension which we must endeavour to understand. For the Word of God is clearly the basis of Church doctrine, and Church doctrine is a decisive witness to the possibility of understanding the Word of God.

The question of the relation between the Word of God and Church doctrine is the cause of an insistent appeal to seek for thorough understanding; this is intensified by the situation of interconfessional dialogue. For the disputed issues in Church doctrine, which here force themselves upon our attention, compel us to consider them in relation to their common ground, for the sake of the clarity of the Word of God. Although many misunderstandings and causes of confusion may be removed in this way, it would be illusory to assume that by proper thoroughness in our theology the Confessional difference itself would be removed. The difference in understanding which underlies the opposition between the Confessions points into the depths of the process of understanding, which more or less baffle the understanding itself. This does not constitute an objection to the attempt to reach a theological understanding, but only points to the difficulty of obtaining the evidence upon which it may rest.

4. *It is the duty of theological discussion to meet contemporary needs.* The formulation of this final introductory point might seem rather sharp. It would be easier to speak about contemporary needs than about what should engage our attention in our theological discussion; but in fact, both are included in our purview. Although theology has little occasion or licence to occupy itself with the fashionable study of the needs of the day, and to engage in the pursuit of temporarily popular ends, yet it should, by reason both of its subject and its mission, be in touch with the present, and be aware of what is of immediate and concrete urgency. Only so may it avoid the danger of degenerating into a disconnected play of ideas, and omitting the 'proof of the spirit and of power'. For theology can only bring its subject into contact with real needs by meeting and engaging itself with them. Yet theology, as the absolute necessity, will find its scope in the need to which it turns its attention. That holds good, *mutatis mutandis*, for all proper theological activity, and is not the preserve of some particular theological discipline, such as Apologetics.

To be aware of this, in my opinion, is of benefit to the interconfessional dialogue. This does not simply mean that attention directed to the clearly obvious fact of the need of divided Christendom, or to the no less obvious need of Christendom faced today by an external threat to its very existence. It is certain that we cannot be made aware, either of the internal division of Christendom, or of the urgent need of realizing the threat to its solidarity, merely by interconfessional dialogue, but rather by every kind of theological activity. Yet all such activity would be vitiated if its motive were directed to specific Christian needs or concerns in preference to other needs, merely with the promotion of Christianity in view. The real need of Christendom is not its own need, but the need of the world. With regard to the inherited Confessional opposition many things could be seen in a different light if it were recognized that the present need was not the pursuit of mutual or united Confessional self-interest, but an acceptance of the mission to the world, and the consequent subordination of Christendom's own need to an increased sense of the importance of human need.

We cannot now discuss in detail what is the contemporary urgent need of the world. We must be content to turn our theological responsibility in this direction, not in the sense of an additional point of view, but because this direction of our responsibility is identical with the matter of theology. In order to avoid misunderstanding it is of course necessary to point out that the realization of the contemporary need, and consequently of the understanding of what is needed to meet it, does not force itself obviously and clearly upon our attention. But we must not be too hasty in making use of the excuse that the world does not recognize what its real need is. In any case, it is only in view of the urgency of the needs, as they come to each man, and in relation to them, that the real need and the true remedy for it can be asserted and analysed. Whether theology is true to its task is proved by its exposing its subject-matter, which is, as we have said, the Word of God, to general experience, so that the Word of God may verify the confused state of experience, and establish itself, by creating faith, as what is really needed as against what is only an apparent necessity, and what is truly contemporary as against what is only contemporary in appearance. In order that this should happen, it will not suffice for theological discussion to accept responsibility for the present need. For what that really is, is just the matter in dispute. In this dispute the Word of God wishes to be grasped as the essential contemporary reality, that is, not as a temporary, passing, and partial meeting of the need, but as the abiding and all-sufficient necessity; its contemporary character deals with the need, and thereby creates true presence, since man's deepest need arises from his refusal to be contemporary, and the deepest necessity of the Word of God is a present which creates true presence.

In the theme of 'the Word of God and Church doctrine', we shall do well to take our bearings from this definition of what the Word of God can do. The more unreservedly we consider what is opposed to it, the more profoundly we may grasp what it can do. Here a situation comes into view which the concept of Church doctrine reaches only indirectly, in so far as it serves the Word of God. For if the distinction between the Word of God and Church doctrine has any real meaning, it clearly consists in the fact that the Word of God is in itself that which is necessarily present, while Church doctrine as such is neither the absolute necessity, nor does it make the present really contemporary. Only in relation to the Word of God, but for that reason in distinction from it, does Church doctrine share in the capacity of the Word of God for necessary presence. Apart from this relation, the view of what necessity is changes from a salutary turning towards the need to be met, into a claim to be met, and the view of what the present is, changes into the claim of an entity in the past. The recognition of this does not diminish the importance of Church doctrine, but its real value and the need of it are acknowledged when we say that that on which man is absolutely dependent cannot be described at will as the Word of God, or as Church doctrine. Only so far as Church doctrine subserves the Word of God does it serve the world in its need. Hence serious attention should also be given to the question whether Church doctrine, even so-called pure, orthodox doctrine, may not be a hindrance to the Word of God by refusing to recognize that distinction, and thereby failing to recognize the real need of the world. Although both are so closely bound together, yet Church doctrine must not be confused with the Word of God, any more than the Church can be confused with God himself.

II

While we have been studying some of the conditions for theological discussion, light has broken on the situation of interconfessional dialogue, and at the same time certain important aspects of our subject 'the Word of God and Church doctrine', have come into view. Looking back, our discussion may seem to have pursued a complicated course; this was due to the overlapping of the various aspects which the problems presented. Yet this complication was not deliberately contrived. On the contrary, it revealed something of the original connection which existed between our task as theologians, our Confessional dialogue, and the fundamental importance of our subject. I hope that my somewhat meditative procedure has not merely brought out disconnected points of view of specialist interest, but above all that it has to some extent succeeded in widening the horizon and establishing an atmosphere in which our meeting may be carried out in such a width of outlook and frankness as befits the subject of our discussion, for which we are all equally responsible.

It now becomes necessary, however, in closer connection with the pattern of the problems involved in our subject, to arrange, investigate, complete, and carry further what has already been delineated. The present setting forbids any attempt at an exhaustive exposition.

1. What exactly does our theme 'the Word of God and Church doctrine' present to us for consideration? What issues are involved in it? What is the crucial question raised by the problem? Clearly the most pressing difficulty requiring explanation is the *distinction* between the two. The question might be raised whether this distinction is of supreme importance. It might be urged that the Word of God is the content of Church doctrine. For what else has the Church to teach; what else gave her the right and title to assume the office of a teacher but the Word of God? Thus Church doctrine would only be the manner in which the Word of God was presented. The distinction would then only concern the content and form of the same thing—as is usually said. In reality there would be identity. At any rate, there ought to be identity, so that the real concern of our theme would not be the distinction, but to stress and preserve the identity. Yet if the occasion calls for emphasis on, and exertions to guard, the identity, this identity is clearly not a matter of course. The possibility, however, of a breach in the identity of the Word of God and Church doctrine, depends on the fact that a difference in their nature already exists which lies too deep to be embraced in the dubious pattern of content and form. Concern that the Word of God and nothing else should be the content of Church doctrine would not in any way compete with our discussion of the distinction. On the contrary, a correct apprehension of the distinction would be the very means of asserting and guarding the unity; while the deepest reason why Church doctrine has lost the sense of unity with the Word of God is because it has blurred the distinction between the Word of God and Church doctrine.

That unity and distinction do not represent rival points of view, but that the conception of the distinction is the correct conception of the way in which they belong together, is an aspect of the problem which is to be met with repeatedly in theology: for example, in the doctrine of Law and Gospel, in Christology, and especially in the relation between God and Man. That in our case there is an essential difference to be considered is shown by the fact in linguistic usage that the concepts of the Word of God and Church doctrine are by no means interchangeable at will; it is further shown by the fact that similarly in linguistic usage, Church doctrine is only one particular way in which the witness of the Word of God takes place, and that not the primary or fundamental way. Admittedly, every attestation of the Word of God could be designated as Church doctrine, in so far as preaching or admonition are doctrine in the broad sense, and in so far as the basis of the Church, and thus its essential utterance, is heard where the Word of God is heard. With regard to Church doctrine, however, when by that the activity of teaching is implied, we are accustomed to make, if not a separation, at least a distinction from preaching and admonition; this is true of teaching, not of the full concrete witness of the Word of God, but the limited concentration of that witness in regulative statements which are generally accepted in the Church.

In order to make this rough distinction more precise, we should first consider the implications of the terminology in which the problem has been stated. Here the distinction takes on a double aspect. On the one hand we have Word, on the other, doctrine; on the one hand there is God, on the other, the Church. It is not easy to penetrate the significance of these terminological contrasts and connections. There is probably no dispute about the distinction between God and the Church as the people of God. But its unfolding in the actuality of the distinction between the action of God and the action of the Church, between the authority of God and the authority of the Church, demands an exposition of the doctrine of the Holy Spirit. The distinction between Word and doctrine has long been a problem. Is not doctrine, at the least, a form of the Word, and is not Word, in respect of its communicative function, doctrine in the broad sense? Nevertheless we here meet with a difference which is hardly solved by the construction of a pyramid of concepts, after the fashion of Arbor Porphyriana.[1] Even if we remember that *doctrina* both in Scholastic and in Reformed usage did not have that doctrinaire overtone which the word usually conveys to us, but rather spills over into the meaning of preaching, the proclaimed Word, we can at least observe various tendencies: Word as defining the actuality of the situation, doctrine as expressing the universal, and moving towards abstraction; Word as the medium of communication between person and person, doctrine as that which subordinates the person to the situation which concerns him. These are inadequate suggestions, which have to be more thoroughly studied, and they call for a comprehensive study of the linguistic problem. Further, we should have to ask—not as the bringing together of unrelated studies, but, by a mutual interpenetration of the doctrine of God as the doctrine of the Holy Spirit, and the linguistic problem—what is involved in the co-ordination of God and Word, Church and doctrine, and in the fact that this co-ordination, whatever qualifications have to be made, is definitely not interchangeable. The far-ranging difficulties and possibilities involved in the development of our theme make it impossible to pursue this line, although it would be indispensable for a thorough working out of the theme.

We shall instead attempt to define more precisely the nature of the problem raised by comparing it with the formula 'Scripture and Tradition' which is the subject of current theological controversy. Do not both statements, 'Word of God and Church doctrine', and 'Scripture and Tradition', mean the same thing? This impression is strengthened if we replace the formula 'Scripture and Tradition', which is commonly felt to be Catholic in character, by the corresponding Protestant formula 'Scripture and Confession'. It should not be forgotten that, in spite of the surprising external resemblance between these two formulas, their meaning is widely different. The formula 'Scripture and Confession' is not to be understood as an antithesis to *sola scriptura*, but as in accord with what could be asserted about the formula 'Scripture and Tradition' by a forced alteration of the meaning of *sola scriptura*. The function of the Confession, at least from a theological point of view, is subordinate to Holy Scripture. The Tridentine ascription 'of equal respect, regard, and reverence'[2] could never be asserted of the Confession on the Protestant view. The general Protestant attitude has been expressed in the *Book of Concord* as follows: 'Such is the distinction laid down between the Holy Scriptures of the Old and New Testaments, and all other writings, and Holy Scripture remains the sole judge, rule, and plumb-line, by which, as the only touchstone, all teachings should and must be examined and tested, whether they be good or bad, true or false. The other creeds and related writings are not judges like Holy Scripture, but only the witness and exposition of the faith, as in every age the Holy Scripture has been understood and interpreted by those living at the time in strict accordance with the articles of faith as laid down in the Church of God, and adverse teaching was by them rejected and condemned.'[3] It is thoroughly Protestant that a significant position should be attributed to Tradition alongside Holy Scripture, although with the express declaration that it is only Church tradition and a witness to Church doctrine, and that it remains subject to the authority of Scripture. The formula 'Scripture and Confession' is thus identical in fact with our theme 'the Word of God and Church doctrine'—at any rate with the presupposition of the Old Protestant Orthodox identification of Scripture with the Word of God. It was not modern criticism which was the first to oppose this identification: the Reformers perceived that the Word of God, strictly speaking, was not writing, but oral speech, the living voice, hence the very Word of God, here and now preached and responded to. Hence, at least in correct Protestant understanding, the formula 'Scripture and Confession' is not simply to be identified with 'the Word of God and Church doctrine'.

We shall not pursue further the problems raised by this aspect of our study, but shall content ourselves with establishing the following position: the Catholic formula 'Scripture and Tradition' is also not to be identified with the formula 'the Word of God and Church doctrine', although in another way. For it is out of the question here to ascribe parity with the Word of God to Scripture, or with Church doctrine to Tradition. This may be made clear by a passage from the *Constitutio dogmatica de fide catholica* of Vatican I: 'In the divine and Catholic faith all those things are to be believed which are contained in the written or transmitted Word of God and declared by the Church, either in solemn decision, or by the regular and universal magisterium, to be believed as divinely revealed.'[4] Although the concept of Tradition overlaps what is merely Church tradition, its central theological significance lies in its application to the unwritten transmission of the Word of God, and therefore to the revelation itself. Yet however much the conception of Church doctrine is related materially to the content of revelation, and thus to the unwritten authoritative witnesses of divine Tradition, nevertheless its distinctive application does not lie in Church witnesses, the authority of which would be of a subordinate and derived nature, but in the fact of its promulgation as that which is contained in the written or transmitted Word of God to be believed as divinely revealed. What is put forward by the Church's doctrinal authority (identical with the so-called active Tradition), is thus necessarily added to the act of revelation as a second authoritative act independently produced by the Holy Spirit. The problem of the Catholic understanding of Church doctrine is in the last analysis centred on this question of its promulgation by the Church, however much the question is also discussed of the authority of the texts in which this promulgation has been made. On the other hand, from the Protestant point of view, the problem of Church doctrine seems to be merely the problem of the authority of the texts, not related to the fact of the authoritative promulgation of what is to be believed divinely revealed by an authority which guarantees the rightness of the judgement.

As our study develops, two questions emerge: the question of the documentary character of Church doctrine, and the question of its authoritative character.

2. With regard to the consolidation of Church doctrine in documentary form, Catholicism and Protestantism, in the modern age, seem to have pursued divergent courses. While Catholicism as a whole has intensified the study of Church doctrine, and has gone forward in its consolidation, in Protestantism the formation of confessions practically ceased with the sixteenth century, apart from a few isolated attempts in the seventeenth century; later the obligatory nature of the confessions was tacitly or expressly abandoned. On the Catholic side there has recently been an intensified study of the problem of the historical character of dogmatic development and of its documentary presentation; while, conversely, on the Protestant side, strong movements towards dogmatic restoration are in evidence. However, not only in spite of, but within such movements Confessional differences make themselves felt. It is no doubt natural that there should be an identification of a fixed confession and Church doctrine. Nevertheless, the loosening or abandonment of the obligatory nature of the Confessions

does not involve the abandonment of Church doctrine in general. Even when its legally tenable aspect is reduced to a minimum, the problem of Church doctrine is not thereby simply eliminated, but continues in many ways to present itself as a problem. Moreover, it asserts its validity in various practical ways, partly through the living use of traditional documents, such as the catechism, books of ritual, hymn-books, and so on; partly through continuing theological studies, preaching and teaching. By such means, in spite of all failures, it has been able to establish the validity of its subject-matter, not, as is too hastily assumed, in any arbitrary subjective fashion, but in fundamental decisions of the Church.

It is perhaps not entirely without foundation to speak of the chaotic state of Protestant doctrine; but, in spite of so much that might give occasion for doubt, it would not do justice to the situation. Granting the presupposition of the fundamental Protestant view, in the sense of Church doctrine, we have only to ask what is to be gained by a fixed obligatory Confession with disciplinary sanctions. It should not be disputed that here we are confronted by tasks and demands which cannot be neglected with impunity. But it is necessary to keep in mind the limits of what is possible, and to serve the Church in the way which makes the Church. The decisive factor is not the formal existence of a binding Confession, but its practical use. Moreover, the consolidation of Church doctrine in no way dispenses us from the task of interpreting and actualizing it. Just as with Holy Scripture the hermeneutic problem arises with the documents of the Church doctrinal tradition. To repeat the words is not enough. On the contrary, the language of tradition must give way to one's own speaking; and it is possible that the element of 'sameness' can only be preserved by 'otherness' in the matter of speech. Moreover, it should not simply be attributable to modernistic tendencies if modern Protestantism recognizes the existence of difficulties in respect to the textual availability of Church doctrine. Undoubtedly, there are certain connections here with the Reformers' position itself. To put it sharply, the problem of Church doctrine in Protestantism is, in a certain respect, the expression of Church doctrine. It may be asserted (though with considerable reserve) that this connection with specific Reformed characteristics can also be seen in the fact that in modern Protestantism the making of confessions and the consequent stabilizing of Church doctrine no longer continues. It would be oversimplifying simply to blame modern men for this, or to place the responsibility for it merely on the divided state of the Church in Protestantism, or on the absence of any authoritative court of appeal. Nor can these oft lamented symptoms be regarded merely as signs of decadence. Moreover, it is no part of the Reformers' understanding of Church doctrine that the making of confessions should be a continuous process. This brings us up against the fact that even the idea of fixed Church doctrine is differently regarded in Protestantism and in Catholicism in consequence of a difference in their Church doctrine.

This can be traced into the realm of terminology, although the origins of different linguistic usage are obscure. It is true that in both Confessions the stabilizing of Church doctrine is described as 'dogma'. But the question arises whether both Confessions use the term in the same sense, or with equal right. Again we observe that on the Protestant side, in modern times, there is an intense dislike of the concept of dogma, as well as a determination, in reaction, to hold fast to dogma, as though the correct Protestant understanding of Church doctrine depended on the use of the term 'dogma'. This situation has now become so complicated that it is hardly possible without misunderstanding to give a brief explanation of it. I am in fact of the opinion that the word 'dogma' is not well suited to designate fixed Church doctrine in the Protestant understanding of it, while its use in the Catholic sense is fully justified. The derivation of the term from the old double meaning of a philosophic tenet, and of a legally binding decree, serves, *mutatis mutandis*, as a starting-point for the Catholic interpretation of the dual authority in Church doctrine, namely, the authority of the subject-matter in question, and the authority of the court of appeal in question. The fact that it is only recently, since the eighteenth century, that the term 'dogma' has come into Catholic usage in the current modern restricted sense, while the earlier historical concept of dogma made a wider use of the term possible, is no reason for denying its predominant use as a technical term for a fixed Church doctrine in the Catholic understanding of the term. In this usage we find expressed the conception of the stabilizing of Church doctrine from the beginning in a definite, authoritative form, guaranteed by an infallible court of appeal. It is wholly appropriate that the Catholic formation of dogma should lead to a dogma in regard to the origin of dogmas. It is similarly in line with this conception of dogma, that, without prejudice to these solemn dogmatic definitions, the process of dogma-making moves on continuously and without limit, in the form of a continuous stabilization of Church doctrine.

In the Protestant usage of the sixteenth and seventeenth centuries dogma was equated with *articulus fidei*, with no suggestion of any defining or promulgating activity on the part of a representative ecclesiastical court of appeal, but, on the one hand, presupposing what is contained in Holy Scripture (cf. Luther in the Schmalkaldic Articles: 'The Word of God and nothing else shall establish an article of faith');[5] and on the other hand, looking towards the liberating assurance for the conscience contained in the affirmations of the Confession of faith (cf. Luther's use of the term dogma in *De servo arbitrio* as the equivalent of 'affirmation' and 'assurance'). It should not be overlooked that, although after the eighteenth century in Protestant usage, too, the term 'dogma' took on the special meaning of an ecclesiastically determined doctrinal position, yet there had once been a time when the usage of 'dogma' referred predominantly to the realm of historical theology. As far as our own linguistic usage is concerned, we are aware of the problem involved in specific dogmas being brought forward. It is not by accident that the idea of dogma is concentrated on usage in the singular. When we speak about *the* dogma of the Church, this no longer implies the existence of an unambiguous body of doctrine, but a theological idea which confronts us with the perpetual problem of the meaning of dogma. Moreover, the situation has given rise to a typical difference in usage. So far as the concept of dogma is used with specific documents in view, and in relation to one's own dogmatic conviction, we limit the word to the dogmas of the early Church, accepted by the Reformation, the Trinitarian and Christological dogmas, which cannot be divorced from the historical fact that they owe their existence to the authoritative decision of an Ecumenical Council, although, for the Reformers, their authority did not rest upon a conciliar decision. In reference, however, to the authoritative witness of Church doctrine since the Reformation, as well as to individual decisions in the course of the shaping of doctrine, the term dogma has been avoided. We speak of the Augsburg Confession, not of the Augsburg Dogma; of the Reformers' doctrine of justification, and not of the Reformers' dogma of justification. Rightly so, since the decisive factor of a decree emanating from an authoritative court is absent in this case.

On the other hand, with the idea of a Confession, the Reformation gained a new guiding concept for stabilized Church doctrine. Confession in this sense is a new coinage of the Reformation, differing in character from the term Profession; the latter means the sworn adherence to a doctrinal formula put forward by the Church, and can also mean the formula itself; while a Confession arises as a responsive recognition of a fact, as ὁμολογεῖν, and can only be used in this sense. Hence, in the concept of Confession, an essentially different understanding of the origin of the Church's enunciation of doctrine, of the nature of its validity, and of its continuance, finds expression. The Confession as an authoritative document of Church doctrine is bound up with a unique situation of decision-making, where what constitutes a Church, distinct, and a real church-community, becomes visible. There is, therefore, sound reason that the making of creeds was confined to the period of the Reformation, since when, in the Protestant world, nothing remotely similar of decisive importance for the existence of the Church has taken place. The Reformers' Confession remains the fundamental statement of the Protestant view of Church doctrine. It is true that it is of the nature of a Confession that personal responsibility plays a necessary part. This implies that the appeal to the Reformation Confession, as the authoritative witness of Church doctrine, involves the duty of independent theological study, both in testing, and in bringing traditional Church doctrine into touch with and recognition by the contemporary world. To regard stabilized Church doctrine as a Confession, however, does not involve a progressive stabilization in the interpretation of the Confession, and an increasing degree of definition with regard to Church doctrine; it involves, rather, concentration on the witnesses which give access to the Reformers' fundamental understanding of the Gospel.

3. In the terminological difference between dogma and Confession

we are confronted in the most characteristic way with the Confessional differences as to the nature of Church doctrine. What I have suggested is only a beginning which would require a comprehensive exposition. We must now, however, turn our attention to the problem of authority, which is so important for the body of problems confronting us, that we might well have concentrated our entire discussion upon it, instead of contenting ourselves with a few scanty remarks on this central problem at the end of a long and tiring approach to it.

The impression, for which Protestantism is to some extent responsible, must be vigorously contested, that it is characteristic of Protestantism, as contrasted with Catholicism, to discredit authority, and that certainty is not acceptable to it, but that uncertainty has actually been elevated to a kind of theological principle. A fundamental aversion is supposed to exist with regard to the phenomenon of doctrine, and Protestantism is supposed to be less inclined to trust the Holy Spirit than is the case with the Catholic Church. Apart from everything that, on a superficial view, may rightly have contributed to this impression, and from details that may conflict with it, in my opinion, if we go to the root of the matter, this ought to be said: what the Reformation, according to its own understanding of its meaning, established, was the acceptance of the claim of overwhelming authority, being seized by the faith that gives assurance of salvation; it established the duty of contending for the pure, saving doctrine, for a new understanding of the doctrine of the Holy Spirit. It is true that authority, certainty, even doctrine, are differently understood here than in the previously predominant conception. However, be that as it may, it must be recognized that the Reformation claimed to be contending for the true understanding of authority, certainty, and doctrine, and in all for the true understanding of the Holy Spirit. It can above all, though not only, be shown in the source of Luther's theology, how everything springs from and centres in the true understanding of the Holy Spirit. It is this which makes the doctrine of justification intelligible. Rightly understood, it is not a symptom of simultaneous atrophy of the doctrine of the Holy Spirit, but, on the contrary, an extreme emphasis on the doctrine of the Holy Spirit, inseparably bound up with the experience of the doctrine, the certainty, and the authority of the word of God.

With regard to the interpretation of authority here presented, for which one would prefer to use the Greek word ἐξουσία, meaning 'full power', the fact is decisive that it contains no implication of a second authority alongside of the Word of God. On the contrary, it is the event of ἐξουσία which is the fact itself which is revealed through the event of the Word of God. What I mean by this must be explained by the exegesis of the great collection of New Testament sayings characterized by the occurrence of key-words such as λόγος (ῥῆμα), πίστις, ἐξουσία, ἐλευθερία, παρρησία, υἱότης,[6] et al., and which is centred in Jesus as the one in whom this ἐξουσία took place, and by appeal to whom it takes place. An essential element in this interpretation of authority is that it is authority revealed by the Word for the Word, and liberates the believer for service. Word and Freedom are essential factors of authority, since it is by this means that God becomes present to the contemporary world, so that in responsible freedom his presence is revealed in the Word. It is of the utmost importance to recognize that the understanding of authority is rooted in the nature of the Gospel itself, and is indeed identical with it.

I can only attempt to give an outline, under three aspects, of what the problem of authority involves within the scope of our theme 'The Word of God and Church doctrine'.

In the first place the criterion of true authority in the Christian meaning of the term—and let us be bold to say, the criterion of true authority in general—is that it does not remain immobile as a mere normative authority, but is a creative authority, empowering, liberating, faith-producing, love-engendering. Where authority stands in opposition to freedom, neither authority nor freedom is rightly understood, and neither has any real existence.

Next, true authority is the identity of two things which usually seem to exist in mutual tension, namely, the authority of fact, on the one hand, which compels recognition, and personal authority, on the other hand, to which obedience is given. The unity of these two is only possible in the Word of God. It might be urged with regard to this, that a firm distinction must be made between person and fact. That is true in so far as the authority of preaching, rightly understood, rests upon what is preached, and not on the personal qualities of the preacher, just as lack of the latter cannot destroy the authority of the fact. On the other hand, the true understanding of authority in the Word of God, because this authority is bound to the Word-event, is inseparable from personal encounter. It is therefore no contradiction if the authority of the person passes into the authority of the fact, that is, into an appeal to the authority which it experiences, that is, which is ascribed to it. This makes it possible to make the standpoint of the authority of an office, or of a body, such as a synod, fully effective. But it must be understood that the responsible pronouncement of the authority depends upon its basis, hence it is never isolated and formal, but only on the basis of authority can authority be claimed for the Church.

Finally, it is, of course, not open to dispute that formal authority in the Church may manifest itself in many ways, for instance, in the influence of a personality, the weight of an overwhelming majority, with which one agrees from love, and so on. But in this connection we find ourselves, as the Church to a large extent does in its external organization, governed by the prevailing social conditions. That has a perfectly justifiable relative claim. But it is limited by the important case where the individual must assert his authority, even against the pressure of the majority and against Church officialdom, for in matters of faith only that has authority which binds and frees the conscience. When, according to Catholic doctrine, we learn that alongside the authority of the Word of God there exists, supporting and validating it, the authority of the magisterium laying down what is to be believed, then any possibility of agreement on this point depends on whether the authority of this Church court of appeal commends itself to the conscience, and on how far it agrees with the character of the ἐξουσία of the Holy Spirit revealed in Jesus. However, in this case it would not be possible to understand in how far we were dealing with two different manifestations of authority.

4. I shall close with a few formal considerations, not by way of summing up the whole discussion, but as a kind of appendix.

a) Church doctrine has not only to be tested as to whether it agrees with the authoritative witness of the revelation, that is, of Holy Scripture, but also if it is responsible, in association with it, to minister the Word of God; that is, that it is authoritative only so far as it sets free for the preaching of the Gospel, and is only rightly understood as a guide to the conscience.

b) Church doctrine in the sense of fixed documentary form is not intended to aim at the most far-reaching and increasing detail in doctrinal statements, in a kind of theological compendium. Strictly speaking, the only business of Church doctrine is to bear witness to what makes the Church a Church. That points to the connection between Church doctrine and the actual existence of the Church community. To ascribe more to Church doctrine than the Confession of what is absolutely essential for the existence of the Church would mean to lag behind that which constitutes the necessity of Church doctrine.

c) It should not be the aim of Church doctrine to establish a normative Church theology. As the formulation of Church doctrine presupposes theology, this implies that it has a duty towards theology. Confessional obligation and doctrinal involvement are only meaningful in so far as they are under obligation to responsible theology. For the stabilization of Church doctrine does not dispense with the necessity of constantly both identifying and distinguishing between the Word of God and Church doctrine, and that is the business of theology.

d) Church doctrine is a unity, since it is the witness of the Word of God. Although it needs to be formulated in articles, it is nevertheless a whole, not as a doctrinal *summa*, but in accordance with the necessity of the Word of God. Whatever has not this absolute character of necessity is not a part of Church doctrine. Therein lies its importance, and that explains its relation to love. Luther has thus expressed it: 'Doctrine should be a golden circle without a break ... For we are made for love and harmony, but abide within the bounds of love ... Let us not play with doctrine ... If we abandon one (article) we abandon all. If they (the opponents) knew what the Word is, they would know that all words are one and that one is all ... If I deny God in one article I deny him in all, for the whole is in each article.'[7]

9

The Mariological Dogma

In the course of its development up to the present the Mariological dogma has passed through three stages. In its first stage it is clearly a part of Christology, and the article of the Creed on the Virgin Birth has no Mariological significance; its bearing is entirely Christological. The Virgin Birth affirms that Christ was born without any taint of original sin, and was conceived, not of human seed, but of God. Nevertheless it is clear that the doctrine of the Virgin Birth involved further problems, for it is not possible to speak about the real Incarnation without introducing the miraculous element involved in the divine nature of Christ. There was a danger that the doctrine of the Virgin Birth might become a breeding-place for a docetic Christology. The danger became in fact a serious one, and the theology of the Church spent much labour in avoiding it without falling into the opposite danger of surrendering the uniquely miraculous character of the birth of Christ. We have only to read the relevant portions of the Scholastic writings to see the ramifications of the problem. For example, such questions were raised as to how the conception took place, how the development of the child in its mother's womb was to be understood, whether the birth involved for Mary the loss of her virginity, and so forth. The aim of the discussion had always a double aspect: it sought to avoid every appearance of docetism, and to present Mary as the true and natural mother of Christ, and the birth as a real birth; on the other hand, it sought to interpret the miracle of what had happened to Mary as an independent miracle, not solely connected with the birth. Hence there was a motive for affirming the virginity of Mary as existing not only before the birth, but both in and after the birth; there was also a concern, in view of the event of the birth, to assert the occurrence of a second miracle in addition to the miraculous conception. The original statement in the Creed which interpreted the Virgin

Birth solely as the miracle of the Incarnation, acquired an importance of its own, so that, side by side with the Incarnation, the virginity of Mary before, in, and after the birth, was presented as a second redemptive fact. In the miracle of the Virgin Birth the event of the Incarnation passed into the sphere of natural historical events as an objective fact, and this objective fact, by the affirmation of the perpetual virginity of Mary, became a second objective fact, separate from and existing independently of Christ himself.

But, and here we come to the second stage of the development of the Mariological dogma, this objectifying of the Incarnation-event by the ascription of perpetual virginity to Mary was also an element in the development of the Christology. We know from the history of dogma that the beginnings of Christological controversy in the narrower sense were focused on the key-word θεοτόκος, which, after the Council of Ephesus in 431, had passed into the vocabulary of dogma. The logic of events which led from the Christology of the early Church to this epithet can be acknowledged. But at the same time the problem arises whether the early Church Christology did not, at this point, come up against serious critical limits to its conceptuality, that is, whether the θεοτόκος was not in essence Monophysite, and legitimized a crypto-docetism; this already existed as an undercurrent in the Christology of the Church; the question further arises whether at least the passionate interest in this θεοτόκος was not an indication that Christology was embarking on a dangerous course. Although Luther maintained as a whole a conservative position with regard to the doctrine of the Virgin Birth, it is nevertheless noticeable that in the last resort it was only a certain positivism of revelation, and not a speculative interest in the doctrine, which determined his view. He took his stand on the relevant passages in the opening chapters of Matthew and Luke, and on the unfathomable purpose of God who could have ordered the event quite otherwise. Thus Luther, in a sermon, could give frank expression to a statement which shows an entirely different attitude to the question of the Virgin Birth: 'It does not matter much whether she be a virgin or a married woman, yet God has willed that she should be a virgin.'[1] If we take the θεοτόκος as it was understood in the fifth century, then not only does the ascription of perpetual virginity appear inevitable, but a special place in the history of redemption is assigned to Mary. Moreover, it will not be disputed that she is not only presented from the point of view of the history of revelation as the mother of Christ, but also from the soteriological point of view as the bearer of salvation; as such she exists ontologically side by side with Christ as the object of veneration for believers as receiving and mediating the prayers of the faithful. The link which the θεοτόκος had established between Christology and Mariology made it possible to develop still further the parallelism between them.

This brings us to the third stage of the dogmatic development. If Mary as the mother of God remained a perpetual virgin (*deipara semper virgo*), then she must have been in the absolute sense immaculate, or sinless. That made it necessary to assert, not only her freedom from actual sins, but that the implication of the Virgin Birth with regard to Christ, namely his freedom from any taint of original sin, must also be asserted of Mary. Although the epithet Immaculate may originally have implied only the actual sinlessness of Mary, the well-known controversy arose in the mid-medieval period between the Dominicans and the Franciscans on the question whether it could be affirmed of Mary that she was also sinless in the sense of being free from original sin, or whether the miracle implied by the Virgin Birth in respect of Christ could have its parallel in the life of Mary, namely that she also might have been born miraculously through an immaculate conception. There can be no doubt that the whole trend of Franciscan teaching on the subject of Mariology and the veneration of Mary was tending towards the Immaculate Conception. Transference of the miracle of the Virgin Birth to the birth of Mary was avoided, but it was taught that in spite of a natural conception, Mary's freedom from original sin was brought about by a special act of divine grace. The Council of Basle had already arrived at a definition of the immaculate conception, but this decision was not recognized by the Roman Church, since it had happened at a time when the Papacy already regarded the Council as schismatic. Sixtus IV intervened in the controversy in 1476 and again in 1483 with a pronouncement which was unambiguous but also very cautious.[2] He only spoke of the conception of one who was immaculate (*conceptio immaculatae*), but nevertheless commended the Feast of the

Immaculate Conception, and forbade opposition to it and to the doctrine underlying it. A final dogmatic decision was not yet promulgated. It was not even arrived at in the Council of Trent, but there it was felt to be enough to issue a decree on Original Sin, with express reference to the Constitutions of Sixtus IV, explaining that the Blessed and Immaculate Virgin was not referred to in the statements about Original Sin.[3] A little later, in refutation of the Augustinianism of Michel Baius, Pius V declared that no one but Christ was free from original sin, and that the sufferings and death of Mary were for her the consequence of original sin.[4]

It was not until after the great crisis of Catholicism in the seventeenth and eighteenth centuries that the doctrine of the immaculate conception was sufficiently developed to become the subject of dogma. The new outbreak of veneration for Mary, stimulated by the manifestations of the Mother of God at the beginning of the nineteenth century, led to the conclusion that this doctrine had already passed long ago from the stage of a common belief through that of a majority belief, and had become a universal belief.[5] The dogmatic definition pronounced by Pius IX in 1854 was startling, not so much on account of its content, as on account of its form; here the Pope assumed the authority which had been accorded to him in Vatican I, of pronouncing an infallible decision on a matter of doctrine without summoning a council. The introductory statement in the dogmatic definition of the Bull 'Ineffabilis Deus' corresponds literally with the form of words used in a canonization, but with the difference that here much more was involved. Mary's freedom from original sin was declared to have taken place at the exact moment of her conception. It was further laid down that this took place by a special act of grace and privilege on the part of Almighty God, hence it was not a physical miracle, but the result of an act of divine grace. Its classification in Christology was ensured by the recognition that this special grace was made possible by the merits of Christ: 'In virtue of the merits of Jesus Christ the Saviour of mankind.'[6] In this way the appearance of an independent Mariology, or of the subordination of Christology to Mariology was avoided. It was not disputed that freedom from original sin is only possible through Christ. Although, in point of time, the immaculate conception of

Mary precedes the merits of Christ, yet logically and theologically these precede the immaculate conception. Moreover, Mary, in spite of the immaculate conception, is what she is only through Christ. We see here how the principle of *solus Christus* is always maintained in theory, yet in such a way that it is presented as the first cause of a second cause proceeding from itself, to hold to which is equivalent to holding to Christ. It is an instructive fact that this third stage of the development of the Mariological dogma did not by any means exhaust all its possibilities.

The further course of the development may be illustrated by some papal pronouncements. Leo XIII, in an Encyclical in 1891, made the following statement:[7] 'The Son of God did not wish to unite himself with human nature without its consent; but this voluntary consent was displayed in Mary as the representative of the whole human race. Hence we cannot participate in the supreme gift of grace which the Lord has brought except through Mary. And the inference is that, as no one can come to the Father except through the Son, so it is hardly (*fere*) possible for any one to come to Christ except through his Mother.' It is, however, significant that this amazing dogmatic statement is qualified by a *fere*. Nevertheless the sequence of these two statements remains: No one comes to the Father except through Christ. No one comes to Christ except through Mary. In the light of corresponding New Testament sayings it must be noted that here Mary is given the place of the Holy Spirit. On the other hand, in the light of the well-known saying of Cyprian, 'He cannot have God as Father who has not the Church as Mother', it must be recognized that here Mary takes the place of the Church. And in fact Leo XIII draws the consequence that Mary is described as the mediatrix of the Mediator. Pius X developed this line further: 'Through the community of suffering and will between Mary and Christ, the Blessed Virgin became the restorer of a lost world, the dispenser of the universal gifts of grace which the death and blood of Jesus have made available for us. Mary has won for us by divine favour the same merits which Christ won by his own worth, and therefore she is the principal dispenser of all the abundant stores of grace.'[8] This parallelism between the person and work of Mary and the person and work of Christ was developed in ever greater detail.

Benedict XV said in 1918: 'She has thus suffered with her suffering and dying Son and has almost died with him; she so completely renounced her maternal rights over her Son for the salvation of men and offered him as an atonement to the righteousness of God, that it can justly be said that together with Christ she has redeemed the human race.'[9] Pius XI said: 'The sorrow-stricken Virgin shared with Christ in the work of redemption. It is a just ascription of praise when to the name of Jesus is added the name of his Mother, our co-redemptrix, the Blessed Mary.'[10] This unbroken chain of papal utterances since Pius IX ends with the Hymn to Mary at the conclusion of the ecclesiological Encyclical '*Mystici Corporis*' of Pius XII, 1943:[11] 'Her most holy soul, above all other souls created by God, was filled with the divine Spirit of Jesus Christ. She gave her assent on behalf of human nature in its totality, so that a kind of spiritual union between the Son of God and human nature might be achieved. By a miracle she gave birth to Christ the Lord, the source of all heavenly life, who, while still in her virgin womb, was crowned as supreme Head of the Church. She presented the new-born Child to those who from among Jews and Gentiles were to be the first to worship him as Prophet, King, and Priest. Her Only-begotten, at his Mother's intercession, wrought the miracle in Cana of Galilee, which caused his disciples to believe in him. Free from personal and original sin, and ever most intimately united with her Son, she offered him, with all her maternal rights and all her maternal love to the Eternal Father, as a new Eve for all the children of Adam, involved in their disastrous Fall. Thus she, already the Mother of our Head according to the flesh, by a new title of suffering and honour, became the spiritual Mother of all his members. Through her prevailing intercession the Spirit of the divine Redeemer, already yielded up on the Cross, was poured out at Pentecost upon the new-born Church in wondrous gifts. Finally, because she had borne nameless suffering bravely and faithfully, above all believers together, she became the true Queen of Martyrs and filled up what was lacking of the sufferings of Christ . . . for his Body the Church. She has guided the mystical Body of Christ, born from the pierced heart of the Saviour, with the same deep maternal love and care wherewith she had cherished the Child Jesus in his cradle, and fed and nursed him at her breast.

'To her undefiled heart we have confidently dedicated all mankind. May she, the most holy Mother of all the members of Christ, shining now in heaven's glory in body and soul, and reigning on high with her Son, ever intercede with him, that rich streams of grace may unceasingly flow from their all-powerful Head upon all the members of his mystical Body. May she with her prevailing intercession, as in the past, so today, guard the Church, and obtain from God for her and for all mankind finally more peaceful times.'

The tendency of this development of the Mariological dogma is quite clear: Mary, the Mother of Christ, the Bride of Christ, the new Eve, answering to the Adam–Christ typology, is *the mythical personification of the Church*, which sees itself as mediating all the gifts of grace. The Church is that which is prefigured in Christ, in that she is the co-redemptrix of all mankind. The Church is not only that which daily accomplishes the sacrifice of the Mass, but has already offered up the Son of God at Golgotha. The Church is thus the mediatrix of the Mediator. No man can come to Christ save through Mary, that is, through the Roman Catholic Church. Yet all this is not explicitly stated, but is symbolized in Mary, and finds its whole metaphysical reality in the person of the divine Virgin.

In all this a grandiose reconstruction of ecclesiology is achieved. The authority of the Church is not only historically anchored in Christ, and in the Apostolical succession from Peter, but also, and more profoundly, in Mary. Mariology becomes the real basis of the ecclesiology. In Mary the Church itself becomes the co-redemptrix. In Mary the Church is adored. In Mary the Church is the Queen of Heaven. The cult of Mary makes it possible, while these consequences are kept out of sight, for the Church, instead of being the place of the cult, to become the object of the cult.

Now at last we can understand the concern to establish the bodily Assumption as a dogma. Here we have to do with something more than the affirmation of a miracle as a dogma. It is a question of the keystone of the ecclesiological structure. Here we have the continuation of what the Vatican Council left incomplete. This difference, too, between Christ and Mary must now be bridged: not only Christ but Mary also has already entered bodily into heaven. For the Church this implies that the resurrection of the dead at the Last Judgement is no longer an element in the eschatology. The Church is already eschatologically complete. The Catholic conception of the Church is thus freed from the last remnant of eschatological tension. For the Church there is no longer any problem of actualizing the historical revelation. The Church itself is the revelation in perpetuity.

This ecclesiological interpretation of the Mariological Dogma has far-reaching implications: Mary is the total synthesis of Nature and Grace. She represents the unlimited activity of revelation in human nature. In Mary human nature is completely elevated to the super-natural level. She is full of all grace. She is the pattern of humanity redeemed by sanctifying grace. In her the Person and Work of Christ are fully reflected. In Christ the divine nature has assumed human nature, but the one Person in two natures is likewise very God; but in Mary the miracle of the Incarnation is displayed in human nature alone, raising it to the supernatural level. Hence in Mary grace has for the first time been realized in humanity and in history. In her, man has become the vehicle of revelation, and thus the historical mediator has become the divine Mediator. Thus from the human standpoint Mary is something between man and God, as the continuing activity of the Incarnation in the sphere of human nature, standing nearer to any one who wishes to come to Christ, binding him to Christ, as the mediatrix of all grace, as the mediatrix of the Mediator, and the co-redemptrix. That is the ultimate reason why Mariology reveals the fundamental structure of the Catholic understanding of the actualiza-tion of the revelation: for Catholic faith everything depends on religious realization, on created grace, on reality raising nature to supernature, on the historical immanence of the revelation, and the mediatorial power of the second cause.

Mary, as the total synthesis of nature and grace, is a unique historical figure, and as such is a metaphysical reality for Catholic faith. But she is much more than that. By virtue of all that is implicit in her, she is the mythical personification of the great entity in which the synthesis of nature and grace is historically active; the entity which the role of Mary as the mediatrix of all grace, as the mediatrix of the Mediator, and as the co-redemptrix, reflects on earth, namely the Church. Mary is not only historically the Mother of Christ, but the continuing actualization in history of the Bride of Christ, and that means the Church. In Mariology the soteriological significance of the Church for Catholic understanding is fully recognizable. The Church is the continuing activity of the Incarnation entering completely into human nature in the course of history. In her alone can Christ be truly apprehended. In her has Christ wholly and abidingly entered into history.

Hence Mariology is the central meeting-point of all the lines of Catholic dogma: Christology and Ecclesiology; anthropology and the doctrine of Grace; natural theology and sacramental doctrine. Hence it follows naturally that the Catholic Church has developed all the logical consequences of the Mariological dogma in our time. In no other dogma could the Catholic Church express more forcibly what she believes. The Mariological dogma implies the reduction to dogma of the fundamental structure of Catholicism.

IO

The Protestant Idea of the Priesthood

About two years ago, on the occasion of 'The Munich University Meeting in Switzerland', the Professor of Fundamental Theology in the Catholic Theological Faculty of the University of Munich, Gottlieb Söhngen, at the invitation of the Evangelical Theological Faculty of the University of Basle, delivered a lecture on 'Law and Gospel'. Although the speaker's theme was a Reformation one, it was not his intention to start a controversy with Protestant theology, but to introduce the Catholic view-point on a subject to which a great Catholic tradition was attached. The speaker suggested that this would benefit both sides, since it would require the ability to translate from one theological language into another.[1]

The situation with regard to the subject on which I am about to address you today is the converse. It is the statement of what might be called a Catholic theme concerning which I am now going to attempt to give a Protestant point of view; for Protestantism too has a significant tradition with respect to this subject. I should be happy if I succeeded in fulfilling in some small degree the function of an interpreter between two very different languages. I do not flatter myself that it is possible, by some small skill in translation, to bring about the disappearance of differences which go back for centuries and are unfortunately very deep. For, with regard to what has been spoken in two languages, it is not only a matter of different words, but of a different spirit. But a readiness both to hear and to understand, and so to be an interpreter between the languages, is able to effect the removal of mutual misunderstandings, and so to clarify the difference without distorting it, that the opposition may come to be realized as a common participation in ultimate truth and seriousness.

Many may think that the difference between the two Confessions on the subject of Priesthood can be disposed of by merely saying that the

Catholic Church has priests and the Protestant Church has not. But such a superficial half-truth must be corrected at the outset on both sides by the preliminary remarks which I prefix to the actual treatment of our subject.

I

The linguistic history of our key-word 'priest' has been somewhat broken. The word 'priest' is derived etymologically from the Greek word *presbyteros*, which came into the language as a loan-word in Reformation circles as a designation of the office of elder in the community. *Presbyteros* means literally 'the elder'. The accent, however, is not so much on age in years, as on pre-eminence in experience, maturity, character, and reputation, and thus on the features which tally with the implication of the Catholic use of the title 'Father'. Priest and presbyter are therefore etymologically synonymous. But if the meaning of these two words has diverged to such an extent that they are no longer interchangeable at will, this is due to a linguistic history disclosing significant developments in the understanding of the Christian faith. For the Catholic priest and the Reformation presbyter are not merely, so to speak, etymological twins, but, although both trace their origin to the primitive Christian office of presbyter, they now express a different conception of this office.

Like all historical events, the rise and development of the relations within the early Christian community presents an intricately interwoven pattern. It would require a separate study to deal with the origin and history of the early Christian understanding of 'presbyter'. We can only briefly suggest that the designation of the leader of a Christian community as presbyter evidently originated in Jerusalem, probably after the death of Peter. Among the Pauline communities this conception was not at first adopted; but later, in the sub-apostolic age, it passed into them from Jerusalem. Its origin is clearly Jewish. Elders had already an important role in the Old Testament, and later, in a changed form, in late Judaism. There were non-priestly members in the Sanhedrin in Jerusalem; and the president of a synagogue could be called a presbyter. The fact that the Christian communities adopted this designa-

tion 'presbyter' for its office-bearers is significant for the following
reason: in so doing they adopted a conception which was not derived
from non-Christian cultic usage of that time. For in the Old Testament
and in Judaism elders were not priests in the cultic meaning of the term
at that time. Similarly, in contemporary Hellenism, 'presbyter' did not
mean a cultic office, but was a title belonging to political or communal
life. So too, the usual early Christian official designations, such as deacon
and bishop, and indeed the self-designation of the Church as *ecclesia*,
were not borrowed from the contemporary cultic vocabulary. In the
Old Testament, in Judaism, and also in heathen antiquity as a whole,
those who functioned as priests in the cultic and religious sense were
called in Greek *'hiereus'*, and in Latin *'sacerdos'*. These titles however
were not borne by any office-holders in early Christianity. The thought
of using such titles was far from their minds. The title 'priest' could be
used of Jesus Christ to indicate his position as 'High-Priest'. But the
word, so used, had no place in the vocabulary of official titles of the
Church. Then, fairly soon, the title of presbyter drew into itself some
features of the priestly character in the cultic sense. The earliest evidence
is in the First Epistle of Clement, in which the office of presbyter is
in some way linked with the idea of sacrifice, and the analogy is
drawn with the Old Testament priesthood. But a considerable time
elapsed—Tertullian is the earliest witness—before the title *'sacerdos'* was
used instead of *'presbyteros'*; then, later on, these terms came to be
used in the Church side by side. Thus, the loan-word 'priest' which was
a product of Christianization has this double background: etymologically it goes back to 'presbyter', and historically at least to 'priest' in the
cultic and religious sense; so that the successors of the 'presbyters' of
the Early Church are described by the same word as is used for Old
Testament or even heathen 'priests', as well as for the priesthood of
Christ.

I have not mentioned these linguistic details with a critical intention
of arguing that 'priest' in the Catholic sense derives etymologically
from the early Christian 'presbyter', and then, through the absorption
of other elements, became 'priest' in the usual sense. I am well aware
that this would be a simplification. On the contrary, I wish to say
something with which I think every Catholic theologian must agree:

when we, as Christians, speak about the priesthood, it does not imply that there is an unbroken continuation therein of the Old Testament or heathen idea of the priesthood. Hence what I suggested about the linguistic history of the words presbyter and priest is an example of something in which we can both equally rejoice, as a sign of how through Christ everything has literally been made new.

For—to remove the most glaring current misunderstandings—on the Protestant side it must no longer be affirmed that the Catholic interpretation of the priesthood is a denial of the sole mediatorship of Christ. For even though we realize that some last differences remain in the understanding of Christ, and that therefore we ask each other whether our partner does not obscure the meaning of Christ by his understanding of priesthood, yet it must be recognized that what each is trying to do is to stress the meaning of Christ. Thus Catholic teaching is of course, to use Karl Rahner's words, that 'the cultic priesthood of the Church is only a ministerial priesthood for and in the priesthood and victimhood of Christ'.[2] In the Catholic interpretation the priest is not a kind of independent mediator between God and man. Through him nothing but the priestly work of Christ is accomplished, which is perpetually striving to be present in the Church as Christ's Body. The idea of the cultic priesthood is thus relativized, or, as Rahner says, even 'invalidated' by its relation to and dependence on the priesthood of Christ. Rightly understood, Christ himself is the Priest in the Mass. The ordained priest only represents Christ. Moreover, the sacrifice of the Mass is not, as is sometimes rashly said, a re-enactment of the sacrifice of Christ on the Cross, but its representation. It is one and the same sacrifice, only differently represented.

Similarly on the Protestant side the argument should not be advanced against the Catholic distinction between clergy and laity that it completely invalidates the biblical idea of the universal priesthood. Both Catholic theology and the Catholic Church are fully cognizant of a priesthood of the laity side by side with the official priesthood. And if we estimate how far the universal priesthood is taken seriously by the extent to which lay activity is admitted in ecclesiastical affairs—though admittedly this is a somewhat superficial standpoint—it will appear that Protestantism can hardly boast of much superiority over Catholicism.

W.G.T.

N

On the other hand it might be suggested that Catholicism should not attribute to Protestantism the conception that by rejecting an official priesthood Protestants also reject the Priesthood of Christ, his vicarious sacrifice, and contemporary participation in it. Nor that the priesthood of all believers is for Protestants the product of anti-clerical animosity, and an attempt to justify religious individualism, making every man his own priest, or to produce a secularist autonomy, so that the world does not need a priestly ministry; to intrude democratic ideas into the notion of the Church, so that even in the Church all authority proceeds from the people, and the Protestant pastor has only the right to speak in the name of the people, and not in the name of Christ. Another idea that should be abandoned is that for Protestants celibacy is to some extent the main objection to the Catholic priesthood, and that by reaching an agreement on this point Church unity would be somehow advanced. I should hope that such ideas are far behind us, whatever support they may have received from a deformed Protestantism. But in the interconfessional dialogue we shall make no progress if we are on the look out for the other's failures, and if we claim that it is from these that his character is to be judged. Rather should we seek to find one another's true character in those untroubled sources in which the statements of our faith had their origin.

Only when the ground has been cleared from the troublesome mutual misunderstandings which have bedevilled the relations between the Confessions will it be possible to recognize the real nature of what divides us. But that means that we must be prepared, not only with regard to the position of the other party, but also with regard to our own, to refuse to be satisfied with pat formulas and slogans, but to submit ourselves completely to the facts of which we have to give an account. In my experience the principal value of the encounter with the other Confessions is that it compels us to reach a deeper understanding of those things which are essential to our own Confession's understanding of the Christian faith. For it is only by ceasing to take things as a matter of course that we reach the beginning of real understanding. Thus shall we at least attempt to make some advance together in our thinking about the question of the priesthood.

II

First of all: What is a priest? I am raising this question intentionally in an entirely general way. Hence we shall, for the moment, leave aside entirely the question of what a priest is in the Catholic or in the Protestant sense, and also, if possible, exclude all Christian features which have anything to do with the question of the priesthood. We shall direct our attention at first entirely to what is usually expected of a priest or the priesthood in non-Christian circles. Of course, we do not claim that such an approach to the subject from the point of view of the comparative study of religion will give us a true conception of the priesthood. We have already suggested that when compared with the non-Christian interpretation of the priesthood the Christian account can only seem strangely broken, and in any case fundamentally altered. That does not mean that no positive light on the meaning of the priesthood is to be expected from a glance at other religions, since in Christianity the situation is totally different. It could lead to some degree of mutual understanding if we could see clearly that some of the points about which we are all agreed are not characteristic of the priesthood in the Christian sense. Here lies the positive value of the approach from the angle of the comparative study of religions: when we speak of priest and priesthood we are dealing with features which are equally Christian and non-Christian. Hence the Christian meaning of the priesthood acquires a sharper definition when it is contrasted with the non-Christian interpretation. But a further step is possible. It is a significant fact that, in spite of profound contrasts and differences between the two interpretations, the same word can be used for both. Hence it is necessary to define clearly certain general characteristics of the priesthood, in order that we may understand why this word has been adopted and claimed for Christianity, and how far the original meaning has been altered or broken.

A broad distinction can be drawn between the Priest and the Prophet. Yet this is not entirely satisfactory, as there is inevitable overlapping. There has been occasionally an over-emphasis on the opposition of the Old Testament prophets to the cult and the priesthood.

Recent research has shown that in many respects the activity of the prophets was bound up with the cultus, and that the indisputable fact of the prophetic criticism of the cult should not be interpreted in an absolutely negative sense. On the other hand, the priests exercised the prophetic function in various ways, in so far as it fell to them to impart divine instruction. We shall therefore not begin from this distinction, but shall turn our attention to the internal pattern of the priesthood with regard to the priest's place, work, and standing.

The priest's *place* was between man and the divinity. He was not, according to the usual view, an intermediate being, neither a man nor a god. He was, rather, a man like other men. It is to some extent misleading to define his place as between man and the divinity, at any rate when we think of his nature as a person. Certainly, as an official person, when his work and standing are taken into account, his place is between man and the divinity. Moreover, it must be emphasized that it is as man that he occupies this intermediate position. For the important point is that he represents man (or a certain group of men), before God. But it also holds good that he represents God before these men. The fact of representation is fundamental for the essential nature of the priesthood. What does this mean? First of all, that the relation between God and man has been broken and is perpetually threatened, needing constant care and cultivation. Furthermore, this activity of creating and maintaining a pattern of order is something quite out of the ordinary, and cannot be carried on by any sort of person; but the representative function must be carried out by those who are entitled and competent to do so. Finally, the representation is always only partial; it depends upon whom, when, and how far, the priest is representing, and thus the limitation holds good so far as man is concerned. But it also holds good where God is concerned. In the usual understanding of the representative activity it is assumed that in the representative of the divinity the divine is partially present, but partially declares its absence. As the representative of God the priest's function is never solely mediatorial, but is also divisive. God is only partially present, and the world is only in a partial degree the scene of his presence. In this connection it would be possible to adduce features of human religiosity which differentiate it from Christian faith. But I must not pursue this subject further.

The *work* of the priest is sacrifice. This is not its only characteristic, but all other activity is directed towards this and coloured by it. The priest's work is cultic, and the ultimate constitutive element of the cult is sacrifice. By reason of the vast variety presented by the comparative study of religions, it is difficult to include under a single common description all that is implicit in the concept of sacrifice. In the Old Testament there are numerous terms used to designate the various kinds of sacrifice, but there is no comprehensive term which embraces them all, Yet, in my opinion, we find the essential feature in the following consideration: sacrifice intensifies the representative element in priestly activity. The cultus is not only a representative activity when the priest is acting vicariously on behalf of someone else, but also when he is acting thus for God; not merely, however, as a cultic action which concerns man, but primarily as one which concerns God. This is, perhaps, an unusual way of regarding vicarious activity. But such an approach can throw a remarkable light on one aspect of it. When the priest's cultic activity relates to God, he is doing something vicariously which God cannot, or will not do, at any rate not unconditionally. When the concept of sacrifice is considered generally from the point of view of comparative religion, it expresses the fact that God is interested in something outside himself, that he is not simply the Giver, but that he needs certain gifts; that he, if not in his own Being, yet for his own satisfaction, is dependent on another. There are transactions within the Godhead which are not set in motion by God himself, but have an external origin, and can thus be performed vicariously. The concept of sacrifice presupposes an idea of God which implies that God cannot love unconditionally; that he is not pure activity, but includes in himself a passive element. He must *be* propitiated. That is a happening which originates outside himself.

But there is still another aspect in which the idea of sacrifice intensifies the idea of vicarious activity. What can give satisfaction to the Godhead? How can it be propitiated? The answer could be: by the satisfaction of its demand. But here precisely lies the mediatorial function of the sacrifice, in that it creates a satisfactory agreement between the claims of God and the claims of man. For example, God has certainly a claim to the whole of the harvest yield. But how could man live if he entirely renounced his claim? Thus the sacrificial offering represents a part of what is claimed. Every sacrificial offering has merely vicarious character. The animal slain as a sin-offering takes the place of a man in his alienation from God. And where human sacrifice is in question, the man is a vicarious sacrifice for others. The intention of the sacrifice is the diversion of the divine claim from one's self, and thus, in all humility, the assertion of one's own claim before God.

Finally, the priesthood is a matter of *standing*. This results from its vicarious character and the necessity that the cultic activity should be permanent; not in the sense of merely being repeated, but as the perpetual repetition of the correct ritual, carried out according to the prescribed tradition. The permanent character of the priesthood not only involves a recognizable distinction from the ordinary, such as dress, mode of life, and privileges. The real significance of the priestly standing in its permanent character lies in its separateness and dedication to God. Thus the priest is in a sense offered up to God, but only within the previously indicated limits, that is, it is his task to offer and to present the sacrifice of another; but he is not required to be a sacrifice himself. The vicarious element in priestly activity is limited by the fact that the priest and the sacrifice remain distinct.

III

We have now to ask what Jesus has done to this view of the priesthood. I can only give a rough outline, needing filling out and correcting in many respects. But it may suffice to emphasize the importance of the question of what change in the priesthood was caused by the appearance of Jesus Christ. As to this it may be said plainly and without any reservation that the priesthood as thus understood came to an end through Jesus. We cannot merely say that this or that feature came to an end or was altered, but that the general pattern of the whole remained the same. It can in fact be said that individual features remained or were modified, but that the general pattern as such has disappeared. This requires some explanation.

I cannot now deal in greater detail with the extent to which the question is affected by the preaching and works of Jesus. Here, obviously, respect for the established order is found linked with critical features. But everything that could have a direct bearing on the question fails to bring us to the point where the real decisions take place. Nevertheless it can already be shown with regard to the historical Jesus how something is to be met with which does not so much touch individual points as shatter the total view. But what happened after the death and resurrection of Jesus is unambiguous. Everything that had been offered in heathen and Jewish priesthood and sacrificial ritual came to an end when Jesus was proclaimed and believed in. Nor do we find these things replaced by a rival priesthood and sacrificial cult of a similar pattern, but, so far as we can speak of priests and sacrifices at all, we find a totally different pattern. This is shown, in the first place, by the fact that any relevant statement is only significant in relation to Christ, and has its exclusive derivation from Christ. Christ is the only Priest. Christ is the only Sacrifice. Only in Christ are vicarious activity and mediatorship between God and man to be found. We must spend a little time over these statements about Christ before we finally deal with the question of the priesthood of which he is the source.

The New Testament evidence must at least be briefly mentioned. Certainly the saving significance of the coming of Christ can be interpreted here with help from ideas connected with priesthood. But there is not a great deal of material. It is the main theme of the Epistle to the Hebrews; but, with the exception of this document, the ascription of the title Priest, or High Priest, to Jesus occurs nowhere else, and the interpretation of the death of Jesus as a sacrifice is of comparatively rare occurrence. The question how far sacrificial terminology is present in the New Testament writings is capable of various answers, and hence the number of relevant passages can vary, according to one's judgement. But this is not decisive. We shall confine ourselves to the question of what becomes of the whole complex of ideas connected with the priesthood when applied to Jesus Christ. The impression is unavoidable that the priesthood is here fulfilled, and has therefore ceased to exist in its earlier form. We recall the emphatic 'once for all' in the Epistle to the Hebrews, which connects the idea of fulfilment with the point of view that the old is now finally settled and done with. But this does not take us far enough. If we were to conceive of fulfilment in such a way as to imagine the whole cultic pattern of the priesthood, as we have just attempted to describe it, being filled as liquid fills a vessel; or, to put it another way, if we were to think of fulfilment as the ideal realization of a prescription, then it would be absurd to describe Jesus Christ as the fulfilment of the priesthood. The idea of fulfilment is only admissible when it is thought of as the total change in the pattern of the priesthood as it occurs when it is *Jesus* who is described as the fulfilment of the priesthood. What we have here is not the fulfilment of an ideal type of priesthood as it has hitherto been, but at most the unsolved problem underlying the existing priesthood has found a definitive answer; by appearing, however, in a totally new light which causes the insolubility of the problem to be recognized. Only then is the new answer seen to be entirely new, and in no way contained in the previously existing problem.

Let us understand this by understanding the death of Christ as a sacrifice, and in order to do so we must make a slight digression. We have already explained the non-Christian conception of sacrifice. Its central point is the appeasement of God. When we speak today of sacrifice, apart from the strict Christian usage, it is with an entirely different connotation. Cultic-religious sacrifice may still exist where the non-Christian religions have not fallen into decay. But where Christianity has not brought this about, this dissolution has resulted from modern secularization, to which all religions find themselves exposed. The question how it has come about that Christian faith and secularization affect one another in a peculiar fashion, at least in a certain respect, must be left aside. But in the language of secularized man 'sacrifice' is a perfectly common word: for example, one says, 'I have sacrificed three hours in discussing a friend's professional troubles'; or, 'So and so, the inventor, has sacrificed his whole fortune in developing a new method of production'; or, 'During the month of February traffic caused a number of regrettable sacrifices'; or, 'So and so has sacrificed everything for this or that cause, idea, or society'. At first sight this half-frivolous, half-serious way of speaking about sacrifice seems confusing, but it is in reality an emasculation of the idea of sacrifice due to the prevailing secularization of life. It is wholly devoid of any reference to God. Even when people speak in that specially tragic way about the sacrifices caused by traffic, they are not thinking about some higher Power appeased by such sacrifices; the most one could say is that in this case men are being sacrificed to the traffic Moloch. Modern man, however, does not see in this some quasi-cultic transaction, but only an example of the fact that we must be prepared to pay a high price for the benefits of mechanized transport. This example also shows that just as there is no reference to God, so there is none to a priest. Who, actually, is sacrificing? With regard to the sacrifice to the traffic, one can only say that it is the community that is making the sacrifice; not, however, in a vicarious sense; but one can say that since it is the community that makes the sacrifice, it is itself as the offerer, at least in a part of itself, at the same time the sacrifice. If we consider the most important implications of this secularized interpretation of sacrifice, we must admit that it suggests an identification of the offerer with the offering, and hence implies self-sacrifice, self-surrender. Thus the surprising fact emerges that here a glimpse is disclosed of the fundamental change in the priesthood and sacrifice which has been brought about by Jesus Christ.

The decisive change lies in the fact that reconciliation is not a transaction directed from man towards God, but, entirely the reverse, a transaction on the part of God directed towards man. Wherever the New Testament speaks about reconciliation between God and man it is always in sharp contrast with non-Christian ideas. Man has not reconciled God, but God has reconciled us, that is, the world, to himself. Thus it says in 2 Cor 5:19, 'God was in Christ reconciling the world unto himself'. Or, similarly, only in Johannine terminology, in John 3:16, 'God so loved the world that he gave his only-begotten Son'. Or, putting it paradoxically, we might say that he sacrificed his only-begotten Son. It is not man who brings the sacrifice to God, but God who brings the sacrifice to men. This sacrificial transaction is the act of love, of surrender, of being for others. Here Sacrificer and Sacrifice are essentially one; not as the surrender of the sinner to the wrath of God, but as God's self-surrender to the sinner. This does not mean that any mention of the wrath of God is replaced by the sentimental plati-

tude of an ever-loving God who need not be taken seriously. But it is
the holy reality of this love that it is a suffering love. And it is the self-
same passion which is revealed to the believer as the love of God,
which is experienced, without understanding, by the unbeliever as the
wrath of God. It is with this love in its totality and its finality that we are
confronted in Jesus Christ. Hence his Passion and death are not in
contradiction with the fact that God was in Christ, but are its direct
consequence: only where God is can this self-surrender involve the
fulness of love; only here can the being for others even to death and the
shedding of blood, be completely endured and confirmed.

Now it is not possible to expound in a short space the Christology
which would elucidate this suitably and protect it from misunderstanding. It only remains to indicate how far in this Christ-event
vicarious activity takes place. The concept of vicarious activity must also
be revolutionized. We cannot say that it is merely a matter of substitution. In Christ we do not have to do with a substitute for God, but
with God himself. And the sacrifice offered by him is not a substitute
for full surrender, but is itself the complete surrender, love in its
totality. Moreover the significance of this sacrificial surrender is not
that it is a substitute for our surrender, but it is intended to set that
surrender in motion. This is the true vicarious activity, the absolute
being for others accomplished in Christ. Vicarious activity in this sense
means keeping a place. Jesus Christ has kept the place where the reconciliation between God and man can take place. So he is the keeper of a
place for God among men, and of a place for men before God. This is
the whole object of his being for others, to awaken faith. For faith
means being before God as those who are loved by God, and therefore
being among men as witnesses of faith, witnesses of the love of God.
This is Christ's vicarious activity, his keeping a place, namely, that he
is for others in such a way that true being for others originates with
him. True being for others, however, is being for God and for one's
fellow-man on the basis of the fact that God is for us.

IV

Hence, what has to be said about the priestly work of Christ and his vicarious sacrifice, in respect of their essential identity, cannot be separated from the fact that where Jesus Christ is concerned faith is also concerned. The work of Christ is the event of faith. This provides the criterion for answering the question how there can be a continuance of the priesthood of Christ in such a way that we can have a share in it. It continues because something has taken place which is essentially a part of the event of faith. This is, in the first place, the communication of faith, not in the sense of the mere communication of statements about faith, but as the imparting of faith itself, a partaking in the love of God and in his grace. This is the result of the preaching of faith, the preaching of the crucified One, in which he comes to us as the risen One. For faith, as Paul says, comes by preaching, and preaching by the Word of Christ. It is not the Word of the Law that communicates faith, but the Word of the Gospel. That is the first thing. The second is the participation, through faith, in the way and work of Jesus Christ. This means, participation, through faith, in the reconciliation accomplished once for all by Christ. This incorporation in Christ is therefore not something added to faith, but participation in the priesthood and sacrifice of Christ is of the very essence of faith. Through faith we are at the place of the reconciliation between God and man. Through Christ, by faith, we all become a sacrifice. For the event of faith for the individual begins in baptism and reaches its goal in death: the death of the old man, and the resurrection of the new. That **this** happens to us is the event of the love of God. This makes us all, by faith, through Christ, priests united in being for others, which gives to the others the decisive thing, by becoming a witness of faith, a witness of Christ; thus the unheard-of thing takes place, that one man becomes Christ for another.

I think that this is the decisive point in the Protestant view of the priesthood of Christ. Yet much still remains to be developed and elucidated. It is unfortunate in a double sense that I have to break off here. For, in the first place, what the Protestant interpretation involves needs clarification as to how the meaning of sacrament and office is based on what has been said. May I be permitted to offer two brief suggestions? In the Protestant interpretation sacrament is inseparable from the Word, and the Word is inseparable from sacrament. But the Word is, as such, sacramental if that is understood to mean that what the Word says it does, and sacrament stresses the sacramental character of the Word. Hence if Christ, as Priest and Sacrifice, is present in the communication of faith, this communication as a whole, Word and Sacrament, is his priestly activity, the representation of his sacrifice; and the office, as the ministry of reconciliation, as Paul says, is in fact a participation in the priesthood of Christ. How else could anything be done in the Church by right and authority, except by the right and authority of Christ, and therefore in his name? But it is precisely for this reason that the office of the Church, in the Protestant understanding of it, is nothing else but the publicly ordered proclamation of the priesthood of Christ, and thus a witness of what the Christian has received in baptism. 'Universal' priesthood is a confusing term, since it refers to a special priesthood. What is active in the various offices and gifts is the one and self-same priesthood.

It may seem puzzling to break off at this particular point, since it now becomes necessary to speak about a subject that cannot be overlooked, namely, the profound difference between the Protestant and the Catholic understanding of the priesthood. I will not make the excuse that I had intended only to deal with the one aspect of the situation. For it is hardly possible to speak unambiguously about this without touching on the other aspect of it, as I have already done indirectly. But to develop this in detail is a task which extends far beyond the limits of a lecture, if it were not to confine itself to a repetition of the formal statements of the Confessional controversy, but to attempt to deal fully with the subject itself. It would involve going very deeply into the subject if one were to attempt to explain the real basis of the Confessional difference without being content to retail partially grasped and half-understood formulas. So modesty is the appropriate attitude towards such an undertaking.

In order that I may not be accused of avoiding the problem of Confessional oppositions, may I put in the form of a question what needs further consideration: How has it come about that, in the Catholic understanding of the priesthood, to a quite surprising degree, importance is attached to these features of the priesthood which I have described as characteristic of the non-Christian priesthood? May it not be, perhaps, that here the radical nature of the break with the past brought about by Jesus has not been sufficiently realized? I might also ask: Is there not here a too narrow, rather than too high a conception of the priesthood and sacrifice of Christ? Is it not here the case that too little, rather than too much stress, has been laid on the fact that God is not seeking to be reconciled, but is himself the reconciler? I might go on to ask in regard to priesthood and sacrifice in the Church whether both have not a more comprehensive and revolutionary character than they seem to have in the Catholic interpretation. At least we Protestants have at heart these questions concerning our Catholic brothers and sisters. They are questions which spring from our candour, responsibility, and love, as sharers in the priesthood of Christ.

II

Word and Sacrament

I

I can only undertake the subject assigned to me under the title: 'Word and Sacrament, A Contribution to the Study of the Difference between the Confessions', with the provision that I am not submitting a thesis, but tentatively raising a question. Slogans such as 'A Church of the Word', on the one hand, and 'A Church of the Sacrament', on the other, distort, and easily render meaningless an essential element of truth in the difference between the Protestant and the Catholic positions. In using the word 'Contribution' I mean something intended to throw light on, and help towards the understanding of, the difference between the Confessions; such a contribution demands the utmost circumspection. Hence we shall begin by considering the situation which confronts such an undertaking, and shall offer some suggestions concerning the various types of audience to which our remarks on this subject must be addressed.

1. The time has passed when it can be thought admissible for the controversy with another Confession to be carried on within the circle of one's own Confession, and for the other party to be judged *in absentia*. The vigorous inter-Confessional dialogue characteristic of our time is of the utmost significance, if only for the discipline of conversation requiring the presence of the partner. This makes self-sufficiency and self-complacency impossible in theological discussions between the Confessions, and changes the internal attitude towards the dialogue within one's own Confession. Yet, before we go on to discuss the character of these two types of audience, there is a third audience to be considered which is actually the most important of all: it is the contemporary non-Christian world, forcing itself upon our attention. An exclusive attitude can exist, even within the so-called Ecumenical

encounter. The meaning of this name implies a world-wide comprehensiveness, but it is no guarantee against an introverted discussion of the Confessional difference without attention being paid to actual contemporary needs. The fundamental division in western Christendom, important as it is, when looked at as a whole, is overshadowed by the modern flagrant contrasts between West and East, white and coloured, Christianity and non-Christian religions, religion and secularistic atheism, or in whatever other terms we may define the great, confused, and overlapping areas of tension now existing.

Consideration of these disturbing problems should not diminish the importance of the one which confronts us by suggesting that Confessional unity is, under these circumstances, at least tactically, if not also factually, bound to come about. On the contrary, the remembrance of our joint responsibility to contemporary humanity in the broadest sense should intensify our sense of theological responsibility to the highest degree. We Christians, Protestant and Catholic, especially with regard to the issues between us, must say, with Paul, that we are debtors 'to Greeks and Barbarians, to wise and foolish'.[1] We owe them the Gospel. We are under the obligation therefore, for the sake of this world to which we owe the proclamation of the Gospel, to take the Confessional controversy seriously, provided that the Gospel in this controversy itself is controversial. Hence the criterion to be applied in respect to what is at issue between the Confessions is that a convincing and authoritative statement should be made of what must be declared in the name of Jesus to be the absolute existential need of contemporary man, Eastern or Western, white or coloured, religious or atheist. Controversial theological questions must be capable of interpretation as existentially necessary questions, and must be so interpreted.

Our theme suggests that the central point of the Confessional controversy about Word and Sacrament, that is, about everything that has been given to the Church, the unique gift that the Church has to give, is the question, How far are Word and Sacrament existentially necessary? United on the point of the *That*, the Confessions join issue on the question of *How* this existential relation between Word and Sacrament is to be understood. The point at issue lies deeper than in any superficial differences as to the number and form of the sacraments and their importance in relation to the Word; it lies in a different interpretation of how Word and Sacrament concern existence, affect or alter it, enter into it, or absorb it; in any case the point at issue is whether Word and Sacrament meet with existence in such a way that it can be defined as Scriptural or Sacramental existence. It serves to lead to a return to the elemental source and to prove the matter in the really serious situation, if the Confessional issues are exposed to the ultimate test of the contemporary critical encounter with Word and Sacrament.

2. The surprising change which has taken place in the relations between the Christian Confessions in general, but notably, although outside any Ecumenical Church organization, in the dialogue between Protestant and Catholic theology, may be connected under the surface with the fact that the changed situation with regard to preaching has given a new impulse to theological thinking on both sides of the Confessional chasm, and has led to the abandonment of the old formulas and categories of Confessional polemics. Yet this aspect is counterbalanced by the opposite tendency to form anti-modernistic associations. At any rate an essential feature on the Protestant side seems to be a leaning towards a neo-Orthodoxy which, in the form of a resolute rejection of the theological errors of the eighteenth and nineteenth centuries and a return to the Reformation, may awaken hopes that a restoration may result therefrom. Not only has the Word of God in concept and content again become central, but also such favoured themes from the Catholic side as sacrament, Church, dogma, and liturgy accompanied by many practical reform movements, even going as far as Protestant monasteries, have had a surprising upswing in Protestantism.

It is questionable whether Protestant theology is primarily so interesting to modern Catholicism because of its restorative tendencies, which go as far as apparent or real Catholicism. 'Neo-Orthodoxy' and 'Restoration' are, moreover, cheap slogans which conceal the manifold variety of the facts. For the rest, the predominant interest in Karl Barth is of primary importance to the more liberal modern interpreters of the dogmatic tradition, i.e. as compared with the traditional Catholic dogmatic style. The careful attention which is being paid to Rudolf Bultmann is, interestingly enough, scarcely any less. Those

French and German-speaking Catholic theologians, however, who have boldly taken upon themselves something new in Confessional history, namely, to learn from Protestant theology in intensive participation, are not Modernists of the old type, although, with regard to the general situation of Roman Catholicism, they correspond to Modernists in the changed state of affairs, and are perhaps to some extent consciously their independent successors. There is a converse movement on the Catholic side unfavourable to the approach to Protestantism. The relation of dogmatic rigidity, shown in the interest in the Bible and the Fathers, and linked up with various efforts at reform, is only one of the faces of modern Catholicism, and certainly not the official one. The extraordinary division, that Roman Catholicism has never diverged so widely from the Protestant view as in the official promulgation of the decree on the Assumption of the Virgin in 1950, while at the same time, in its theological activity, it has never been so receptive to the Protestant view as in our time, does not detract from those latter signs which are so welcome to us.

Yet it warns us to sober judgements, and above all to a realistic interpretation of the recent Catholic controversial literature which is of such epoch-making importance in certain respects for the Confessional dialogue. The first impression may be that we have here occasional refined and graceful interpretations, deceptive rather than productive of any bridge-building over dogmatic differences. This would be an over-hasty and unjust estimate. We see here very important hermeneutic events, in which the careful reader will find himself more completely confronted with the real Catholic attitude. Recognition of this does not involve a wholesale renunciation of any criticism of this literature and its hermeneutics. When, for example, Hans Urs von Balthasar can see no insuperable opposition between Karl Barth's interpretation of the revelation and that of Vatican I;[2] or when Hans Küng finds a fundamental agreement between Barth's doctrine of justification and the Tridentine, going so far as to say that, 'It is precisely in the doctrine of justification, where the Reformed theology began, that there is fundamental agreement between Catholic and Protestant theology';[3] or when Peter Lengsfeld, with reference to the relation between Scripture and Tradition, declares that there is a noticeable drawing together between the two camps, and with regard to the disputed question of '*sola*' and '*et*' claims that it is 'Today generally regarded as out of date';[4] or when a surprising relaxation in the hitherto opposed attitudes with regard to Word and Sacrament has taken place, —a matter which concerns our subject, and about which more will be said—we must thankfully acknowledge that, in spite of all criticism, which must still be noted, here the interconfessional dialogue is served, not by eirenic mollifications, but by a realistic sharpening of the issues. Moreover, according to the opinion of the authors quoted above, the Confessional difference is not simply disappearing, but is shifting from traditional inadequate formulas and worn-out doctrinal decisions to what is more and more firmly held before Protestants as the real points at issue, namely, the doctrine of the Church.

Protestant theology must welcome this challenge to a radical re-assessment of the Confessional difference, and to a deeper interpretation of the authoritative documents to which it owes its origin. It would be rash to imagine that the difference was about to be sur-mounted. It would be an unexpected advance in understanding if the Confessions were able to agree about the real difference. For, apart from the secondary features which constantly conceal the essential factor, features which are of such immense importance in so intricate a structure of tradition as are the great Christian Churches, there also exists along with a genuine readiness to take part in dialogue, a mutual lack of understanding and misunderstanding which is almost a part of the structure of the difference between the Confessions. This difference, which involves a far-reaching difference in language, is itself a her-meneutic matter, and extends even to the means of understanding. Here is no excuse for resignation; it pledges us rather to such an approach that in the encounter with the other Confessions we should at the same time, without reservations, attack the problems of our own Confession. For comprehension of the Confessional difference in-volves also the theological understanding of our own Confession. Interconfessional discussion must be accompanied by inner-Con-fessional discussion.

These preliminary remarks have enlarged the field of our discussion beyond the ability of the following outlines to cover. But why should I conceal the gap between task and fulfilment? For in such matters the man who knows, knows that it is inevitable, while the less experienced man must at least recognize the fact.

II

The traditional conception of the distinction between the Protestant and the Catholic doctrine of Word and Sacrament can be summed up under the following main points of view.

1. It is indisputable that in the duality of Word and Sacrament we have the two means by which the salvation revealed in Jesus Christ is imparted in the Church; we have likewise their inseparable unity, as they stand side by side, but directed towards the same purpose, to be an inwardly related and conjoined means of grace. Thus, fundamentally, the Word precedes the Sacrament, and in the Sacrament itself the Word has a determinative function. Nevertheless in the understanding of their diversity in unity the Confessional opposition appears, and in a much more important regard than, say, in the number of the sacraments. For the significance of the reduction of the sacraments from seven to two, namely, Baptism and the Lord's Supper, and the different understanding of these two, in the first case apparently unimportant, in the second fundamental, become fully apparent only from the standpoint of the Confessional difference with regard to Word and Sacrament.

While, according to Protestant doctrine, the whole Gospel is contained in the Word itself, and Gospel is essentially the spoken Word; according to Catholic doctrine the advent of grace in its real and full meaning is bound up with the sacraments. In the Protestant view *solo verbo* is the decisive word; but this in no way excludes the sacraments in the Protestant understanding of them; on the contrary, it includes them in so far as they are only another form of the Word; the distinctive promise which they offer is none other than that of the Word itself. Important as they are, they cannot compare with the Word in the strictest sense as necessary for salvation. This is why there can be no Protestant doctrine of the sacraments apart from a doctrine of the Word, and strictly speaking the distinction between Word and Sacrament is only of secondary theological significance, that is, with respect to the full meaning of the Word of God. In the Catholic view, on the other hand, the decisive word is *solo sacramento*. Of course that does not exclude the Word. It has an indispensable function for the action of grace, yet only preparatory, introductory, and following. Real grace in the full meaning of the word, justifying grace and sanctifying grace, is exclusively imparted sacramentally, a fact which only emphasizes the sole exception that, in case of need, an expressed wish for the sacrament (*votum sacramenti*) may suffice. Hence, in the strict sense the sacrament is necessary for salvation. The doctrine of grace is essentially a sacramental doctrine, and this can be expounded without direct teaching from the Word. For the function of the Word in the sacrament is not to address a person, but to consecrate the elements.

2. These different conceptions embrace a far wider range of dogmatic considerations, which alone make it possible to understand how all this has come about. The Protestant *solo verbo* has its counterpart in *sola fide*. It is generally assumed that these basic formulas of the Reformed doctrine of justification only exclude good works in the usual sense as the ground of justification. But only in relation to Catholic sacramental doctrine do the principles of *sola fide* and of *solo verbo* receive their precise meaning in theological controversy; for according to Catholic teaching as well, the principle of *sola gratia* has an unconditional validity. Works are in no way regarded as an alternative means of salvation side by side with grace. Nevertheless, the sacramental interpretation of grace allows the point of view of works to find an entrance into the doctrine of grace in a twofold aspect. The sacraments work *ex opere operato*, in virtue of their own efficacy as such; not, indeed, without a certain disposition on the part of the dispenser and the recipient. The usual Protestant criticism of this interpretation of the way in which the sacraments operate as 'magical' or 'mechanical' is unjust at least to the theological interpretation of the matter, in which two points of view are strangely intermingled: objectively the sacraments are divine acts of grace, and as works carried out by human action are *eo ipso* works acceptable to God.

This blending of grace and the work of man in the operation of the sacrament is in accordance with the understanding of what is given in the sacraments. It is, in essence, a quality of grace appropriated by man: a created supernatural reality, imparting an inward inclination to and capacity for works carrying grace. Since the sacrament alone confers this so-called 'habitual' grace, the sacrament becomes the ground of meritorious works, which, being the effect of grace, in turn affect grace. Hence the sacramental grace conferred upon man is in reality the capacity to love, without which the faith produced by the Word alone, even mere imparted faith, is dead, but through which it becomes a living faith. Love is, in the Aristotelian sense, the 'form' of faith. On the other hand, according to the Reformed doctrine, the sacrament can only be interpreted on the ground of faith. The *sola fide* principle is directly antithetic to the *opus operatum* mode of activity, on the one hand, and to the principle of faith working through love (*fides caritate formata*), as the effect of the sacrament, on the other hand. The sacrament does not become what it is merely through faith, any more than the Word preached does; each of them, as the Word, is God's act. Hence the saving effect of the sacrament depends wholly on its reception in faith that here the recipient meets with the Word of promise, for the strengthening of this faith. The sacrament does not lead away from the relation between World and Faith; it confirms the recipient in it and ensures his continuance in it.

The Confessional difference with regard to Word and Sacrament is certainly easier to understand in ecclesiology than in soteriology. Rooted in the Catholic conception of the sacraments are the distinction between Clergy and Laity, the twofold power of the Church, as the doctrinal and administrative authority, and possessing authority to ordain; also canon law, the clerical life, and religion, in short, the interpretation of the Church as the original sacrament,[5] whose nature finds expression in Mariology.[6] On the other hand, all the Protestant objections to, and divergence from, the Catholic understanding of the Church go back to the principle of *solo verbo–sola fide*.

III

1. The Catholic theologian van de Pol, in a phenomenological study of Protestantism,[7] has attempted to show that the fundamental feature

in the traditional discussion of the disagreement between the Confessions is a difference in their understanding of reality. From the outline of the situation, such as we have just given, he takes as the basic pattern of the Confessional opposition, 'That the character of revelation for the Reformed Christian is *a revelation of the Word*, for the Catholic Christian, on the other hand, it is *a revelation of Reality*.'[8] 'Whatever else may be present as dogmatic, theological, ecclesiastical, liturgical, or other differences between the Catholic Church and the Reformation, may be traced back to this basic and principal difference that, according to the Catholic Church, revelation is the breaking through of a supernatural divine *Reality in the sense of being* (*seinshaft*) in visible form, in the midst of our earthly reality; while, according to the Reformation, it means that God has spoken to man through his Word.'[9] It is true that Protestantism also speaks of 'reality', in a theological regard, and sometimes most emphatically. But, in accordance with its basic understanding in terms of the Word, Grace, Election, Justification, New Birth, and so forth are 'Not reality in the sense of being, but in a relative sense, that is, in the sense of a new relation with God, which is certainly very real.'[10] 'What has come to us in revelation is not a new Reality in the sense of being; but the fact that the atonement accomplished by God is also a reality for me is proclaimed both by preaching and by sacrament. As proclamation, both preaching and sacrament are the proclamation of the Word of God. Revelation in the form of the sacrament has also the character of a revelation of the Word, but not as in the Catholic Church a revelation of Reality in the sense of being. Word and Faith change nothing in the order of existence, but in the relation between God and man . . .'[11] Van de Pol finds a break here between the Christology as it is to be found, in agreement with the Catholic Church, in the Reformation, and that which resulted for the Protestants. 'The Incarnation, in Reformed Christianity, has become a single isolated event, an occurrence which is not continued in the supernatural life . . .'[12] of believers.' '*The distance between God and man* was, in the Reformation point of view, only once done away in Christ, but it continues to exist in the relation between God and the believer.'[13] On the other hand, the Catholic believer has as his immediate object the reality of the Catholic Church,[14] in which he, as it says in the Encyclical '*Mystici Corporis*', 'sees Christ himself'.[15] 'The Catholic's act of faith is directed towards . . . a supernatural reality of being, which is a given unity. Every feature of it is indispensable: the Apostolic Chair, the living Magisterium, ordination and the other sacraments, grace, the Mother of God and the Saints.'[16] According to van de Pol it is not faith in Christ, but faith in the Church as a super-natural sacramental reality in a 'mystically real', sense of being, which really separates the Confessions.[17] The separation from the Catholic Church is therefore not the consequence, but was already the cause, of the Reformation. 'Seen from the Catholic point of view, it is clear that Luther would never have been troubled with his problems, nor arrived at his new conception of the righteousness of God, and the doctrine based on it of "Justification by faith alone", if he had not already lost his faith in the Church as a supernatural reality, and in the sacramental mediation of the atoning work of Christ in and through the Church. The loss of faith in the specific Catholic sense had already taken place.'[18] Now, however, 'Instead of the sacramental link . . . there is the personal relation to God by faith'.[19] 'Instead of the objective reality of the Church, there is "the Word", the Gospel, the Good News.'[20] Instead of sanctifying grace, there is faith,[21] which is 'more something *possessed in hope* than in reality'.[22]

A closer scrutiny shows that there are serious weaknesses in this carefully constructed conception of van de Pol, which, however, does actually bear on the problem at issue. I shall now single out three aspects of this. The unity in faith in Christ asserted by van der Pol[23] is, as he has evidently failed to notice, decisively called in question in one of the few passages in which he expressly refers to a Reformation text.[24] He quotes the well-known saying of Luther in the *Tractatus de Libertate Christiana*, about the union of the soul as a bride by faith with Christ as the Bridegroom, whereby the exchange is effected, 'That Christ has the sins, death, and hell, but the soul has grace, life, and salvation.'[25] On this van de Pol remarks, 'It is clear from the words "that Christ has the sins, death, and hell", that Luther is here not speaking in the real sense of being. Hence one cannot understand his assurance that Christ dwells in us by faith, lives in us, and is one with us, as ending in a mystical union of grace in the existential sense of being.'[26] To this the only reply is 'Certainly not!' But that is just why the Christological basis of *sola fide* should be seriously considered, since it indicates a profound Confessional difference in the understanding of the dereliction of Christ on the cross, and consequently in the understanding of Christ's real humanity. To follow this up would require, in the second place, a more careful consideration of the theological use by van de Pol of the banal ontological terminology, which in any case is left unexplained. Not to escape from the Scylla of these catch-words in order to fall into the Charybdis of their Protestant transvaluation into 'Personalism against Ontology', but to consider the ontological problem on the level of language and word, and thus to discard a false alternative and push on to the essential hermeneutic decisions. All should be agreed on the necessity of this task. Thirdly, it seems to me to be in the interest of Catholic theology that a more discriminating analysis of the relation between Word and Sacrament, and of its consequences for the problem of Confessional differences, should be undertaken, than van de Pol has done; it must be said that he seems to be insufficiently aware of the increasing urgency of this task for Catholic theology.

2. In an essay entitled *Priest and Poet*, Karl Rahner has written, 'To the poet is entrusted the Word. Alas, that there should be no theology of the Word! Why has no one yet set about gathering together, like Ezekiel, the scattered members on the fields of philosophy and theology and spoken over them the Word of the Spirit, so that they may arise up a living body!'[27] It is a surprising thing to hear the call for a theology of the Word from the mouth of a Catholic theologian; all the more convincing is the internal movement from which the cry emanates. In the writings of Rahner, which must command our respect, there is ample evidence of the seriousness of his desire, never more vividly expressed than in the essay 'The Word and The Eucharist' which appeared in 1960.[28] 'It is really astonishing', he says, 'that we Catholics provide no space, no systematic place for a theology of the Word in the average theology of our schools, in the Latin manuals etc. . . . Thus a theme which appears to be highly relevant remained to a great extent unnoticed in the Catholic theology of the last few hundred years.'[29] Among the reasons why Catholic theology seems to be changing today, he mentions significantly in the first place—(I may recall the

introduction to my lecture)—the contemporary need of preaching, out of which grows the 'need of a theology of preaching'. 'But a theology of preaching cannot but force us to take up a theology of the annunciation of the Word of God.'[30] Rahner's approach differs from what we have seen of van de Pol's. Precisely for the sake of the ecclesiology he does not start from the alleged matter, of course, but more subtly and acutely from the unity of Word and Sacrament and then goes on to the possibility of distinguishing between them. He begins with a thesis about the Word of God, which he explains as being identical with the definition of the sacrament. He says, It 'is the salutary Word, which brings with it what it affirms. It is itself therefore the salvific event, which ... displays what happens in it and under it, and brings about what it displays. It renders the grace of God present.'[31] He goes on to say 'It is perfectly legitimate and objectively perfectly justifiable to subsume the whole Sacrament under the concept of the efficacious *Word*.'[32] 'Grace is present always and everywhere from beginning to end, from the first Word of preaching to the Sacrament inclusively, in the form of the Word.'[33] It does not diminish the significance of such statements, but only clarifies them in terms of the theological context from which they come, when he asserts that, 'The supreme realization of the efficacious Word of God ... is the Sacrament and only the Sacrament',[34] and more specifically, 'The Eucharist is in all truth the Sacrament of the Word absolutely, the absolute call of the Word anywhere.'[35] We can recognize how the road leads from a wholly unfamiliar starting-point, through newly discovered territory, to debouch with certainty into the explicit dogma and reality of the Catholic Church. Moreover, even the marking out of boundaries against Protestantism ultimately issues in an agreement with van de Pol's basic idea when Rahner indicates the real source of the objection to Transubstantiation in the following words: 'It is an effort to confine the action of God to the purely divine sphere; it does not intervene to change anything where the things of the world are— the bread, morals, the grave, and so on. It remains somewhere beyond the experience of unbelief, which is quite true, but it also remains outside worldly reality itself; God's in his heaven; but nothing happens where the bread is.'[36]

3. The break-through of Catholic theology into a theology of the Word, and the express self-understanding of the so-called Church of the Sacraments—without prejudice to what is right in this—as the Church of the Word of God,[37] is already making its presence more extensively felt. Several other publications could be mentioned in addition to the one referred to by Rahner.[38] For example, as a bridge to van de Pol's distinction between a revelation of the Word and a revelation of reality, a discussion of Lengsfeld's much more careful distinction between verbal tradition and tradition of reality might be rewarding.[39] Yet, in my opinion, certain structural questions have been most instructively dealt with in a recent Catholic publication on our subject: this is Otto Semmelroth's book, published in 1964, *Wirkendes Wort. Zur Theologie der Verkündigung* (Effective Word. Towards a Theology of Proclamation). We cannot now deal in detail with its stimulating ideas on the meaning of the Word, but must confine ourselves to the connection of such a theology of the Word with the Catholic interpretation of the sacraments.

Semmelroth makes use of an almost identical distinction to that of van de Pol between a revelation of the Word and a revelation of Work; although he insists on their inseparable unity in duality: not actually as two modes of the divine revelation, but as two essential elements in *one* act of revelation.[40] For the Word is also Work, and the Work is also Word. It holds good of the revelation-event that Word and Work are closely interconnected; in Aristotelian terminology it is to be understood that God's Work is the material, and the Word the formal, element in revelation. They are related as body and soul. The distinction between them only serves to clarify their connection. Hence a mere 'attribution of Word and Work to Preaching and Sacrament respectively is no longer possible.'[41] But here Semmelroth adds to his more exactly expounded distinction between Word and Work, another which supplies the key to his dogmatic pattern, namely the distinction between Word and Response. Although he does not explicitly affirm the connection between these two distinctions, he does imply that the closest connection exists both between God's Word and his Work, and between God's Word and man's response. If I understand him rightly, he claims that under the category of Work the situation is indicated that God's revelation does not occur one-sidedly as his Word alone, but that he realizes himself in the human response; thus the Work of God manifests itself as the responsive Work of man, so that the Work of God consists in setting in motion man's response to the Word of God. From this Semmelroth arrives at a surprising interpretation of the relation between Word and Sacrament. It would be natural to think of the characteristic Catholic interpretation of the relation as a movement of divine activity directed towards man exclusively from above. On the contrary, in Semmelroth's view, this descending line belongs to the Word of preaching, while the actual characteristic of the Sacrament is to be found in its creation of man's response, thus making possible the performance of meritorious works. The Christology upon which this is based is as follows: the Word of preaching is directly co-ordinated with the event of the Incarnation, and is, to that extent, the self-mediation of God to man; while the Sacrament is directly brought into relation with the Sacrifice on the Cross, and thus with the meritorious activity of Christ as the God-man. Certainly none of these elements should be isolated from one another, but all must dialectically, as Word and Response, be held together: Incarnation and the Cross, Preaching and Sacrament, and thus also Faith and Merit. 'What a man does in faith when he receives the Word Incarnate proceeding from the Father, and when he partakes in the sacrifice as he eats the sacramental food, belong dialectically together; it is at the same time the hearing of the Word, and the participation in the Response.'[42]

The somewhat arbitrary and unconventional line of thought pursued by Semmelroth is sure to provoke much criticism from the Catholic side, but will hardly give occasion for the censure of the Magisterium. In his theology of preaching, which may be described as the unity in duality of Word and Response, there is no mistaking the unchanged difference between Catholic and Protestant Confession. 'Set against the one-sided emphasis at the Reformation on the preaching of the Word of God as the sole means of salvation, there is the complementary emphasis, not as a one-sided counter-argument, on the Sacrament, whose importance lies in the fact that the Word of God makes possible and calls for a genuine response from man in the sacrifice of the God-man. When Protestantism maintains that the Word and its reception by faith is the only way of obtaining the salvation offered by God, it leaves us with an inadequate understanding of the saving significance of man's response and of a personal encounter between God and man. The Reformation is in danger of regarding the relation between God and man only in the sense of the line descending from above to man below, and of neglecting the response rising from man below to God above.'[43] At the point where the Work of God becomes one with the Word of God, including in its totality both Word and Response, the Church itself is the Word of God. Exhibiting in its polarity both sides of the dialogue,[44] it appears as 'the very embodiment of salvation',[45] 'a divinely animated Reality',[46] 'the original Sacrament'.[47] Although, judged by Catholic standards, it borders on heresy to speak of the efficacious grace of preaching, and the usual interpretations of the distinction between Word and Sacrament according to various forms of causality,[48] or various kinds of grace,[49] and even as a climax in Rahner's sense[50] are abandoned, yet, from the viewpoint of the dialectical united activity of preaching and sacrament, the whole of Catholic doctrine emerges undiminished. For the preaching of the Word of God only produces divine grace in respect of that united activity of Word and Sacrament. 'The condition of receptivity produced in man by the preaching of the Word of God, the gift of God ... is the material cause of salvation, which then through the life of the sacramental indwelling of God as its formal cause, inspires the actually sanctified man. Since the preparation of the material cause takes place through the preaching of the Word of God, even if not through that alone, this too has a large part in producing the condition of grace in man, even if the real formal cause of justification has not yet been given.'[51] Thus as, in contrast to *sola fide*, love producing faith (*caritas formans fidem*) is definitely affirmed to be in principle the formal cause of justification reserved for the Sacrament,[52] so too, it is a matter of course that, in contrast to *solo verbo*, he holds firmly to the sacramental hierarchical structure of the Church: so that 'the actual preaching of the Word of God possesses increased efficacious activity of grace, the more its connection with the Sacrament is not only put into effect, but also made visible'.[53] Important as it is in theological controversy to concentrate on clarifying theological issues, and not on details of Church order, it can also be a source of illumination if the concrete consequences of fundamental issues are brought out. Semmelroth concludes his theology of preaching with the following explanation: 'The preaching of a priest, who is both commissioned by the Church, and through sacramental ordination possesses authority to perform the sacramental representation of the sacrifice of Christ, is more sacramental in character, and hence, other things being equal, possesses more efficacious grace than the preaching of a layman. This efficacy of the priest's preaching should be more productive of grace when it takes place in actual connection with liturgical worship than without, as in teaching and lecturing, although these are properly connected with the sacraments, and therefore are not lacking in the efficacy of grace.'[54]

IV

If we ask how far the Confessional dialogue has succeeded in overcoming the difference between the Confessions, the cautious answer would be that it has changed nothing. If this holds good with regard to the most forward-looking movement in Catholic theology, what can be hoped for from a Council? Although it is a mistake to indulge in extravagant expectations, yet actually much has changed. Instead of occupation with matters of secondary importance and the rigidity of irrelevant polemics, we find a serious endeavour to understand the real nature of the difference between us; and instead of formally repeating the doctrines which divide us, we find a present sense of responsibility for the interpretation of them. This change for the better involves, and this is not a contradiction, a factual difficulty. Traditional arguments lead nowhere; they prove to be ambiguous, or turn unexpectedly against one's own position. As Protestant theologians and as Protestant Christians, it is our responsibility to probe our faith more deeply, to express it more clearly, and to expose it without reserve to experience. I shall now indicate the task which our subject involves in the form of three briefly outlined theses:

1. *Protestant theology must give a fresh interpretation of the doctrine of the*

Word. It would be a mistake to suppose that the doctrine of the Word of God had of course been Protestant theology from the time of the Reformation, and had been renewed as the result of theological changes four decades ago. There has been (it is supposed) no lack of this kind of theology, while in Catholic theology a doctrine of the Word of God has been lacking. Much more necessary for Protestant theology (it is supposed), as a counter-movement to the efforts of Catholic theology already alluded to, is the supplementing and correction of a one-sided doctrine of the Word: by a stronger development of the doctrine of the Sacraments, as the most striking example of which we may refer to Peter Brunner's[55] doctrine of Worship; or it may be by a historical theology of the facts, in whose name Wolfhart Pannenberg has recently challenged the doctrine of the Word;[56] or by the practical carrying out of religion which clothes the naked Word and brings the salvation-event into contemporary life. Here is a danger of which Karl Barth rightly warns us, feeling the necessity of a sharp distinction between God's Word and man's response; he finds Rudolf Bultmann liable to this danger, and wittily, though it seems to me wrongly, characterizes his position as the 'existentialist translation of the sacramental doctrine of the Roman Church'.[57] The mention of these inter-Protestant controversies, together with the recent increase of questions in Catholic theology, shows how necessary it is that the Protestant doctrine of the Word of God should realize its responsibility to explore in a fresh direction certain central aspects, such as, Word and Revelation, Word and Work, Word and History, Word and Existence, Word and Reality.

2. *The Protestant doctrine of the sacraments has as its exclusive object a more accurate conception of the* 'solo verbo–sola fide' *principle*. This does not imply any depreciation of the sacraments, but on the contrary, it aims at a correct understanding of them, as against the danger of spiritualistic and sacramentalist enthusiasm. From a doctrine of the sacraments shaped under the influence of the Reformers, the interpretation might have been expected to take a converse direction, and that, developing from the relation of Word and Faith, the sacraments would be added to the basic Protestant view. This view contains something of the truth.

Nevertheless, as the result of the prevalence of this one-sided attitude, the doctrine of the sacraments has acquired a joyless apologetic note; not only so, but the doctrine of the Word is exposed to the danger of losing its distinctive character. Moreover, the further danger arises of an over-emphasis on the doctrine of the sacraments compensating for a lack in the doctrine of the Word. It seems to me that the task which today confronts Protestant theology is to arrive by means of the sacraments at a clearer recognition of the nature of the Word, not only as it is in the sacraments, but as it seeks to make its true character apparent in all the various forms of its presentation: its foundations in history, its character as an event, its externality, its communal character, its determinate character, its concern with the whole man, its eschatological significance. We shall only find joy in the sacraments when we expect nothing from them save the Word of Faith.

3. *The existential meaning of the difference between Catholicism and Protestantism confronts us with the alternatives: supernatural perfectibility, or the assurance of faith based on the Word.* Instead of explaining once more from the dogmatic point of view the detailed suggestions which I have already made towards the understanding of the difference between the Confessions, I shall refer by way of illustration to that short but weighty account of a dialogue which Dietrich Bonhoeffer recalls in one of his last letters. He was discussing with a young French pastor what their real purpose was in life. 'He said he would like to become a saint. I think it is quite likely he did become one. At the time I was very much impressed, though I disagreed with him, and said I should prefer to have faith, or words to that effect. For a long time I did not realize how far we were apart. I thought I could acquire faith by trying to live a holy life, or something like it. It was in this phase that I wrote *The Cost of Discipleship*. Today I can see the dangers of this book, though I am prepared to stand by what I wrote.

'Later I discovered and am still discovering up to this very moment that it is only by living completely in this world that one learns to believe. One must abandon every attempt to make something of oneself, whether it be a saint, a converted sinner, a churchman (the priestly type, so-called!), a righteous man or an unrighteous one, a sick man or a healthy one. This is what I mean by worldliness—taking life in one's stride, with all its duties and problems, its successes and failures, its experiences and helplessness. It is in such a life that we throw ourselves utterly in the arms of God and participate in his sufferings in the world and watch with Christ in Gethsemane. That is faith, that is *metanoia*, and that is what makes a man and a Christian.'[58] I am of the opinion that just so far as we take into consideration that world-wide audience of which we spoke at the beginning, and in our theological controversies keep in mind the contemporary need, we shall have no cause to be ashamed of this Gospel. We should not go on owing the Gospel to the world.

The Protestant View of the Sacraments

I

Two suggestions may help towards answering the question of how to arrive at a theological definition of the special character of the sacraments.

1. The first suggestion is to be taken from that in the Reformers' position which seems to make the significance of the sacraments a problem. If the Gospel is orally delivered, in accordance with the fact that the divine event of revelation is God's Word, and if 'Word' here is not used symbolically, but in the strictly literal sense, then the question arises what further should the sacraments be. The Protestant doctrine of the sacraments seems to involve the dilemma that, either through a purely symbolical interpretation the sacraments lose their value and become superfluous; or they are understood as being in some way supplementary to the bare spoken Word, so that the Reformers' principle of *solo verbo–sola fide* is called in question. The actual relation to the sacraments in the life of the Protestant churches always tends towards one of two extremes: either to an unintelligent, indifferent, and purely traditionalist attitude towards the sacraments; or to an extremely high evaluation of their importance, under the influence of the Catholic attitude, and in ignorance of their meaning in Protestantism.

It seems surprising that to take the *solo verbo–sola fide* seriously is the starting-point for the understanding of the sacraments, which brings out their special character. Yet, if the sacraments are to be understood neither as a symbolical substitute for the Word-event, nor as a supposed outbidding of it, but as the very Word-event itself in the strict sense, then we have a clear indication how the special character of the sacraments may be defined. In that case the special character of the sacraments cannot consist in a breaking-away from the bare Word-event, but must be based on the way in which the sacrament-event is identical with the Word-event. Thus the sacraments cannot exhibit anything which has theological importance which is not already implicit in the Word-event of the Gospel. Any reference to specific features of the sacraments must be subject to the limitation that these are also contained in every form of oral proclamation of the Gospel. Yet this does not imply such a complete identification of Word and Sacrament as to deprive the latter of its special characteristics. For what is implicit in the Word-event as such, is in a special respect emphasized in the sacraments in a way which is not possible in general in the bare utterance of the Word. Thus the fact that the Sacrament in its various aspects emphasizes in a unique way what is the nature of the Gospel as a Word-event, is a decisive clue to understanding how the special character of the Sacrament may be defined, not only without prejudice to the Reformers' *solo verbo–sola fide*, but even as a means of understanding it.

Everything which, following this suggestion, can be brought forward as an aid towards the definition of the special character of the sacraments, contributes, in keeping with the nature of the sacrament, only to the formation of a deeper conception of what the Gospel as the Word-event really is. The sacraments ensure, in a special respect, the right understanding of the Word-event as such. This gives them in fact a certain precedence, a factual, though not absolute, irreplace-ability.

At the same time the situation involves a certain weakness and vulnerability. The strength with which the sacraments emphasize certain aspects of the Word-event is as it were at the expense of certain weaknesses, which are the reverse side of the strength. We do no service to the significance of the sacraments by ignoring their inherent dangers. A similar situation exists with regard to the various oral forms which the Word-event can assume. Who would dispute the fact that preaching gives rise to concern about the non-accidental inherent weaknesses which are the other side of its strength?

Such reflections should not cause surprise. If the easily misunder-stood formula 'Word and Sacrament' is taken to mean that the various forms of the oral presentation of the Gospel, together with the two sacraments of Baptism and the Lord's Supper, are all modes in which the one and self-same Word-event finds expression, and that *solo verbo* does not therefore mean *sola praedicationes*; that the validity of the sacraments is never to be understood as a *solis sacramentis*, nor as a *solo verbo* corrected by *et sacramentis*, but can only be expressed by the *solo verbo* itself, then the idea cannot arise that the sacraments conflict with the forms of oral preaching, and that conversely, the latter conflict with the validity of the sacraments; the real situation is that each belongs to, and refers to, the other. Only such a doctrine of the sacraments would be relevant as was congruent with the oral proclamation of the Gospel, and which took into account that the sacraments refer to the oral preaching and are connected with it.

2. By way of giving sharper point to this one basic suggestion, a further suggestion may be offered, agreeing with the well-known statements of Luther in his Maundy Thursday sermon in 1523;[1] this is that something apparently takes place in the celebration of the sacraments which is based on the preaching, but usually remains concealed. The occurrence of the confession in the celebration of the Sacrament, where the individual emerges from the mass, is interrogated and answers, and thus identifies himself with the heard Word, is by no means the only aspect of the special character of the sacraments which calls for discussion; but it affords an indication where the heart of the matter lies. The explanation which the Word-event as such receives in a certain respect in the event of the Sacrament is to be broadly understood as meaning that here, from various angles, the *situation* of the Word of God comes into clearer focus. This provides a key-word whose elucidation can be helpful. A slogan, of course, is of little value, and may do more harm than good. In any case it needs much hard work if it is to make any useful contribution to the subject.

II

Two critical limitations may help to bring nearer the gain in interpretation which awaits us here. The two key-words chiefly used in the Tradition determined by Augustine regarding the special character of the sacraments were 'sign' (*signum*), and 'visible word' (*verbum visibile*).

1. The use of '*signum*' rests on a twofold relation between the Sacrament and the Word. It is based in the first place on the distinction between *signum* and *verbum*. According to this distinction it is characteristic of the Sacrament to make use of its property of visibility, either merely in respect of the consecrated Elements, or in respect of the rite as a whole, to indicate what the Word says in a symbolic way, to emphasize and make it sensible. The indication of the relationship here involved is connected with the other distinction between the sign (*signum*) and the thing (*res*) symbolized. Here it is clear that in *signum* we have to do with a fundamental hermeneutic idea, and also that *verbum* itself can, in its function as the spoken element in the ritual, express its meaning. Thus, in the special character of the Sacrament, there is a recapitulation of the essential nature of the Word, yet in such a way that through the doubling of the significant relation we reach a deeper realization of the ultimate insufficiency of the Word. Seen in the light of that hermeneutic significance, it is not merely accidental for the Sacrament to be so interpreted that the weakness of the merely significative Word should be supplemented by an unspoken, or at least indirectly spoken, *signum*, which as an efficacious symbol of grace (*signum efficax gratiae*) is superior to the Word, replacing it by an immediate contact with the thing itself (*res*). First, consideration must be given to the development of the Catholic doctrine of the Sacrament from this very instructive point of view, that it is an attempt to overcome the inadequacy of the significative interpretation of the Word. Its effect is, indeed, exactly the opposite to that which we find in our study of the Reformed position. Instead of the special character of the Sacrament consisting in its function of revealing a special aspect of the Word-event as such, its effect turns out to be a substantiation of the insufficiency of the Word. If the thing (*res*), namely grace (*gratia*), is to be really attained, it should not be in verbal form, since that prevents the possession of the thing (*res*) itself. The word (*verbum*) in its function as a symbol (*signum*) refers to the thing (*res*), but also separates it and places it at a distance. The Sacrament, on the other hand, leads us on from the Word-situation.

2. The other Augustinian term '*verbum visibile*' seems to be congruent with the Reformation doctrine of the sacraments, and provides

a formula which makes it possible to understand the Sacrament as Word. It is, no doubt, true that the Sacrament in a certain way makes the Word, as we have to do with it, visible; it has a representative function, and thereby remains attached to the Word. Hence the use of the term *verbum visibile* enables us to advance a step further in working out the special character of the Sacrament in its relation to the Reformers' understanding of it. Yet the interpretation of the Sacrament as *verbum visibile* remains inseparable from its background of a hermeneutic signification. Through the visible character of the sacramental signs the Word is undoubtedly reinforced in its function as a sign and made more explicit, but its significative character is, nevertheless, maintained. The fact that the Word itself is an event is concealed by the fact that for its visibility it depends upon some kind of cultic ritual. For the event of the cultic ritual is itself either merely significative; or, if it is to be efficacious, it goes beyond the Word, surpasses it, by allowing the Word to become an event, and adds the event to the Word which, as such, is not an event, and thereby creates a situation which the Word could not do.

III

When the Reformers took their starting-point with the Word of God, they introduced as determinative a view of the Word as having the nature of an event. When I say that the Reformers interpreted the Word in a historical sense, the etymological connection between the verb *geschehen* and *geschichtlich* (historical) will at once occur to the mind. The reference to the verb *geschehen* focuses our attention upon the many meanings implied by the word 'event', especially the Word-event. I shall endeavour to take a comprehensive view of the many aspects of the point of view which we are to consider, by making use of the idea of the 'situation'.

It would need a consideration, which cannot be undertaken here, of the history of the word 'situation' in order to avoid the impression of arbitrariness in any view of the word, and, in so far as it departs from the accepted linguistic usage, to test it by a critical analysis of linguistic tradition. At any rate the popular understanding of the word 'situation'

must be refuted: this is clear in view of the fact that the usual interpretation of 'situation' as implying a point of time, a momentary
occurrence, a break in the continuity of history, does not stand up to a
closer reflection of what 'situation' is. Certainly 'situation' implies a
definite location, and it can be thought of in spatial terms, although the
use of the word 'situation' in relation to location in time, to the
historical situation, has become thoroughly established. Yet if a description is being given from a purely local point of view, as, for instance,
of the 'situation' of a building-site, then this is not thought of as an
isolated fact, but as something which presents many aspects to be
considered: how it lies in relation to the sun, to what winds it is
exposed, whether it has a good view, whether there is a spring in the
neighbourhood, how far it is from the nearest town, what shopping
facilities there are, and so forth. Hence 'situation' means the concrete
connection of individual details, and the use of the term for a historical
situation is not a random one; for, even in the example just given,
factors are at work which determine the nature of the situation:
effects, occurrences, the sunshine, the direction of the wind, the way in
which the surroundings come to view, concern for the water-supply,
the fact that the close proximity of neighbours may be disturbing, or
that too lonely a site may be undesirable, wider roads may be necessary,
and so forth.

It is obvious that Word and Situation belong together as soon as
Word is not defined in the abstract sense as indicative of the timeless
content of an idea, but concretely of being spoken in time; hence when
it is used as a time-word, that is, a verb, referring to the Word as an
event. But it is also necessary to guard against merely placing Word and
Situation in an external relation; but care must be taken to ensure that
the essential nature of their connection is taken into account. Hence it
can be said that Word is the definition of a situation; situation is the
illuminated historical present which has come to speech.

Many further points of view press for notice, which lead to a more
concrete understanding of the nature of Word and of situation, as soon
as we consider the inner relation between Word and situation, a relation which is not merely something added to the nature of the Word,
or to the nature of the situation, but rather belongs to the nature of

both, so that in respect of the situation the nature of the Word is disclosed in terms of the situation, and the nature of the situation in terms of the Word. It might be suggested, not as a hard and fast definition, that situation is the nature of the Word, and Word is the nature of the situation. We may accustom ourselves to thinking of the Word as the Word-event by considering the relation between Word and situation from the following angles.

1. *Word originates in situation.* Since it takes place in time, the Word, when it occurs, does not only belong to a particular situation, but is caused by the situation and illuminates the situation. It is usual to think of this relation between Word and situation for the most part as exercising a limiting effect, and diminishing the meaning of the Word. We speak of a word as conditioned by time, or we may attempt to free a word from the situation in which it is enclosed. But even when it is a question of the universal, timeless truth of a word, which can be simply separated from the situation in which it was spoken, it is still, as an event, a word in a particular situation. That this is so is revealed by the fact that the utterance of a universal, timeless truth can be completely meaningless and irrelevant, or it can hit the nail on the head, and that means that it can be completely one with the situation. It is a mistake to suppose that its apparent liberation from a situation is the ideal and freest condition under which a word may make its appearance. On the contrary, the full force of a word is realized, the more it is implied in the situation, takes up the situation into itself, and, as transmitted, is in a position to transmit the situation, to bring along with it the situation from which it originates. What the authority of the Word is, is disclosed only from the point of view of the situation. An authoritative Word is one which meets the situation in the fullest sense, one which exactly fits the time. Moreover, the problem of the transmissibility of an authoritative Word is the problem of the transmissibility of the unity of the Word and the situation, and therefore of the transmissibility of the situation through the Word. This means that it is not the bare fact of the occurrence of the Word that is transmitted, but that which has been made an event through the Word. The exposition of this particular point of view, that the Word originates

from a situation, introduces two further angles of this matter of the Word-event which make possible and require a comprehensive study.

2. *Word finds a situation already there.* The situation disclosed may be one which is, perhaps, obstinately opposed or closed to the Word. Although its very irrelevance may bring into relief the vitality of the Word as it confronts its opposition and contradiction, yet its irrelevance can only become meaningful if it is in a particular aspect completely appropriate to the situation. It can be shown by random examples from everyday life that the Word cannot be considered apart from the situation in which it occurs and which it finds already there, but its essential relevance is revealed in the peculiar blending combined with difference of Word and speech. As speech, Word is connected with and refers to speech already uttered, and even as a contradictory Word is an intelligible Word. Nevertheless the fact that the Word always finds a situation already there which it cannot search out at will, so that it often degenerates into mere chatter or silence, showing the insurmountable cleavage between Word and situation, is something which discloses a further point of view.

3. *Word changes a situation.* It even creates a situation. A single word can completely alter my position. This can be most clearly seen when there is no change in the external circumstances, but the situation becomes completely different, so that I now realize its true character, because the Word has now reached me in my situation and freed me from its compulsion by reconciling me to it; I might say with Kierkegaard, it makes me contemporaneous with myself.

When theology is taken seriously as a theology of the Word of God, and the aim is to let the Reformers' principle of *solo verbo–sola fide* be the hermeneutic key to a real understanding of the theological position, then it will be of decisive importance to have taken into account the relation between Word and situation. I shall now give a brief outline of the way in which this opens up the doctrine of the sacraments.

IV

The understanding of the sacraments occupies a central position in the Christological, soteriological, and ecclesiological doctrinal complex. Moreover, it may often seem as though the abstract interest concentrated on the soteriological details may conceal the ecclesiological significance of the sacraments, and vice versa. It is indeed a criterion of the correct hermeneutic attitude towards the doctrine of the sacraments that the Christological, soteriological, and ecclesiological aspects of the sacraments should be regarded as a unity. How far is the Word as a starting-point congruent with this position?

We said that the special character of the Sacrament can only be defined on the principle of *solo verbo–sola fide* in such a way that the Sacrament-event understood as the Word-event throws into sharp relief definite aspects of the Word-event, which are, however, implicit in every form of the Word-event. On a superficial view we may seem to be on the wrong track in suggesting that the sacraments make specially clear the relation between Word and situation. Whether it is regarded as an advantage or a disadvantage of the sacraments, it is true that, in comparison with preaching, they are remarkably superior to the situation. While preaching must always wear a fresh aspect, and in many respects is extremely dependent on the situation, the liturgical form peculiar to the Sacrament can and must always be repeated in the same way without diminution or addition. Similarly, in preaching the problem of authority is acute, because the Word-event is so closely related to the situation; whereas the celebration of the Sacrament is independent of the authority of the celebrant, or rather, the authority demanded by the Sacrament is of an entirely different order from that of the authority of preaching, since the authoritative character of the Sacrament-event seems to be detached from the question of the situation. It would be erroneous to conclude from this difference that the distinction consisted in the fact that by its involvement in the situation, the event of preaching revealed the extent to which the Word-event is conditioned by the human and historical situation; while the sacraments, being apparently independent of the situation and timeless, reveal more clearly that in them we have to do with the Word of God. On the contrary, it is the bare spoken Word which, by reason of its marked involvement in the situation, is the occurrence of the Word of God, the Gospel in the strict sense. In any case, as a starting-point for a theological consideration of the relation between Word and situation, we must take account of the various ways in which the bare spoken Word can occur, for they include all the aspects of the relation between Word and situation. This does not, however, exclude, but rather, of necessity, includes the doctrine of the sacraments, since particular aspects of the Word as a situation, and of the situation as spoken Word, are here sharply defined and are a principal help towards the understanding of the Word-event.

1. It is a special characteristic of the sacraments that they emphasize in a very definite way the basic situation out of which the Gospel arises. It is an evasion of problems connected with the *Christological* basis of the sacraments to say that they were expressly ordained by Jesus. The truth that Jesus is the foundation of the Church does not depend on whether Jesus did or did not found it by an express act. The founding of the Church in Jesus is to be understood on the basis of what came to speech in him as a person, and came to speech in him with such authority that it could be repeated. It is not a command of Jesus, but Jesus himself, crucified and risen, that is the foundation of the Church. The same is true of the sacraments. They come from Jesus in such a way that they are the witness that he himself is the sum and substance of the Gospel. This is why Baptism and the Lord's Supper are the only sacraments, because they alone can be regarded as witnessing to the fundamental situation of the manifestation of Jesus. His course begins with baptism and ends with the giving of his body and blood for us. Similarly the sacraments, in their chief difference from one another, namely in the time factor, emphasize the fact that, on the one hand, the ministry of Jesus as the original situation of the Gospel is absolutely unique, and, on the other hand, that it makes possible a perpetual repetition.

2. The *soteriological* relevance of the sacraments is congruent with their Christological relationship. They are related to the fundamental situation of mankind: man is destined to be born and to die; he must

undergo that strange passage between the two, in that, as he enters into life, he begins to die, and that by death alone he enters into life; just as he is nourished from day to day as he fulfils his life's journey as *homo viator*. Only a weak abstraction can regard this as an individualistic approach to the sacraments. The temporal nature of the interval between birth and death, between death and life, is the world's sign-manual, and can only be understood as a tension involving Creation and Eschatology. Herein lies the truth of the eschatological connection with the often mentioned bodily character of the sacraments. The sacraments emphasize, as they alone can, that the Gospel reaches us in our bodily historical existence as an eschatological Word, that is, it makes our world-situation an eschatological one, reveals it as eschatological.

3. Finally, this soteriological relationship of the sacraments coincides with their ecclesiological relevance. They show what has always taken place in the Word-event, but now becomes unmistakably determinative of the situation. Anyone who has been met by the Word of God, laid hold of by the Word of God, is once for all designated, incorporated in Christ, even if he should become a severed, dead member. Such is the situation under the Gospel, that throughout his whole life the baptized person may claim to be an heir of promise through baptism which is the evidence that he has once for all been chosen to be a member of the body of Christ. It is also the situation under the Gospel that our joy in the fact that Jesus is for us does not isolate us, but is a feast of fellowship, fellowship in receiving, fellowship in thanksgiving; it is the Eucharist.

These are seminal suggestions towards a doctrine of the sacraments which may have value for ecclesiology, not in competition with the interpretation of the Church as the authoritative Word-event, but as an exposition of this starting-point.

Notes

ESSAY 2

Confessional Study: Task and Method

A Report given at a conference for Ecumenical studies in Heidelberg, on March 1st, 1952.

1. Cf. my article: 'The Historicity of the Churches and their Message as a Theological Problem.' SgV 207/208, 1954, p. 86.

ESSAY 3

The Problem of the Confessions

A Report given at a conference for Ecumenical studies in Heidelberg on March 1st, 1952.

1. *Rechtgläubigkeit und Ketzerei im ältesten Christentum.* BHTh 10 (1934) 1964[2].

ESSAY 5

Has the Opposition of the Confessions a Philosophical Side?

The above is only a reference to an unjustly forgotten book on the Confessional problem. The slightly revised paper is from a series of lectures given in Oct. 1957 at a Confessional-study seminar of the Evangelical Union held in Esslingen on the subject 'The Place of Philosophy in the Discussion between Catholicism and Protestantism'.

1. E.g. van de Pol: *Das reformatorische Christentum in phänomenologischer Betrachtung*, 1956, see p. 204ff. Approaching the subject from a different angle, but in the end not so different from van de Pol's fundamental thesis, is Hans Urs von Balthasar's study of the Confessional dialogue from the point of view of the different thought-forms, in *Karl Barth: Darstellung und Deutung seiner Theologie*, 1951.

2. ChrW. 1917, 832ff.   3. Kaftan, 398.   4. *Loc. cit.*

5. *Loc. cit.*   6. *Ibid.*, 18.   7. *Loc. cit.*

8. *Ibid.*, 254.   9. *Ibid.*, 13.   10. *Ibid.*, 14.

11. *Ibid.*, 16.   12. *Loc. cit.*   13. *Ibid.*, 14.

14. *Ibid.*, 18.   15. *Loc. cit.*   16. *Ibid.*, 4.

17. *Ibid.*, 22.

20. *Ibid.*, 14f.

23. *Ibid.*, 163.

26. *Ibid.*, 173.

29. *Ibid.*, 33.

32. *Ibid.*, 225.

35. *Ibid.*, 242.

38. Kaftan, 21.

41. *Ibid.*, 254.

44. *Ibid.*, 400.

47. *Ibid.*, 274.

50. *Ibid.*, 229.

53. *Ibid.*, 63.

18. *Ibid.*, 20.

21. *Ibid.*, 85.

24. *Ibid.*, 265.

27. *Ibid.*, 187.

30. *Ibid.*, 281.

33. *Ibid.*, 6.

36. Cf. *ibid.*, 276, 330.

39. *Ibid.*, 399.

42. *Ibid.*, 2.

45. *Ibid.*, 255.

48. *Ibid.*, 22f.

51. *Ibid.*, 255f.

54. *Ibid.*, 19.

19. *Ibid.*, 14.

22. *Ibid.*, 86.

25. *Ibid.*, 188.

28. *Ibid.*, 29.

31. *Ibid.*, 44.

34. *Ibid.*, 184f.

37. Mirbt No. 616.

40. *Ibid.*, 2.

43. *Ibid.*, 20.

46. *Ibid.*, 22.

49. *Ibid.*, 2.

52. *Ibid.*, 24.

ESSAY 6

'Sola Scriptura' and Tradition

A preparatory study for the Fourth World Conference for Faith and Church Order in Montreal 1963. It first appeared in: *Oekumenischer Rat der Kirchen. Kommission für Glauben und Kirchenverfassung: Schrift und Tradition. Untersuchung einer theologischen Kommission.* Edited by Kristen E. Skydsgaard and Lukas Vischer. EVZ-Verlag, Zurich, 1963, pp. 95–127, 172–183. Reprinted with the kind permission of the EVZ-Verlag, Zurich.

1. In the following pages I have elaborated certain points of view which I set forth in 1956 in a lecture on *'Sola Scriptura'*. This received a certain amount of publicity in a duplicated form issued by the diocese of Rottenburg and the Evangelical Academy of Bad Boll under the title of *'Schrift und Tradition'. Ein interkonfessionelles Gespräch*, and was occasionally quoted in current literature. The present elaboration of the theme replaces the earlier form. The format of this book has made it necessary to keep source-references and documentation within definite limits, and to forgo any extensive discussion of what others have said on the subject.

2. The most comprehensive survey is in A. Michel: Art. Tradition, in DThC XV (1946), pp. 1252–1350. Cf. also: J. Beumer: *Die mündliche Überlieferung als Glaubensquelle.* Handb. d. Dogmensch., edited by M. Schmaus and A. Grillmeier, Bd. I, fasc. 4, 1962.

3. It is noteworthy, for instance, that in the *Vocabularius theologiae* of Johannes Altenstaig, 1517, there is no entry *'traditio'*; and in L. Schütz's *Thomas–Lexikon*, under the heading 'traditio' in the sense of tradition, besides two passages which speak of the tradition of sacred Scripture (S.Th. 2, IIq. 140a. S2.c.gent.IV, 34),

only a single passage is referred to, dealing with an individual question of the celebration of the Mass, and speaking in the most guarded way of the argument from an Apostolic tradition supplementing Scripture, in reference to John 21:25; S.Th., III.q.83a. 4 ad 2.

4. Cf. J. de Ghellinck: ' "Pagina" et "Sacra Pagina", Histoire d'un mot et transformation de l'objet primitivement désigné.' In *Mélanges A. Pelzer*, Louvain, 1947, pp. 23–59.

5. Cf. e.g., J. Beumer: 'Das Katholische Schriftprinzip in der theologischen Literatur der Scholastik bis zur Reformation.' *Scholastik* 16, 1941, pp. 24–52. Y. Congar: 'Traditio und Sacra doctrina bei Thomas von Aquin.' In *Festschrift J. R. Geiselmann*, 1960, pp. 170–210. B. Decker: 'Sola Scriptura bei Thomas von Aquin.' In *Festschrift A. Stohr*, 1960, pp. 117–129. J. R. Geiselmann: 'Die Heilige Schrift und die Tradition'. In *Quaest. disp.* 18, 1962, esp. 222ff., on the question of the sufficiency of Holy Scripture. On Thomas cf. esp. S.Th. Iq.1a.8 ad 2: 'The authorities of canonical Scripture (sacred doctrine) may be rightly and necessarily used in argument; but the authorities of other doctors of the Church may be rightly made use of, but only as probable. For our faith contends for the revelation made to the Apostles and Prophets, who have written canonical books, but not for a revelation, if there be such, made to other doctors.' For the need of a Creed alongside Holy Scripture, cf. S.Th.2, IIq. 1a.9 ad 1: '. . . It was necessary that a clear summary of the teachings of Holy Scripture should be made, which should be presented to all for belief; which indeed is not something added to Holy Scripture, but rather taken from Holy Scripture.'

6. W. Maurer: 'Luther's Verständnis des neutestamentlichen Kanons.' *Fuldaer Hefte* 12, 1960, pp. 47–77, esp. 53.

7. Denz. 783–786. With regard to the contemporary discussion about the interpretation, Geiselmann's essay makes it clear that the '*et*' of the decree (in written books *and* unwritten traditions'), was not to be understood in the sense of 'partly—partly' of the draft. On the point, cf. esp., J. R. Geiselmann: 'Das Konzil von Trient über das Verhältnis der Heiligen Schrift und der nicht geschriebenen Traditionen. Sein Missverständnis in der nachtridentinischen Theologie und die Überwindung dieses Missverständnisses.' In *Die mündliche Überlieferung. Beiträge zum Begriff der Tradition*. Edited by M. Schmaus, 1957, pp. 123–206.

8. A. Sperl: 'Melanchthon zwischen Humanismus und Reformation. Eine Untersuchung über den Wandel des Traditionsverständnisses bei Melanchthon und die damit zusammenhängenden Grundfragen seiner Theologie.' FGLP 10. Reihe. Bd. XV, 1959. P. Frankel: *Testimonia Patrum. The Function of the Patristic Argument in the Theology of Philip Melanchthon*. Geneva, 1961.

9. The formulations at the end of the first and second parts of the Augsburg Confession are particularly characteristic: 'This is practically the central element in our teaching, in which nothing can be seen which is not in accord with the Scriptures, or with the Catholic Church, or with the Roman Church, so far as may be seen from our writers.' (*Die Bek. Schriften der ev.-luth. Kirche*, 1952², 83c, 7–11) . . . 'it seemed necessary to say these things, in order that it might be understood that in our teaching and ceremonies nothing has been accepted contrary to Scripture or the Catholic Church, since it is clear that we have most carefully guarded against any new and wicked teachings creeping into our churches' (*op. cit.* 134, 17–23).

10. I have dealt with this more fully in: 'Die Geschichtlichkeit der Kirche und ihrer Verkündigung als theologisches Problem,' SgV.207/8, 1954, esp. pp. 31ff. WuG pp. 351ff, 381ff. 'Wort Gottes und kirchliche Lehre', MdKI 13, 1962, pp. 21–28, 155–174. 'Theologie und Verkündigung' (HUTh 1) 1962, 3ff. Art. Tradition VII. Dogmatisch, RGG³ VI (1962), 976–984, esp. 979ff .

11. E.g., *Studium Generale* 4, 1951, H.6. G. Krüger: *Geschichte und Tradition*, 1948; now also in G. Krüger: *Freiheit und Weltverwaltung. Aufsätze zur Philosophie der Geschichte*, 1958, pp. 71–96. R. Wittram: *Das Interesse an Geschichte*, 1958, esp. pp. 95ff. H.-G. Gadamer: *Wahrheit und Methode, Grundzüge einer philosophischen Hermeneutik*, 1960, esp. pp. 261ff., 275ff.

12. Most instructive is the study by B. Altaner: 'Zur Frage der Definibilität der Assumptio B.V.M.' in *Theol. Rev.* 44, 1948, pp. 129–140; 45, 1949, pp. 129–142; 46, 1950, pp. 5–20. A summary in 'Das neue Mariendogma im Lichte der Geschichte und im Urteil der Ökumene', ed. Fr. Heiler. *Ökumenische Einheit*, 1951, Heft 2, pp. 49–60.

13. Cf. K. Rahner: 'Über die Schriftinspiration'. *Quaest. disp.*, 1958, p. 7f. Id. 'Was ist eine dogmatische Aussage?' Cath.15, 1961, esp. pp. 180, 182 (reprinted in K. Rahner: *Schriften zur Theologie* V, 1962, pp. 54–81 Eng. Tr. *Theological Investigations* Vol. 5, Baltimore, Helicon Press and London, Darton, Longman and Todd, 1967, pp. 42–66). Id. Art. Hl. Schrift und Theologie, in *Handbuch theologischer Grundbegriffe*, ed. H. Fries, II, 1963, pp. 517–525. H. Küng: *Rechtfertigung. Die Lehre Karl Barths und eine katholische Besinnung*, 1957, pp. 116f. P. Lengsfeld: *Überlieferung, Tradition und Schrift in der evangelischen und katholischen Theologie der Gegenwart*, 1960, pp. 187ff. O. Semmelroth: *Wirkendes Wort. Zur Theologie der Verkündigung*, 1962, p. 106.

14. K. Barth: KD.II,2, 1946, pp. 533–563. Cf. H. Diem: *Theologie als kirchliche Wissenschaft. Bd. II Dogmatik*, 1960³, pp. 160–162.

15. It would, of course, be necessary to distinguish between the actual part

played by oral transmission and the reasons for the pre-eminence accorded to it. With regard to the Old Testament and Judaism cf. among others, J. van der Ploeg: 'Le Rôle de la Tradition orale dans la transmission du texte de l'AT.' *Revue Biblique* 54, 1947, pp. 5–41. H. Ringren: 'Oral and Written Transmission in the O.T.' *Studia Theologica* 3, 1949, pp. 34–59. B. Gerhardsson: *Memory and Manuscript. Oral Tradition and Written Transmission in Rabbinic Judaism and Early Christianity.* Acta Sem. Neotest. Ups. 22, 1961. With regard to Greek literature, R. Harder: 'Bemerkungen zur griechischen Schriftlichkeit', in R. Harder: *Kleine Schriften*; ed. W. Marg, 1960, pp. 57–80. With regard to the notion of succession connected with oral tradition in the Greek philosophical schools, see L. Koep: Art. Bischofliste (AIII), RAC II, pp. 409f., and H. v. Campenhausen: 'Kirchliches Amt und geistliche Vollmacht in der ersten drei Jahrhunderten.' BHTh 14, 1953, pp. 174f.

16. H. v. Campenhausen, pp. 172ff.

17. H. v. Campenhausen, pp. 215ff., e.g. Strom. I, 13, 2, 'Secrets such as the doctrine of God are only preserved orally, not committed to writing.' In Clement, connected with the idea of oral transmission, we find such various aspects as the idea of the discipline of the arcana, the pedagogic training of souls implied in the personal relationship between teacher and scholar, the conjecture that it is not merely a question of imparting knowledge, but that life and spirit can only be transmitted through life and spirit, as well as the hermeneutic point of view, that actual transmission, including Scriptural—for Clement is a thoroughly 'Scripture' theologian—must take the form of interpretation.

18. With regard to what follows, see S.Th. I. II q.106, a.1., 'Whether the new law should be a written law.'

19. In S.Th. III q.42, a.4. Thomas speaks, in a discussion of the question whether Christ should have committed his teaching to writing, in relation to Christ himself, referring to Pythagoras and Socrates, of the superiority of oral teaching as 'the more excellent mode of teaching.' But the views here advanced are not helpful for the understanding of the Gospel and a theology of preaching.

20. WA 10,1,1; 17, 7–12 (1522).

21. WA 10,1,1; 625, 625, 19–627, 3 (1522). Cf. also WA 10, 1,2: 34, 27–35, 3 (1522) 10,3; 305, 1–8 (1522) 7; 526, 12–24 (1521).

22. Cf. my book, *Theologie und Verkündigung*, HUTH 1, 1962, pp. 110f. =Eng. Tr. *Theology and Proclamation*, London, Collins and Philadelphia, Fortress Press, 1966, pp. 114f.

23. For a classical example, see R. Bultmann: *Die Geschichte der synoptischen Tradition* (1921) 1957[3].

24. WA 10,1,1; 627, 1–21 (1522).

W.G.T.   Q

25. Loci theol., loc.1, *De script.s.*, cap.2, q.3, ed. Cott.II,30. Cf. my book, WuG p. 328.

26. P. Lengsfeld (see p. 240, n. 13) p. 102f., 104.

27. Cf. Joh. Wolleb's formulation, in *Christianae theologiae compendium* (1626): 'The witness of the Church is prior in time; but that of the Holy Spirit is prior in nature and efficacy. We believe the Church, but not on account of the Church; but the Holy Spirit is believed for his own sake. The witness of the Church declares τὸ ὅτι (that which is); but the witness of the Holy Spirit demonstrates τὸ διότι (why it is). The Church advises; the Holy Spirit convinces. The witness of the Church is an opinion; but the Scriptures produce knowledge and well-grounded faith.'

28. A. Ritschl: 'Über die beiden Prinzipien des Protestantismus', ZKG 1, 1876, pp. 307–413 = Ges.Aufs. I, 1893, pp. 234–247. Cf. G. Gloege: Art. Schriftprinzip. RGG³ V, pp. 1540–1543.

29. Cf. B. Hägglund: *Die Heilige Schrift und ihre Deutung in der Theologie Johann Gerhards. Eine Untersuchung über das altlutherische Schriftverständnis.* 1951.

30. This, for example, is what Joh. Wolleb means in *Christ. theol. comp.*: 'The question whether the Scriptures or the sacred books are the word of God is unworthy of a Christian man. For as in the schools we do not dispute with any one who denies the basic principles, so we should judge it unworthy to listen to any one who denies the basic principle of the Christian religion.'

31. Joh. Gerhard (Loc. theol., Prooemium de natura theologiae, 19, ed. Cott. II, 8), says by way of summary: 'The principle of supernatural theology is sufficiently and rightly described as the divine revelation which today is only to be found in the sacred writings, i.e., in the prophetic books of the Old, and the Apostolic books of the New Testament; hence we say that the written Word of God, or, which is the same thing, Holy Scripture, is the sole and rightful principle of theology. It should however be observed that we are not here concerned with the principle of "being" but of "knowing". God is the principle and prime cause of theology, since from him both end and means arise; but the principle of knowledge in theology is the Word of God.'

32. This corresponds to the distinction which Thomas draws between the material object of faith, and the formal reason of faith as an object, S.Th. 2. II q.1, a.1.

33. With regard to the positive hermeneutic meaning of the term 'prejudgement' cf. H.-G. Gadamer: *Wahrheit und Methode*, 1960, pp. 255ff.

34. To emphasize this is the object of Luther's preface to the New Testament: 'Take heed that thou so direct thy attention to the books of the New Testament that thou mayest learn to read them in this fashion.' WADB 6; 10, 6f. (1522). The practice of affixing such prefaces is not a new thing. Luther follows,

although critically (cf. WADB 6; 8,5=9,5), the example of Jerome's preface to the Vulgate.

35. WADB 6; 12f. Both in the German New Testament of 1522, and in the edition of the Bible of 1546.

36. WADB 6; 10, 6–35. This passage from the preface to the New Testament is omitted from 1534. Cf. however, the preface to the Epistle to the Romans: WADB 7; 2,3f. (1522)=3,3f. (1546). also the beginning of the preface to the Epistle to the Hebrews, WADB 7; 344, 2–4 (1522)=345, 2–4 (1546): 'So far we have had the authentic main books of the New Testament. But the four following books have formerly worn a different aspect ...'

37. With regard to the Ep. to the Hebrews: WADB 7; 344, 4–19 (1522)= 345, 4–19 (1546). With regard to the Eps. of James and Jude: WADB 7; 384ff. (1522 and 1546). But it should be observed that alongside the well-known characterization of the Ep. of James as 'an Epistle of straw' (WADB 6; 10, 33f. 1522), we are told: 'This Epistle of St. James, although depreciated by the ancients, is one which I love and esteem, since it puts forward no man-made law, and lays stress on God's Law.' WADB 7; 384, 3–6 (1522)=385, 3–5 (1546). On the Rev. of John: WADB 7; 404 (1522), in 1530 replaced by an entirely different preface (*op. cit.* 406ff.).

38. Denz.783. The question of equality in connection with the relation of the canonical writings to one another had also been discussed; but had been left undecided with regard to the meaning of 'equal authority'. H. Jedin: *Geschichte des Konzils von Trient*, Bd.II, 1957, pp. 45f. R. Geiselmann: *Die Heilige Schrift und die Tradition*. Quaest. disp. 18, 1962, p. 280. On the other hand loud voices were raised, insisting that 'with equal reverence' only expressed the equality of written and unwritten traditions, H. Jedin: *op. cit.*, p. 60.

39. Cf. K. Rahner: 'What is a dogmatic statement?' Cath. 15, 1961, pp. 161–184 (see p. 240, n. 13). Rahner explains the 'unique, once-for-all position of the Holy Scriptures' as follows: 'Their statements are part of the unique historical event of salvation, upon which all proclamation and all subsequent theology depend; they are, in this wholly specific sense, true as theology and true as absolutely binding theology. They are not only a statement of faith, but are the abiding ground of all other statements in the future; they are the transmitted thing, not the unfolding tradition of the transmitted thing.' (p. 180). To the question in what form the 'original statement of faith as *norma normans non normata*, both the statement demanding faith and the modern non-obligatory statement of faith, is given', Rahner replies, 'simply and plainly', 'in Holy Scripture'. He also remarks with regard to this: 'Even if we in the Catholic Church still, and today more than in the last century, leave entirely open the disputed question whether the Tradition, which according to the

Council of Trent is a standard of our faith and of the doctrinal teaching of the Church, is basically and in the abstract a material source for the content of the faith in addition to Scripture, or is merely a formal criterion of the purity of the faith, after the material content of the Apostolic preaching has been adequately laid down in written form, we can still answer our question: "The Holy Scriptures". The reason for this is simple. Even if we assume the existence of a source alongside Scripture, which might attest for us material elements of the faith which were not also to be found in the Scriptures, yet such a source of tradition would not be of such a kind as to contain only the divinely guaranteed authentic witness of the actual revealed Apostolic tradition with no admixture of any human tradition.' (p. 181) '. . . Christians are in general agreement, at least in essentials, that in the Holy Scriptures the Church *has* received the authentic and completely historical written record of the Apostolic kerygma . . . Nowhere else does the Church possess such an objective standard, if she will, out of the actual totality of her tradition, admit the gift of discriminating between what is the genuine revealed element in this tradition, and what is merely human tradition, as has been the case from the beginning of the Church. Hence, in so far as there is an objective *norma normans, non normata*, and this is identical with Scripture and with that alone, a norm moreover primarily intended for the believing consensus of the whole Church and for the doctrinal authority of the Church, and not for the individual (nor for his struggle against the believing consensus of the whole Church authoritatively attested by the magisterium), such a norm is the original Word of revelation and faith in the Church and for the Church, essentially distinct from every later theological statement of the Church and in the Church . . .' (182). See also, Karl Rahner: *Über die Schriftinspiration*, Quaest. disp. 1, 1958. O. Semmelroth: *Wirkendes Wort. Zur Theologie der Verkündigung*, 1962, p. 33, 'Scripture and Tradition do not stand in the same relation to the Word of God. With regard to their content they both contain God's Word, that which God has spoken. But Holy Scripture as an inspired book *is* God's Word, it does not only contain it. For God is its Author, which cannot be said about Tradition.'

40. E.g., the formulation of Nicaea II: Denz. 308.

41. As in Session IV of the Council of Trent: 'Written books and unwritten traditions.' Denz. 783.

42. Advice such as that given by P. Lengsfeld (see above p. 240, n. 13) at the Conference of Evangelical Theologians with regard to the rejection of the distinction between 'divine-apostolic' and 'ecclesiastical' traditions, might have been more kindly received if the obligation had been borne in mind to pronounce on the question of the verifiability of this distinction.

43. H. Jedin (see above p. 243, n. 38), p. 50.

44. Cf. in the Tridentine decree (Denz. 782), the statements: 'By the removal of errors the purity of the Gospel in the Church is to be preserved', as well as: 'This truth and discipline is contained in written books and in unwritten traditions . . .'

45. The statements of K. Rahner quoted above on pp. 243-4, n. 39, tend in the same direction.

46. At the Council of Trent (Denz. 783) stress was laid on the historical once-for-allness of the revelation, and at the same time the unbroken movement of tradition up to the present time was emphasized: . . . 'by unwritten traditions which were received from the mouth of Christ himself by the Apostles, or, dictated by the Holy Spirit, were handed down by the Apostles, as if by hand, they have finally reached us.' Further: . . . 'the traditions themselves, relating both to faith and to morals, dictated orally by Christ, or by the Holy Spirit, have been preserved in unbroken succession in the Catholic Church . . .'

47. The Council of Trent (Denz. 783) has no comprehensive term for 'written books' and 'unwritten traditions'. The same is true of the Constitutio dogmatica de fide catholica, cap. 2 De revelatione, of the First Vatican Council. The appendix, 'De fontibus revelationis', Denz. 1787, is an addition by the editor. The use of the term 'two sources of revelation' predominates. For the more recent dogmatic literature, cf. e.g., P. M. Nicolau, S.J., in: *Patres S.J. in Hispania professores, Sacrae Theologiae Summa I,* Madrid 1955, Tract. In. 57: 'The treatise concerning the sources of revelation, or concerning Tradition and Scripture, is the foundation of dogmatic theology . . .' M. Schmaus: *Katholische Dogmatik I,* 1953[5], p. 107: 'The objective tradition in the strict sense is a source of faith independent of Scripture and of equal value.' Similarly the *Kath. Katechismus der Bistümer Deutschlands* (1955) Nr. 51: 'Not all the truths which God has revealed are written in Holy Scripture. Many were only preached by the Apostles, and were then transmitted by the Church as a precious heritage. We call them oral tradition, or the inherited teaching. Most of these truths were committed to writing shortly after the time of the Apostles by holy and learned men (Fathers of the Church). Holy Scripture and the legacy of teaching are the two sources of faith. Under the guidance of the Holy Spirit the Church preserves them uncorrupted and from them draws its teaching,' J. R. Geiselmann (see above p. 239, n. 5) p. 9, describes this formulation of the relation between Scripture and Tradition in the *Einheitskatechismus* as 'unfortunate'. He himself speaks of the 'two forms' under which the Gospel promulgated by Jesus Christ, proclaimed by the Apostles, has been transmitted as the sole source of salvation (p. 271).

48. Both at the Council of Trent and at Vatican I the statements about

Scripture and Tradition (Denz. 785, 1727), and about Scripture and Church as the final authority on interpretation (Denz. 786, 1788) stand side by side, without any consideration of the connection between them. It is obvious, however, that this connection exists and requires explanation; and that therefore the Church's interpretation, above all with its power as the final authority, belongs to the content of tradition, and that tradition has hermeneutic importance.

49. Cf. e.g., K. Rahner's reservation in the passage quoted above on p. 244, n. 39: he says that Scripture alone is the objective *norma normans, non normata*: 'a norm primarily intended for the believing consensus of the whole Church and for the doctrinal authority of the Church, and not for the individual (nor for his struggle against the believing consensus of the whole Church authoritatively attested by the magisterium) ...' O. Semmelroth (see above, p. 240, n. 13) p. 106f.: 'The substance of the faith revealed by God is contained in Holy Scripture in so far as it is imparted and interpreted through the living tradition of the Church under the guidance of the Holy Spirit. Conversely, it can be said that the divine revelation has been given to us through the living tradition in so far as it carries Holy Scripture in its hands, and brings to light from its depths what the divine inspiration of the Spirit has hidden there. What tradition has transmitted to subsequent generations, to interpret and bring to light, is Holy Scripture and that alone. For Holy Scripture is formally the Word of God which constitutes the content of the transmitting and proclaiming activity of the Church ... And if the Church today bases her preaching and doctrinal decisions expressly on Holy Scripture, even where that does not appear to be fully justified from a purely textual point of view—as in the case of the last two Marian decrees—such a decision bears only in part the aspect of a valid proof, but in part it seems much more to be a confession that the Church does not proclaim her own, but God's Word, which Jesus Christ bequeathed to his Church. In its preaching the Church interprets Holy Scripture under the guidance of the Holy Spirit who indwells the life of the Church and alone is capable of drawing out all that lies in its depths, all that he himself by his inspiration has laid down and revealed in the words of Holy Scripture.' Can what has just been said mean anything else than the claim that in a given case interpretation can be a substitute for interpretation, and that the semblance of an interpretation may suffice to satisfy the demand for interpretation?

50. Denz. 1788 ... 'That in matters of faith and conduct pertaining to the building up of Christian doctrine, that should be regarded as possessing the true meaning of Holy Scripture which is held by Holy Mother Church, whose function it is to decide what is the true meaning and interpretation of the Holy Scriptures; and therefore no one shall be allowed to interpret Holy Scripture

itself so as to conflict with this meeting, or with the unanimous agreement of the Fathers.'

51. Cf. my Essay: 'Wort Gottes und Hermeneutik', ZThK 56, 1959, pp. 224–251; reprinted in WuG pp. 319–348.

52. *Form. Conc. Epitome* (Die Bek. Schr. d. ev.-luth. Kirche, 1952², 769, pp. 19–40): 'In this way the clear distinction is to be maintained between the sacred books of the Old and New Testament and all other writings, and Holy Scripture alone is to be recognized as judge, standard, and rule, to which, as to a touchstone, all decisions are to be submitted and judged, to determine whether they are pious or impious, true or false. But other creeds and other writings, of which we have just spoken, do not possess judicial authority, for this honour is to be ascribed to the sacred writings alone; nevertheless they bear witness to our religion and expound it, and show how on certain occasions of controversy in the Church of God the sacred writings were understood and explained by learned men who lived at that time; they also show for what reasons dogmas discordant with Holy Scripture were rejected and condemned.'

53. Cf. the material in Fr. Kropatscheck: *Das Schriftprinzip der lutherischen Kirche*, Bd. I. Die Vorgeschichte. Das Erbe des Mittelalters, 1904. An article from the Taborite Confession of 1431 is particularly impressive: 'Holy Scripture is the rule of faith, from which, rightly understood, all convincing proof should be drawn, and by which every controversy about faith or conduct should be finally settled; since it is the first and most generally accepted principle of doctrine and of the knowledge of the faith; authority should be ascribed to no other writing beside it, nor any authority admitted contrary to it . . .' *op. cit.* p. 82.

54. See above p. 239, n. 5. In this connection the Scholastics quote *Augustine Ep. ad Hier.* 82, 1, 3, MPL 33,277=CSEL 33,354: 'I have learnt to give this reverence and honour only to those books of the Scripture which are called canonical, and to believe firmly that no author has erred in anything that he has written in them. But with regard to others I say that however pre-eminent in sanctity and learning they may be, I do not therefore accept as true what they may have thought or written.' E.g., Thomas, S.Th. I q.1, a.8.

55. WAB 1; 171, Nr. 74, pp. 72–74 (Letter to J. Trutfetter v.9.5. 1518) . . . 'I learnt from thee first of all that faith should only be given to the canonical books, all the rest should be read with judgement, as the blessed Augustine, and indeed Paul and John, advise.' This corresponds exactly with William of Ockham, *Dial.* p. 411: 'It is necessary to give the firmest faith only to the canonical books which are contained in the Bible' (Kropatschek 314). On the problem of 'Scripture and Tradition' in Nominalism, see now H. A. Oberman:

The Harvest of Medieval Theology. Gabriel Biel and Late Medieval Nominalism.
Cambridge. Mass. 1963, pp. 361–422.

56. WA; 95–101.

57. *Ibid*, 96, 4–6: 'I do not intend, moreover, to bow to the authority of any father, however holy, unless he has been approved by the judgement of sacred Scripture . . .'

58. *Ibid.*, 96, 10f.: 'What is authoritatively laid down in the canons is quoted by every one orally or in writing, but understood by few: The Holy Scriptures may not be subject to private interpretation.'

59. WA 56; 157ff.

60. WA 7; 97,36–98,3. Cf. e.g., the concluding passage in a disquisition on the pride of heretics in the first preface to the Psalms (1513–15), which sounds like an early warning to himself: 'Do not therefore believe and cast everything into doubt, looking for some new teaching: this is the most serious temptation of a master. Take heed, therefore, O man; but learn in humility to be wise, and do not, as a new author, overstep the bounds which thy fathers have laid down. But ask thy father and he will tell thee. For God has placed the spirit of the law, not in letters written on papyrus, on which the heretics rely, but in men whom he has placed in offices and ministries, that instruction might be sought from their mouth. Otherwise what could be easier for the devil than to seduce him who attempts to be his own instructor in the Scriptures, rejecting the ministry of a man? One word wrongly understood can throw the whole of Scripture into confusion' WA 3, 578, 38–579,7. Luther has underlined the last sentence. Cf. U. Mauser: *Der Häresiebegriff des jungen Luther* (Diss. Tübingen), 1957.

61. WA 7: 96, 11–20.   62. *Ibid.*, 96, 21–25.   63. *Ibid.*, 96, 25–34.

64. *Ibid.*, 97, 1–3: 'The Scriptures are only to be understood by that Spirit by whom they were written, a Spirit which it is nowhere more possible to find present and living than in those sacred writings of his which he has written.'

65. *Ibid.*, 97, 5–9.   66. *Ibid.*, 97, 11–13.

67. *Ibid.*, 97, 16–22: 'Why is it not permitted today to study only or primarily the sacred writings, as it was permitted for the early Church? Scripture ought to be the judge of this opinion, which cannot be done unless we have given Scripture the first place in everything, as the Fathers did . . .'

68. *Ibid.*, 97, 23–34: . . . 'That it may, by itself, be its own interpreter, the most certain, the easiest, the most accessible, proving all things, judging, and illuminating . . .'

69. *Ibid.*, 97, 24–35. Luther is dealing with Ps. 119, 130 and 160: 'Light and understanding come, in part, through the words of God alone, as by . . . the first principle . . . from which the approach to light and understanding should begin. The Word of God must thus be used as the first principle by which all

words are to be judged. Hence the Psalm goes back to the source and teaches that the words of God must be studied first and solely; but the Spirit will come of his own accord and drive out our spirit, so that we may theologize without danger.'

70. *Ibid.*, 97, 36–98,3.

71. *Ibid.*, Cf. 97, 5f. 34f. 99,1 and 100, 18–24 '. . . that, just as they (sc. holy men and Fathers of the Church) laboured at the Word of God for their time, so let us too labour at it for our age . . . It is enough to have learnt from the Fathers how to labour at the Scriptures with zeal and diligence . . .'

72. *Ibid.*, 97, 43f., see above p. 248, n. 69.

73. WuG (see above p. 247, n. 51) pp. 333f.

74. Taking a broad view, we may consider the various conditions under which the spoken word has been heard and received in a situation identical for speakers and hearers, a situation in which identity of language has played a part. This does not exclude the possibility that the Word may so change the situation as to create a new situation.

75. See above p. 248, n. 66; also nn. 67 and 69. Cf. also *ibid.*, 98, 4–7: 'There are therefore first principles of Christianity, the Words of God alone; but all human words are conclusions drawn from these, and to be referred back to their source and judged by it . . .' *ibid.*, 98, 11–17 '. . . the divine Words are more accessible and more certain than any human words; they are not learnt through human words, but human words themselves must be learnt, tested, laid bare, and confirmed by them.'

76. WA 18; 606,1–609,14; 653, 13–35 (1525). On this cf. R. Hermann: *On the Clarity of Holy Scripture. Studies and Discussions on Luther's Doctrine of Scripture in De servo arbitrio*, 1958.

77. WA 606, 16–21; 653, 31–33.

78. *Ibid.*, 603, 6–8.

79. *Ibid.*, 653, 28–35: 'For Christians should, in the first place, be most firmly convinced that the Holy Scriptures are a spiritual light far brighter than the sun, above all in those things which pertain to salvation or need . . . that is our first principle . . .'

80. *Ibid.*, 606, 22–39: '. . . Take Christ from the Scriptures, what more will you find in them? All the things contained in the Scriptures are presented, in some places perhaps still obscure because of unknown words. . . . The same thing indeed, most clearly declared to the whole world, is spoken in the Scriptures, sometimes in plain words, and sometimes still hidden in obscure words . . .'

81. 'The clarity of Scripture has a double aspect, as also its obscurity: one is external, in the word as ministered, the other exists in the attitude of the

recipient . . .' *ibid.*, 653, 13–28: . . .'spirits are searched out or tested by a double judgement. The one is internal, because by the Holy Spirit or by a special gift of God, anyone, illuminated concerning his own salvation, judges and discerns with the utmost certainty the teachings and meanings of all . . . this is a matter of faith and is necessary even for the individual Christian . . . the other is an external judgement, by which, not only for ourselves, but for others and for their salvation, we judge all spirits and teachings with the utmost certainty. This judgement is exercised in the ministry of the Word and in public office, and is the special prerogative of leaders and preachers of the Word . . .'

82. In the linguistic usage of the word '*Sache*' it is permissible to use the same word to express the usual distinction between 'content', or 'object', on the one hand, and 'task', 'competence', 'function', or 'office', on the other. The inseparable connection between the two is a consequence of the nature of speech. Hence it is no mere play on words to indicate this connection in speech.

83. See above p. 122ff.

84. Here we might recall the usual distinction made in Catholic Dogmatics between *regula fidei proxima* and *regula fidei remota*. This does not simply correspond with what has been said above, since, at any rate in the traditional pattern of doctrine, a distinction is made between Tradition and the doctrinal authority of the Church. Thus Scripture and Tradition as the two sources of revelation are the *regula fidei remota* in distinction from the teaching office of the Church as the *regula fidei proxima*. The classical statement of this interrelation is to be found in *Vat. I Const. dogm. de fide cath. cap.* 3 (Denz. 1792): . . . 'In the divine and Catholic faith all things are to be believed which are contained in the Word of God, written, or in tradition, and are promulgated by the Church, either by special decree, or by its ordinary and universal magisterium, to be believed as divinely revealed.' Cf. e.g., I. Salaverri, 'De ecclesia Christi', in: *Patres S.J. in Hispania professores, Sacrae Theologiae Summa*, Vol. I (Madrid 1955), Tract. II, n. 780f. See also the next note.

85. To complete it we might insert, 'of the individual'. But can we separate responsibility from conscience? The problem is not made more complicated if we oppose the suspension of hermeneutic responsibility to 'the subjective arbitrariness of the individual'. Moreover, we meet with a vivid recurrence of the problem in the pronouncement in the Encyclical '*Humani generis*', AAS 42, 1950, 567–569: . . . 'This sacred Magisterium should be, in matters of faith and conduct, the ultimate and universal standard of truth for every theologian; since to it the Lord Christ has entrusted the whole deposit of faith, to wit, the Holy Scriptures and the divine tradition, to be guarded and protected and interpreted . . . It is also true that theologians should ever return to the sources

of divine revelation, since it is their function to decide why those things which are taught by the living Magisterium are found either expressed or implied in the Holy Scriptures and in the divine Tradition ... For together with these sacred sources God has given to his Church the living Magisterium, in order that those things which are contained in the deposit of faith, even obscurely and implicitly, may be illuminated and explained. The divine Redeemer has not entrusted this deposit for authentic interpretation to individual believers nor to theologians themselves, but to the Magisterium of the Church *alone*.' This '*particula exclusiva*', which I have italicized, is the exact antithesis of '*sola scriptura*'.

86. See above p. 110ff.

87, Cf. my publications: 'Kirchengeschichte als Geschichte der Auslegung der Heiligen Schrift' SgV 189, 1947. See above pp. 11–31. 'Die Geschichtlichkeit der Kirche und ihrer Verkündigung als theologisches Problem.' SgV 207/8, 1954, esp. pp. 81ff.

88. See above pp. 249-50, n. 81.

89. See above p. 249, n. 80. WATR 2; 439, 25f. (Nr. 2383): 'Christ is the mathematical point of Holy Scripture.' On the Christological bearing of Luther's early exegesis, cf. E. Gogelsang: 'Die Anfänge von Luthers Christologie nach der ersten Psalmenvorlesung', AKG 15, 1929, and my Essays: 'Die Anfänge von Luthers Hermeneutik', ZThK 48, 1951, pp. 172–230, esp. pp. 129ff.; 'Luthers Psaltersdruck vom Jahre 1513, ZThK 50, 1953' pp. 43–99, esp. pp. 80ff. On the point that Christ is the subject of Scripture, is decided the question of the unity and intelligibility of Scripture. See the statement in the first preface to the Psalms (1513/15), WA 3; 356, 35–57: ... 'All the words of God are one, simple, identical, true, since they all meet in one, however many they are. And all the words which meet in one are one word.' WA 4; 439, 20f.: '... in Christ all words are one word, and outside Christ they are many and empty ...'

90. In our 'historical' way of thinking, the term 'sources' means whatever discloses and leads back to the past as such. Cf. e.g., J. G. Droysen's definition, in *Historik* 1958³, p. 37: '... Anything which a study of the past of earlier times provides by way of a description or recall of that past, we call a "source".' The original meaning of the term, not only in theological usage, was the contemporary disclosure of 'the original, undistorted truth', 'the primal founts of pure and fresh water from an invisible depth'. (Gadamer [see above p. 240, n. 11] p. 474). In considering the difference in interest, the common element should not be overlooked: the unconditioned superiority of the sources over that which comes from them. 'In the fountains fresh water is always flowing, and this is true of the spiritual sources in the tradition. Their study is precisely

so rewarding, since they always yield something different from what has hitherto been received from them.' (Gadamer, p. 474.)

91. WA 6; 516, 30–32 (1520): 'For neither does God deal otherwise with men than by the word of promise. Conversely, neither can we deal with God otherwise than by faith in his word of promise.' The insistence on this fundamental relation between word and faith appears in connection with the controversy about the Roman conception of the Mass. WA 6; 515, 27–29: 'From these it may be seen that nothing is needed for a valid Mass but faith which holds fast to this promise, believes that Christ is true in these words of his, and does not doubt that these immense benefits are given to him.'

92. WADB 7; 384,22–386,2 (1520)=385,22–387–2 (1546): 'For it is the duty of a genuine Apostle to proclaim Christ's passion, death, and office, and to lay the foundation of faith in the same ... And all genuine books agree in this, that they all proclaim and magnify Christ. Moreover, the true touchstone, by which all books are judged, is whether they glorify Christ or not, since all Scripture presents Christ ... What does not teach Christ is not Apostolic, even were S. Peter or Paul to do so. Conversely, what proclaims Christ is Apostolic, even if Judas, Annas, Pilate, and Herod were to do it. But this James no longer does so, for he magnifies the Law and its works ...'

93. WA 39,1; 47, 3f. 19f. (1535): 'Scripture is not to be understood as against, but for Christ, hence it either refers to him, or is not to be reckoned true Scripture ... For if opponents have pleaded Scripture against Christ, let us plead Christ against Scripture.'

94. WA 6; 560,33–561,2 (1520): 'For the Church is born by faith from the word of promise, and is fed and preserved by the same, that is, that she herself owes her existence to the promises of God, and not that God's promise proceeds from her. For the Word of God is incomparably far above the Church, in that she, as a creature, has no power to decree, arrange, or act, but only to be the object of decree, arrangement, or action. For who begets his own parent? who has first brought his own author into existence?'

95. Cf. the close connection between the doctrine of the clarity of Scripture and the affirmative and assurance character of faith, in the Introduction to the *De servo arbitrio*, WA 18; 603,1ff. (1525) 603,28f.; 'Take away affirmations, and you have taken away Christianity.' 604,33: 'For what is more wretched than uncertainty?' 605,32–34: 'The Holy Spirit is not a sceptical spirit, nor has he written doubts and opinions in our hearts, but affirmations more certain and assured than life itself and all experience.'

96. There is an unsurpassable statement in the beginning of the *Invocavit-Predigten* 1522, WA 10, 3; 1,6–2,2: 'We are all together doomed to death and no one dies for another, but every one in his own person faces death for himself.

We can cry out in protest. But every one must rely on his own resources in the time of death. I will not be with you then, nor will you be with me. In this situation the main thing for every man must therefore be to act as a Christian, to understand and be prepared ...'

97. See above pp. 250-1, n. 85.

98. I am well aware of the changed position of the doctrinal authority with regard to the reading of the Bible by the laity, and of the Catholic Bible Movement. This enhances the extent to which various levels exist in the Confessional situation. Superficially Protestant controversy may feel bewildered at the statement in the German Diocesan Catechism (1955), no. 51: 'I will buy myself a New Testament, or have one given to me; it shall accompany me throughout my whole life.' What we have now to do is to work out the essentials of the situation; the context shows that no objection exists to what is contained in the above statement. What internal Catholic changes may result from an increased contact with Holy Scripture is not a subject for speculation.

99. The conclusions drawn above on pp. 125ff., need not on this account be retracted; they will however be regarded as an issue of theological controversy. Although the concept of the purely interpretative function of the Tradition, looked at from the point of view of the general pattern of Catholic doctrine, seems the more consistent, it must however be regarded, from the Protestant point of view, as an attempt to legitimize the complementary function of the Tradition.

100. See above pp. 102f., 104–8.

101. See above p. 125ff.

102. Cf. my art. in *Hermeneutik*, RGG³ III, pp. 242–262. G. Hornig: *Die Anfänge der historisch-kritischen Theologie. Johann Salomo Semmlers Schriftverständnis und seine Stellung zu Luther.* 1961.

103. Cf. WuG (see above p. 247, n. 51), p. 322, n. 7.

104. The connection asserted between the general doctrinal conception of tradition and what may be called, putting it briefly, the Catholic doctrinal principles summed up in the formula 'Scripture and Tradition', still needs thorough testing and clarification. This must include the very difficult connection between the basic tendency expressed in the formula 'Scripture and Tradition', and the attitude to early interpretations of significance and metaphysics.

105. EvTh 11, 1951/52, 13–21. Reprinted in E. Käsemann: *Exegetische Versuche und Besinnungen* I, 1960, pp. 214–223.

106. *Op. cit.* p. 221.   107. See below p. 148.

108. Cf. the discussions on historical and dogmatic theology in my book

Theologie und Verkündigung, HUTh 1, 1962, pp. 10–18=Eng. Tr. *Theology and Proclamation*, pp. 22–31.

109. In what follows I am making use, occasionally word for word, of my article, 'Tradition VII dogmatisch,' in RGG³, 976–984, although I have not been able to deal fully with all the points there raised.

110. Mark 7:1–13 par.; Gal 1:14; Col 2:8.

ESSAY 7

The New Testament and the Multiplicity of Confessions

From a lecture on *Dogmatik I* in the Summer term in 1962.

1. 'Begründet der neutestamentliche Kanon die Einheit der Kirche?' EvTh. 11, 1951/1952, pp. 13–21. I am quoting from the reprint in: E. Käsemann, *Exegetische Versuche und Besinnungen* I, 1960, pp. 214–223.

2. *Ibid.*, p. 215.   3. *Ibid.*, p. 216f.   4. *Ibid.*, p. 219.
5. *Ibid.*, p. 220.

6. They have already been quoted above on p. 143, and are here merely referred to. Käsemann, *op. cit.* p. 221.

7. *Ibid.*, p. 223.   8. *Ibid.*, p. 221.   9. *Ibid.*, p. 221.
10. WA 18; 603, 18f. BoA 3; 98, 14f.
11. *Ibid.*, p. 221.   12. *Ibid.*, p. 222.   13. *Ibid.*, p. 222f.
14. *Ibid.*, p. 223.

ESSAY 8

The Word of God and Church Doctrine

Delivered at a working-party of Protestant and Catholic theologians at Lucerne, Oct. 4, 1961. First published in *Materialdienst des Konfessionskundlichen Instituts Bensheim*, 13th year, pp. 21–28.

1. In the medieval philosophical schools use was made of a kind of 'genealogical tree' to represent in schematic form the various methods of definition; it illustrated the progressive divergences from the conception of categories to the concept of the Individual. The basic textbook was Porphyrys's (d. 304/5 B.C.) Introduction to Aristotle's doctrine of the Categories.

2. The Council of Trent, Session IV (1546), with regard to the relation between the revelational truth of the written and the unwritten tradition, defined that the Church 'accepts and honours with equal pious readiness and reverence the books of Holy Scripture and the oral Tradition'. (Denz. 783).

3. BSLK 769, 19–35.

4. 'With divine and Catholic faith everything is to be believed that is con-

tained in the written and oral Tradition of the Word of God, and is declared by the Church, whether in formal decision, or by the regular general magisterium, to be believed as the revelation of God.' (cap. 3, Denz. 1792. This article is also to be found in the CIC under canon 1323.)

5. BSLK 421, 24f.

6. Word, Faith, Authority, Freedom, Boldness, Sonship.

7. Comm. on c.5:9 of the Ep. to the Galatians. WA 40,2; 47f.

ESSAY 9

The Mariological Dogma

First appeared in ZThK 47, 1950, 383–391. The following considerations are only a marginal comment on the question of Mariology. They were offered at the winter session of 1949–1950 as a lecture on Confessional studies and only represent an extract from my treatment of Mariology. I have limited myself particularly to the expression of a point of view which in my opinion has not received sufficient attention hitherto in the literature. In so doing the intricate pattern of motives which appear in Mariology should not be disputed and harmonized in favour of some agreed attempt at a solution. Only by a comprehensive study of the subject from the point of view of comparative religion, religious history, the history of dogma, the history of interpretation, church-politics, and other related disciplines, is it possible to arrive at a satisfactory over-all picture. The occasion of this study explains why it contains no reference to the intervening events, and why there is no discussion of what has been written since then on this subject. It would, moreover, be a task in itself, on the basis of a critical study of Protestant opinions on the Mariological dogma, to give a picture of the contemporary theological situation.

1. WA 15; 411, 21–23.   2. Denz. 734–5.   3. Denz. 792.
4. Denz. 1073.
5. B. Bartmann: *Lehrbuch der Dogmatik I* (1923⁶), 455.
6. Denz. 1641.   7. Denz. 1940a.   8. Denz. 1978a.
9. Denz. 1978a, n. 2.   10. *Ibid.*
11. Denz. 2291; I am quoting the authorized German translation.

ESSAY 10

The Protestant Idea of the Priesthood

A lecture given to the Catholic People's High School at Zurich, March 1, 1959.

1. Cf. G. Söhngen: *Gesetz und Evangelium. Ihre analoge Einheit*, 1957, p. Vf.

2. K. Rahner: *Schriften zur Theologie* Vol. III, 1957², p. 296. Eng. Tr. *Theological Investigations* Vol. 3, Baltimore, Helicon Press and London, Darton, Longman & Todd, 1967, p. 249.

ESSAY 11

Word and Sacrament

An address delivered at the Academic Festival of the 55th General Assembly of the Evangelical League on Jan. 9, 1962 in Kiel. First published in the Yearbook of the Evangelical League, 1963, *Im Lichte der Reformation*. Bd. VI. Vandenhoek & Ruprecht. Göttingen. 1963.

1. Rom 1:14f.

2. Hans Urs von Balthasar: *Karl Barth: Darstellung und Deutung seiner Theologie.* 1951, p. 320: 'No real contradiction can be found between what Barth has said in his anthropology about the possibility of human nature recognizing God in the concrete order of revelation, and the statements of the Vatican Council. Moreover, when Barth, in every step of his reasoning, maintains the existence of an all-embracing supernatural power, and bases creation on Jesus Christ, while the Vatican Council, occupied with the refutation of a particular heresy, announces a particular truth, no irreconcilable contradiction exists there.'

3. Hans Küng: *Rechtfertigung. Die Lehre Karl Barths und eine katholische Besinnung.* 1957, p. 276.

4. Peter Lengsfeld: *Überlieferung. Tradition und Schrift in der evangelischen und katholischen Theologie der Gegenwart.* 1960, p. 159.

5. Cf. O. Semmelroth: *Die Kirche als Ursakrament.* 1953. K. Rahner had already coined the epithet 'original sacrament' (*sacramentum radicale*) for the Church in a cyclostyled manuscript, *De penitentia tractatus historico-dogmaticus.* Innsbruck, 1952, quoted by O. Semmelroth, p. 238, n. 35. Also K. Rahner: *Kirche und Sakramente, Questiones disputatae* 10, 1961.

6. Cf. my Essay, 'Zur Frage nach dem Sinn des Mariologischen Dogmas' in ZThK 47, 1950, pp. 383–391, printed above pp. 181–9.

7. W. H. van de Pol: *Das reformatorische Christentum in phänomenologischer Betrachtung,* 1956.

8. *Op. cit.*, p. 259. The italics are van de Pol's, as are those in the following quotations.

9. *Ibid.*, p. 270.   10. *Ibid.*, p. 269.   11. *Ibid.*, p. 286f.

12. I have omitted the word 'and' here. It is a printer's error in van de Pol which spoils the sense.

13. *Op. cit.*, p. 273.

14. *Ibid.*, p. 304: 'Everything depends on whether the reality of the Catholic

Church which is the proximate object of the Catholic faith, is or is not acknowledged and accepted as the reality of revelation.' In my opinion this is inac-
curately expressed. According to the correct wording of Catholic doctrine,
the material object of faith is formally revealed truth, the formal object of faith
is the authority of God who reveals it. Cf. *Vatic. I, Const. dogm. de fide cath.c.3.*
(Denz. 1789): 'The Catholic Church professes this faith, which is the source of
man's salvation, to be of supernatural efficacy, by which, assisted by divine
grace, we believe in the truth of his revelation, not because of the intrinsic truth
of things perceived by the light of natural reason, but on the authority of God
himself the revealer, who can neither be deceived nor deceive.' On the other
hand, the Church is 'the proximate *rule* of faith', in distinction from Scripture
and Tradition as 'the remote rule of faith'. Cf. e.g. on this distinction, I.
Salaverri in Vol. I of *Sacrae Theologiae Summa* (Madrid, 1955) p. 762 N. 780:
'The concept of a rule of faith is related to the preceding, and therefore theologians are accustomed to call Scripture and Tradition the remote rule of faith,
but the Magisterium of the Church the proximate rule of faith.' N.781: 'Scripture and Tradition are therefore the remote and objective rule of faith, since
from them, as from springs, the Magisterium draws those things which it
presents to the faithful as things to be believed. But the Magisterium is the
proximate and active rule of faith, since from it the faithful learn directly what
they ought to believe concerning those things which are contained in the
sources of revelation, and what to hold concerning those things which have a
necessary connection with revealed truths.' The dogmatic basis of the distinction between the remote and the proximate rule of faith lies in the fact that a
distinction must be made between the revelation as such, and its promulgation
by the Magisterium of the Church. *Vatic. I. id.* (Denz. 1792): 'In the divine and
Catholic faith all things are to be believed which are contained in the Word of
God, written, or in tradition, and are promulgated by the Church, either by
special decree, or by its ordinary and universal Magisterium, to be believed as
divinely revealed.' As a commentary on this cf. A. Aldama in Vol. III of *Sacrae
Theologiae Summa*, p. 792.N. 142: 'But note that there it is not a question of the
divine faith simply (for which the first might suffice), but of the divine *and
Catholic* faith. Therefore the same object which had been revealed by God, and
that publicly, and which henceforth was already a sufficient object of divine
faith, receives something new from without, namely, the institution of the
Church. But this does not change the motive of divine faith, but is merely its
condition, making us more certain that God has indeed spoken. Many things
therefore can be believed by divine faith, which cannot be believed by the
divine and Catholic faith; but not conversely. The object of the divine and
Catholic faith is called *a dogma of faith.*'

15. Van de Pol, p. 274. The passage from the *Mystici Corporis* to which van de Pol refers is in AAS 35, 1943, p. 238: 'As then such a firm and undivided love dwells in our hearts and day by day increases, we learn that Christ himself must be seen in the Church. For it is Christ who lives in his Church, who teaches through her, governs, imparts holiness; it is Christ also who in various ways manifests himself through his various associated members.'

16. Van de Pol, p. 308.   17. *Ibid.*, p. 448.   18. *Ibid.*, p. 391.

19. *Ibid.*, p. 390.   20. *Ibid.*, p. 391.   21. *Ibid.*, p. 405.

22. *Ibid.*, p. 415, with the addition: 'the last understood empirically, existentially, realistically.'

23. *Ibid.*, p. 448.

24. Together with the question of fact, this observation calls for a close critical examination of van de Pol's method. He sharply distinguishes between the Christianity of the Reformers, to which he confines his attention, and all the other forms of Protestantism, which, compared with the Reformed, 'have forfeited the right to that name, (61). He does not attribute Protestantism's loss of its character to a turning towards Orthodoxy, or to Pietism, or to the Enlightenment, but, in accordance with the significance which he attaches to the ontological point of view for a Confessional understanding, to Kant; that means, according to van de Pol, a transition from Realism to Idealism; from an objective, ontological (*seinshaft*) view of reality, to a 'phenomenalist' view. 'God becomes a creation of the human mind.' (197). 'Man has become autonomous, even in matters of religion . . . Thus modern theology of the nineteenth century is in direct contradiction with the witness of Holy Scripture and the original preaching of the Church, it is also in direct opposition to the preaching of the Reformers . . . Both Holy Scripture, and the way in which the Reformers understood it, present a realistic attitude. The reason why the theology of the nineteenth century, with all its adherence to the traditional forms and expressions, came into diametrical opposition to the genuine Christian and Reformed understanding of the revelation, lay in the sphere of philosophy.' (198) Hence it was to be expected that van de Pol would take his account of Reformed Christianity from Reformation sources. Apart from general remarks about the Reformers, he bases his account on the writings of Karl Barth and Emil Brunner, as well as on some of the Dutch theologians of the same school. Their stand against Neoprotestantism seems to justify this proceeding. But have they really revived the theology of the Reformers? Van de Pol himself is obliged to be sparing in his praise of Barth and Brunner: 'They have not touched the real root of the disease. They accept the "Copernical revolution", which entered into history through Kant's epistemology; they regard it as an achievement which can never be surrendered; they wish to heal the disease without attacking its

cause.' (199) Hence the question arises, 'Whether a theology which clearly starts from the assumption of the correctness and irrefutability of the Kantian hypothesis can really be Reformed in the original sense.' (194) If, nevertheless, van de Pol adheres so closely to Barth and Brunner, he must be aware at what point, as the result of the Kantian infiltration, this revival of Reformed theology parts company with the genuine Reformed theology. According to van de Pol that is the case with regard to the natural knowledge of God, where both Barth and Brunner, in spite of their disagreement on this point, do not manifest agreement with Scripture so much as with philosophic presuppositions. Since, from a purely philosophical point of view, they think realistically, but from an epistemological point of view, on the other hand, they think idealistically, subjectively, and phenomenologically, their turning to the God of revelation is a leap, separating faith and reason, theology and philosophy, and allowing no connection between a natural knowledge of God and a knowledge by faith. (199) Yet, is this really so divergent from the genuine Reformed position? Van de Pol himself refers occasionally, without any differentiation, to the hostile attitude of the Reformers to philosophy (43f) ... 'the Reformed Christian would attribute "the force of logic" rather to the Devil than to the God and Father who reveals himself in Jesus Christ.' (226) This, then, is the reason why van de Pol does not confine himself to a discussion of the Reformers on the question of an understanding of the truth and reality of the Confessional difference. 'The Reformers had not yet explicitly raised the question of the Biblical conception of truth and reality; modern Reformed theology has been the first to raise the question of the conception of truth and reality of the nineteenth-century Protestant, and at the same time, Catholic theology according to the particular Reformed, that is, Biblical, understanding of truth and reality in the revealed sense' (200f). Here van de Pol involves himself in a contradiction. On the one hand he emphasizes the internal Protestant contrast in the understanding of reality: between the genuine Reformed realistic, existential, ontological understanding of reality, and the epistemological mode of thought introduced by Kant. The new Reformed theology of Barth and Brunner, although permeated by Kantianism, goes back to the biblical realism of the Reformers, at least in relation to the facts of revelation. On the other hand, according to van de Pol, the deepest root of the Confessional difference, and not only of the internal Protestant difference, is to be sought in the understanding of reality. Clearly, then, a revolution in the conception of reality must be assumed to have already taken place in the Reformation. The nature of the revolution will differ according to one's view of Protestantism, but it will not be of the Kantian kind. Or finally should both positions be connected? Van de Pol once suggests, in disagreement with his usual statements on the point, that demythologization seems to be the ultimate consequence of the denial by the Reformers of a realistic understanding of the reality of revelation. 'Once Christ is no longer seen in the Church, once Christ is no longer adored in the most holy Sacrament of the Altar, the Catholic faith is, in principle, surrendered, and the way opened leading step by step to denials, until it ends in the "demythologizing of Christianity" and the total denial of the divinity of Christ and the supernatural character of the revelation.' (274)

25. WA 7; 54,31ff.; 55,1f.; 'Christ has the sins, death, and hell; the soul has grace, life, and salvation.'

26. Van de Pol, p. 451. He does not raise the question whether what correctly means 'existence' (*sein*) here, can only be interpreted on the basis of the event which Luther expounds as 'the sweetest spectacle . . . not only of communion, but of saving warfare, and victory, and salvation, and redemption': WA 7; 55, p. 7ff.

27. Karl Rahner: *Schriften zur Theologie*. Bd. III. 1957², p. 349f.=Eng. Tr., p. 294f.

28. In *Aktuelle Fragen zur Eucharistie*, ed. M. Schmaus, 1960, pp. 7–52; printed in Karl Rahner: *Schriften zur Theologie*. Bd. IV. 1962², pp. 313–355= Eng. Tr., pp. 353–286. Most of it (pp. 313–338=Eng. Tr., pp. 253–281) is devoted to the question, '*Word and Sacrament in general*'.

29. *Op. cit.*, p. 315=Eng. Tr., p. 255.

30. *Ibid.*, p. 315f.=Eng. Tr., p. 255f.

31. *Ibid.*, p. 321=Eng. Tr., p. 260. A comparison may be made of the definition of the distinction between the sacraments of the Old Covenant and those of the New in the Decree *Pro Armenis* of the Council of Florence (Denz. 695): 'The former (i.e., the sacraments of the Old Law) were not the cause of grace, but typified that grace could only be given through the passion of Christ; but the latter, i.e., our sacraments, both contain grace, and confer it upon those who receive them worthily.'

32. *Op. cit.*, p. 330=Eng. Tr., p. 266.

33. *Ibid.*, p. 354=Eng. Tr., p. 286.

34. *Ibid.*, p. 329=Eng. Tr., p. 265.

35. *Ibid.*, p. 351=Eng. Tr., p. 283.

36. *Ibid.*, p. 379f.=Eng. Tr., p. 306f. in an essay on '*The Presence of Christ in the Sacrament of the Lord's Supper*.

37. *Op. cit.*, p. 317: 'Catholic theology, has no more than the Magisterium, ever been able to accept the formula that the fellowship of Protestant Christians constitutes the Church of the Word, while we Catholics are the Church of the Sacraments. . . . But Protestant theology is now beginning to take the Sacraments seriously again, and to see their essential and irreplaceable sig-

nificance for Christian existence. And we Catholics are reflecting more expressly on the fact that we are the Church of the Word of God.'

38. E.g., K. H. Schelkle: 'Das Wort in der Kirche'. ThQ. 133, 1953, pp. 278–293. By the same author: *Jüngerschaft und Apostolat.* 1957. H. Schleier: *Das Wort Gottes, Eine neutestamentliche Besinnung.* 1958.

39. Peter Lengsfeld, see above, p. 256, n. 4, esp. pp. 64ff., 209ff.

40. Otto Semmelroth: *Wirkendes Wort, Zut Theologie der Verkündigung.* 1962, p. 54.

41. *Ibid.*, p, 184.	42. *Ibid.*, p. 126.	43. *Ibid.*, p. 59.
44. *Ibid.*, p. 177.	45. *Ibid.*, p. 219.	46. *Ibid.*, p. 217.
47. See above p. 256, n. 5.	48. *Op. cit.*, p. 203.	49. *Ibid.*, p. 238.
50. *Ibid.*, p. 180.	51. *Ibid.*, p. 205.	52. *Ibid.*, p. 204.
53. *Ibid.*, p. 244.	54. *Ibid.*, p. 245.	

55. Peter Brunner: 'Zur Lehre vom Gottesdienst der im Namen Jesuversammelten Gemeinde'. *Leiturgia* I. 1954, pp. 83ff.

56. His contributions to: *Offenbarung als Geschichte*, ed. W. Pannenberg, KuD. Beih. 1, 1961, pp. 7ff, 91ff.

57. KD IV, 1, p, 858f.

58. D. Bonhoeffer, *Widerstand und Ergebung*, 1951, p. 248f. Eng. Tr. *Letters and Papers from Prison*, London, SCM Press, 1953, p. 168f, Fontana Edition, 1959, p. 124f; as *Prisoner for God*, New York, Macmillan Co., 1957.

ESSAY 12

The Protestant View of the Sacraments

From an address on Ecclesiology given in the summer semester, 1963.

1. WA 12; pp. 472–493.

INDEX

Index